Meeting the Needs of Multiethnic and Multiracial Children in Schools

Francis Wardle

Red Rocks Community College

Marta I. Cruz-Janzen

Florida Atlantic University

PEARSON

Boston • New York • San Francisco
Mexico City • Montreal • Toronto • London • Madrid • Munich • Paris
Hong Kong • Singapore • Tokyo • Cape Town • Sydney

We wish to dedicate *Multiethnic and Multicultural Children in Schools* to our children, the future of the multiethnic and multiracial movement in this country and the world: Eva DeLourdes Janzen and Maia Shali, Eirlys Celeste, Kealan Andreas, and RaEsa Joan Benjamin-Wardle.

Series Editor: *Traci Mueller*
Series Editorial Assistant: *Krista Price*
Senior Marketing Manager: *Elizabeth Fogarty*
Senior Editorial-Production Administrator: *Beth Houston*
Editorial-Production Service: *Walsh & Associates, Inc.*
Composition and Prepress Buyer: *Linda Cox*
Manufacturing Buyer: *Andrew Turso*
Cover Administrator: *Kristina Mose-Libon*
Electronic Composition: *Publishers' Design and Production Services, Inc.*

For related titles and support materials, visit our online catalog at www.ablongman.com

Copyright © 2004 Pearson Education, Inc.

Between the time Website information is gathered and then published, it is not unusual for some sites to have closed. Also, the transcription of URLs can result in typographical errors. The publisher would appreciate notification where these errors occur so that they may be corrected in subsequent editions.

Library of Congress Cataloging-in-Publication Data

Wardle, Francis, 1947–
    Meeting the needs of multiethnic and multiracial children in schools / Francis Wardle, Marta I. Cruz-Janzen.
        p.   cm.
    Includes bibliographical references and index.
    ISBN 0-205-37608-8
    1. Racially mixed children—Education—United States.   2. Racially mixed children—United States—Ethnic identity.   3. Racially mixed children—Race identity—United States.   4. Multicultural education—United States.   I. Cruz-Janzen, Marta. II. Title.

LC3621.W37 2003
371.828—dc22   2003053679

Printed in the United States of America

10   9   8   7   6   5   4   3   2   1   07   06   05   04   03

Photo credits: p. 6, Kealan Wardle; all other photos, Francis Wardle.

Contents

Foreword by Maria P. P.
Root   vii

1 *Multiethnic and Multiracial Children*   1

Who Are the Children?   2
Personal Journeys   4
No Longer Invisible   7
Diversity in the Classroom   8
   Multicultural Education   9
   Increasing Advocacy   12
   Interracial Parents   13
Needs of Multiethnic and Multiracial Children   13
   Responsibility of the Schools   15
Conclusion   18
Questions/Projects   19
Resources   19

2 *Traditional Approaches*   20

Single Race/Ethnicity Approach   21
Diversity within Traditional Racial Groups   22
Race, Ethnicity, and Culture   24
   Understanding Race, Ethnicity, and Culture   25
   The Process of Assimilation   26
   What Is Race?   28
   What Is Culture?   28
Group Membership   29
   Non-Whites   32
   Group Acceptance and Multiethnic/ Multiracial Identity   32
Getting on the Same Page   33

Diversity and Culture   33
Race and Ethnicity   35
Approaches to Teaching Multicultural Education   36
   The Five Dimensions of Multicultural Education   36
   Approaches to Multicultural Education   40
Reforming Multicultural Education   43
   The Problems with Traditional Approaches   43
   Multicultural Education That's Truly Multicultural   45
Conclusion   46
Questions/Projects   46
Resources   47

3 *Historical Developments*   48

Development of a Racial System   50
   Colonialists   50
   Preoccupation with Race   50
   Racial Boundaries   52
   Immigration Acts and Court Rulings   53
   False Equality   54
Origins of U.S. Racism   54
   Racial Hierarchies   55
   Proving Racial Superiority   56
   Irish Americans   56
   Today's Racism   57
Rejection of Racial Mixing   57
   Negative Influences   58
   Japanese Racial Purity   59
Latinos   60
   The Term "Hispanic"   60

Immigration   *62*
   Japanese American
      Immigrants   64
   Opposition to Non-White
      Immigrants   67
   Puerto Ricans and Filipinos   68
   Civil Rights Movement   68
   New Restrictions   69

Racism and Segregation   *69*
   Legal Segregation   70
   World War II   70

Changes and Improvements in
Education   *71*
   Desegregation   71
   Language Proficiency and the
      Rights of Disabled Students
      71

Multiracial and Multiethnic
Children in Schools   *72*

Multicultural Education   *74*

Conclusion   *74*

Questions/Projects   *75*

Resources   *75*

4   *Categorizing People*   *76*

Understanding Race, Racism,
and Categorizing People   *78*
   Slavery   79
   Categorizing People   80
   Shifting Identities   80
   Justifying Racial Labels   82
   Current Racial Categories   82

The Ethnic Category:
Latino   *85*

The Race Myth   *87*
   The Theory of Hybrid
      Degeneracy   87
   The Problem with Race   88
   Passing as White   88
   Multiethnic and Multiracial Native
      Americans   89
   Supporting the One-Drop
      Rule   90

After the Civil War   *91*
   Attempts to Classify Blacks
      Differently   91
   Hardening of the Lines   92
   Mainstream Whites   93

Categorizing People in Other
Nations   *93*
   South Africa   93
   Latin America and the
      Caribbean   94

The Legacy of Slaves and
Slave Owners   *96*

Maintaining the Color
Line   *97*
   Group Solidarity   98

Today's Multiracial and
Multiethnic Children   *99*
   Where Do We Go from
      Here?   99
   New Visibility   100

Conclusion   *100*

Questions/Projects   *101*

Resources   *101*

5   *Identity Development of*
Multiethnic and Multiracial
Children   *102*

Identity Development:
A Definition   *102*

Identity Development
Models   *103*
   Poston's Model   108
   Jacobs's Developmental
      Model   108
   Phinney's Model of Ethnic Identity
      in Adolescents   109
   Kerwin-Ponterotto's Model
      110
   Root's Approach   111

Wardle's Developmental and
Ecological Model of Identity
Development   *112*
   Developmental Stages   112
   Stage I: Early Childhood   113
   Transition Period   115
   Stage II: Adolescence   115
   Ecological Components   118
   Family   120
   Group Antagonism   122
   Cultural Contexts   123
   Community   125
   Integrating the Ecological
      Components   126

Conclusion   *126*

Questions/Projects   *127*

Resources   *127*

6   *Families and Communities*   *128*

The Multiethnic and Multiracial Family   *129*
  The Child's Ethnic or Racial
    Identity   129
  Religion   132
  Selecting Schools and Early
    Childhood Programs   134
  How Schools Can Support
    Multiracial and Multiethnic
    Families   135

Different Family Structures   *138*
  Transracial Adoption   138
  Foster Families   141
  Blended Families   142
  Single-Parent Families   144
  Grandparents Raising
    Children   145
  Teen Parents   146

Conclusion   *147*

Questions/Projects   *148*

Resources   *148*

7   *Curricular Approaches*   *149*

Early Childhood (up to 8 Years Old)   *149*
  Goals for Early Childhood
    Curricula   150
  Learning Environment   151
  Curricular Content   151
  Curricular Materials   152

Late Elementary (8 to 11 Years Old)   *153*
  Goals for the Late Elementary
    Curriculum   154
  Learning Environments   154
  Curricular Content   156
  Curricular Materials   156

Middle School   *161*
  Goals   161
  Learning Environment   162
  Curricular Content   162
  Curricular Materials   163

High School   *164*
  Goals   165
  Learning Environment   166
  Curricular Content   167
  Curricular Materials   168

Hidden Curriculum   *169*

Multicultural Model   *170*
  Race/Ethnicity   170
  Culture   172
  Gender   173
  Ability/Disability   173
  Community   173
  Family   174
  Socioeconomic Status   174
  Application of the Model   176

Conclusion   *177*

Questions/Projects   *177*

Resources   *177*

8   *Instructional Strategies*   *178*

The Impact of Standards on Instruction   *179*

The Influence of the Teacher   *180*
  When the Teacher and Parent
    Disagree   182
  Teachers and the Hidden
    Curriculum   182
  Role of Teachers' Ethnicity and
    Race   183
  Teachers as Products of
    Culture   184
  Addressing Bias and
    Prejudice   185
  Understanding Racism   186
  Changing Teachers'
    Attitudes   187

Biased Instructional Materials   *188*
  Forms of Bias in Curricular
    Material and Programs   188
  Culturally Authentic Bias   192
  Making Learning
    Meaningful   193

*Specific Suggestions for
Instructional Techniques*   *194*
   Support Different Learning
     Styles   194
   Support Healthy Racial Identity
     Development   194
   Provide Adult Role Models and Use
     the Community   197
   Treat All Children as Unique
     Individuals   198
   Don't Allow Biased Behavior or
     Language   198
   Provide Small Groups and
     Cooperative Learning   199
   Provide Lots of Opportunities to
     Explore Race and Racism in
     This Country   199
   Don't Stereotype Any of Your
     Students   199
   Create Appropriate Instructional
     Materials   200

Conclusion   *201*

Questions/Projects   *201*

Resources   *201*

9   *Teaching Teachers*   *202*

*The Nature of Public
Education*   *203*

Preparing Future Teachers   *204*
   Looking the Monster in the
     Eye   204

Teachers of Teachers   205
Critical Pedagogy   207
Curricular Content   208

*Sociopolitical Construction of
Multiethnic and Multiracial
Persons*   *209*
   Multiethnic and Multiracial
     Students Need to See
     Themselves in Their
     Curricula   211
   Teachers Need to Affirm
     Multiethnic and Multiracial
     Students' Strengths   212

*What Teachers Must Know and Be
Able to Do*   *213*

*Twenty-Five Recommendations for
Teachers, Education Professors,
and Educational Leaders*   *216*

Conclusion   *220*

Questions/Projects   *221*

Resources   *221*

Appendix A   **Age-Related
Issues for Interracial and
Interethnic Families**   **223**

Glossary   **229**

References   **234**

Index   **241**

Foreword

What began as an unmapped personal journey for these authors transformed their professional work as educators, psychologists, and researchers. Oftentimes the scouts on the lookout trail have the good fortune of seeing and experiencing aspects of life for which they have no template. If the adventurer can temporarily suspend a desire to make things fit into existing schemas, he or she is in the position to create new questions, grapple with new realities, and consequently enhance his or her critical thinking about the issues that surround us.

The combined professional and personal experience of Drs. Wardle and Cruz-Janzen delivers a road map pushing readers and educators to embark on a transformative journey rarely mapped in multicultural education and its training. They examine and educate us through the experiences of children of culturally, ethnically, and racially mixed heritages. In doing so, they are certain to challenge even longtime multicultural experts to broaden how we think and approach multicultural education.

The authors provide a crash course on understanding the developmental needs of multiethnic, multicultural, and multiracial children. They also are sensitive to delving into the contexts within which these children emerge, which also reminds the reader to critically think about diverse family constellations. Different models of multiracial identity development are reviewed. Materials that are difficult to find are included within their chapters, further making this book a special resource.

Most readers, be they student or educator, will find a new world and way of experiencing traditional multicultural education that can only transform us. The information, questions, and features within and across chapters deepen our understanding of how racial and cultural xenophobic laws and traditions have limited engaging a growing number of multiethnic and multiracial students—children who do not belong solely to one of the traditional racial groups created by the federal government.

With almost 7 million persons checking more than one race in the 2000 Census, and over 40 percent of this sample being persons under 18 years of age, this book is timely. The authors also push us to think beyond biracial or bicultural terms. Recent census figures support their urging us to look forward. For most "two-race responses," the largest portion was a traditional category such as Black or Asian or White with "other." The "other" has often been someone who already does not neatly fit into the conventional race framework. Thus, with our youngest group of children we are beginning to see a visible cohort of children that may opt to be multiethnic and multiracial in their expressions, behaviors, and thinking.

While the authors use racial terms as labels at times, they start where many of us understand this language. Then Wardle and Cruz-Janzen push the envelope of typical awareness. They clearly are the harbingers of questions and information in a changing climate of race and culture ripe for redress and new ways of thinking, talking, and educating.

Although this book is geared toward the educational field, parents of multiethnic and multiracial children will find much affirmation, information, and hope in these pages. Parents must guide their children on a journey that they have not traveled themselves. The first roadmaps for parents and educators are just emerging and they are not "one-size-fits-all." Critical thinking remains imperative. Parents and educators need to know that they are only guides in this process, though critical. Children are influenced outside the family by peers, community, and religion, which are filtered through their temperament, talents, and learned and developed capacities for resilience. Orienting children who do not identify as multiethnic or multiracial to valuing diversity and mixed-race identity provides a positive environment for all children.

The authors have done an excellent job of reminding us of the dynamic nature of culture and the socially constructed and therefore dynamic nature of ethnic and racial identity. Not all children in the same family will identify the same. Whereas research and clinical literature on multiethnic and multicultural children suggest that labels are important, they are important to affirm that different ways of being do exist and these have expanded over the last few generations. However, they are not a guarantee as to where the child will land. Opening up their options, however, may reduce some of their struggle to fit in.

The power of education is to offer ways of understanding the world to our children, the adults and leaders of the future. Drs. Wardle and Cruz-Janzen synthesize an enormous amount of information from different fields. They further our critical thinking about multicultural education by making visible multicultural, multiethnic, and multiracial children.

Maria P. P. Root, Ph.D., author of *Racially Mixed People in America*, and *The Multiracial Experience*, both published by Sage, and *Love's Revalution: Interracial marriage* (Temple University Press).

Acknowledgments

We would like to thank all those people who have supported our efforts in writing this book, including a vast array of people who share our views, support our commitment to create change, and believe in the right of multiethnic and multiracial children to have their full identity supported by society and our schools. Specifically, we wish to acknowledge the patience, goodwill, and undying support of our spouses—John H. Janzen, and Ruth Elaine Benjamin Wardle, the reviewers of the manuscript—Dorothy Hewes (San Diego State University), Edith King (University of Denver), Solange Lopes-Murphy (James Madison University), and Kathleen Lutz (The College of St. Scholastica)—and our Allyn and Bacon editor Traci Mueller.

1

Multiethnic and Multiracial Children

The number of mixed-race babies is increasing at a faster rate than the number of single-race babies (U.S. Bureau of the Census, 1992). Since the early 1970s, the number of single-race babies has grown by 15 percent, while the number of multiracial babies by more than 260 percent, according to the National Center for Health Statistics. This increase translates into over 100,000 births per year since 1989, a total of more than 1 million first-generation biracial births in the last ten years (Root, 1996). Increases in multiethnic and multiracial births include a variety of combinations of first-generation biracial births—Japanese/mainstream White babies, Native American/non Native American babies, and other Asian American and Pacific Islander interracial babies—and, of course, Black/mainstream White babies (Root, 1996). Further, the 2000 Census—the first to allow people to select more than one ethnic or racial label—reported that 6.8 million people checked more than one box when asked to identify their race. Many believe this is a conservative number, because many individuals of mixed heritage still prefer a single race and ethnic identity.

The increase of multiethnic and multiracial births is a result of a variety of factors. In 1967 the landmark U.S. Supreme Court decision *Loving v. State of Virginia* overturned the several remaining state laws against intermarriage; by 1991 more United States citizens approved (48%) than disapproved (42%) of interracial marriage (Gallup Poll, 1991), a shift from a 72 percent disapproval rate in 1968. The civil rights movement and resultant legislation led to people from a variety of racial and ethnic groups interacting with each other in jobs, schools, colleges, and neighborhoods. A natural outgrowth of this integration between the racial and ethnic groups has been interracial and interethnic relationships, marriages, and children.

The focus of this book is to explore ways schools can meet the needs of the ever-increasing number of multiethnic and multiracial children and their families in our P–12 programs (Preschool through twelfth grade). While multiethnic and

1

multiracial children are a relatively new population in our schools, children of color are not. Our discussion will be within the broad framework of meeting the needs of all children of color—teacher training; curriculum development, content, and instruction; approaches to tracking; special education and gifted programs; and parent involvement and community partnerships. We believe these agendas go together and that any approaches to serving children of color and/or multiethnic and multiracial children that conflict means there is something inherently wrong with the approaches. Providing the highest quality education for children of color, and responding appropriately and proactively to the special and unique needs of multiethnic and multiracial children and their families, are totally consistent.

FOCUS QUESTIONS

1. Why are the educational concerns of multiethnic and multiracial children an issue for today's educators? And, are the educational concerns of multiethnic and multiracial children different from those of single-race, minority children? If so, how?

2. When schools collect required Office of Management and Budget (OMB) ethnic and racial statistics, where do these children belong? Further, how can teachers and administrators be sensitive and supportive to children of mixed heritage when collecting this information?

3. What is the identity of multiracial children—that of their minority, or lowest status parents, that of their White, or highest status parent, or a combination of both? Are there a variety of choices for these children?

Who Are the Children?

Children of one Black parent and one mainstream White parent are the most obvious—and most visible—mixed race/ethnicity children. Because they represent both ends of our racial hierarchy and challenge our country's deep-seated system of separating people by race (Banks & Banks, 1997), they are the most discussed example of multiracial children. However, multiethnic and multiracial children come in all sorts of racial, ethnic, tribal, and national combinations. Just a few examples are Navajo (Dine) and Black, Korean and Puerto Rican, German and Black, Jamaican and Jewish, Asian Indian and Vietnamese, Japanese and Latino, and Black Foot Indian and Polish. These are first-generation children. Think of the rich and varied combinations for children with one parent who is Asian/Black and the other who is Irish/Latino, or parents who are Pueblo Indian/Latino and Polish/West Indian. Of course, categories such as Latino, West Indian, Asian Indian, or even African American are themselves multiethnic and multiracial, based on a history and movements of people across the world. Actually, most mainstream White people are multiethnic or multiracial, also! Add to these combinations foreign multiracial and multiethnic children—

Brazilians of Indian/Portuguese/German or Black/Indian background, Puerto Ricans of Black/Latino heritage, and South Africans of White/Black and Indian (Asian) heritage—and you get the picture! In fact, the other day when Francis Wardle was visiting the Seminole Reservation in Oklahoma, a young lady declared, "I'm part Lakota Sioux, part Cherokee, and part unregistered Seminole—I'm really mixed!"

Some of these children are, strictly speaking, **biracial**—with parents from two distinct races, and some **biethnic**—children from two ethnic groups, for example, non-Latino White (in this book referred to as mainstream White) and Latino White. The initial interest in multiethnic and multiracial children focused on children whose parents crossed **traditional Census categories** to marry and have children—thus these children were all technically biracial or biethnic. However, after more careful study, it soon became apparent that (1) biracial and biethnic children of the 1960s were now having their own children, and (2) as the strict racial and ethnic boundaries of past thinking were being challenged, more people who simply accepted a single racial or ethnic label began to embrace their full heritage. Thus the language to describe children of mixed heritage is now more accurately multiethnic and multiracial.

In this book we use the terms **multiethnic** and **multiracial** to represent people whose acknowledged identity includes two or more of the U.S. government Census categories. As described by the 2000 Census, these categories are White (non-Latino), Latino/Spanish/Hispanic, Black (not Hispanic), American Indian or Alaska Native, and Asian (U.S. Bureau of the Census, 2000). Clearly, most minorities in this county are multiracial, many Latinos by definition are **mestizo** (White and Indian), **mulatto** (White and Black), or a combination of all three. But, until this country rejects its entrenched reliance on racial labels (Banks & Banks, 1997), there is a need to define children of different racial and ethnic parentage as multiracial and multiethnic. While we recognize that the category is fuzzy, we also recognize that the boundaries between traditional racial and ethnic groups are becoming unclear (Root, 1996).

We also include in this category a group of children who are being labeled **third-culture children**—children with two or more racial/ethnic backgrounds and two or more national citizenships (West, 2001). Recently, the U.S. government dropped its insistence that people who become U.S. citizens must reject their former citizenship, resulting in an increasing number of children being raised with dual citizenship. For example, Francis Wardle's children have both U.S. and British passports.

Multiethnic and multiracial children's cultural contexts differ greatly from each other, depending on the kind of community they live in, the values and traditions their parents and extended families pass on to them, the religion and educational levels of the parents, and family expectations for their children. While it is always dangerous to stereotype any child or family based on race/ethnicity/culture, it's simply impossible and disingenuous to do so with multiethnic and multiracial children.

Personal Journeys

Both authors of this book are personally involved in multiethnic and multiracial issues. Marta I. Cruz-Janzen was born and raised in Puerto Rico. She is married to a mainstream White man who is part Dutch, English, and Scottish. Marta's mother is White and her father Black. Despite the widespread misconception in the U.S. mainland that all Latinos/Puerto Ricans are racially mixed, Puerto Rico and most Latin American nations are racially divided and stratified, with Blacks

Chapter Feature
Eva

Marta and John faced incredible challenges raising their daughter Eva. They emphasized her legitimate multiracial and multiethnic heritage while struggling to combat the racial harassment she was constantly subjected to. As she grew, Eva's phenotype changed dramatically. Sometimes her Black heritage was apparent; at other stages it was not. Most people assume that she is the biological child of John because of the closer physical resemblance to him rather than to her biological mother. Eva is very light-skinned with natural blonde hair and medium brown eyes. John has blonde (now becoming white) hair and blue eyes. Eva is also tall and heavy-boned while Marta is 5'1", petite, and brown-skinned with black hair and eyes. John is 6'3". Throughout her schooling Eva found herself classified and reclassified differently by school officials and classmates. She was often in tears from the cruel remarks and rejection. She was often told that she was Black because her mother is Black; she was even told that being Puerto Rican did not make her or her mother any less Black because in the United States anyone who is Black, regardless of nationality, is simply Black—period.

In middle school and high school the situation became extremely uncomfortable and painful as classmates and teachers constantly challenged her racial and ethnic identity. Latino classmates would tell her that she was not like them because she was Black; African Americans would either tell her that she was not Black enough and/or that she was ashamed and used her Latino/Puerto Rican identity to deny her Blackness. In middle school Eva wanted very much to fit in with the Latino kids and struggled to be as Latina as possible, even more than her friends. She dyed her hair black and took Spanish classes. In high school she found herself rejected by Latinos and struggled to fit in with the Black kids. One day she even begged Marta not to allow John to come to a school function so her Black friends would not see him.

Eva has grown very aware of the different treatment she receives when people realize she is not White, and particularly when they realize that she is part Black. Today she continues to dye her hair brown, "Because it makes me look less odd"—and surrounds herself with multiracial and multiethnic persons and couples.

Marta, John, and Eva.

and Indians at the bottom of the social scale and Whites at the top. Between Blacks and Whites there are multiple stratified layers of racially mixed groups. Within the Puerto Rican community, both on the island and the U.S. mainland, Marta is considered mulatto. Because of her education and social standing, she is most often elevated to **trigueña** (wheat-colored).

Both of Marta's paternal grandparents are Black. They completed high school, considered a significant accomplishment among their generation, especially for Black Puerto Ricans. They were middle class, owned a home in a predominantly White community, emphasized education, and sent their children to college. Because of the family's social standing, they were not considered Black. Since they had no White ancestry and therefore could not be considered mulattoes, they were officially reclassified as mestizos, even though there is no Indian heritage in the family lineage. Marta's mother is considered White Puerto Rican even though her grandmother was pure **Taino Indian**. The family prefers not to discuss that part of their heritage. The rest of the family is White from Spain and Russia. Marta's daughter is multiracial; her biological father is biracial of White Cuban background on the mother's side and Black/African American and Native American Indian on the father's side.

Chapter Feature
Student Profile: RaEsa Joan Benjamin-Wardle

RaEsa is the fourth child of Ruth Benjamin-Wardle and Francis Wardle.

Age: 17

School: George Washington High School in Denver, Colorado.

Program: International Baccalaureate Program—an international high school curriculum based in Cardiff, Wales, used in schools throughout the world. Many students in these programs are third-culture children.

Interests/Hobbies: Lacrosse, French, art, fashion.

Mother: Ruth Benjamin-Wardle, MED, Special Education, and Licensed Family Therapist. Ruth is Black and Chickasaw Indian. Neither of Ruth's parents had a college degree, but grandparents on her mother's side were college graduates. Ruth grew up in Kansas City and Oklahoma. She was raised Catholic and attended Catholic schools until college. Her interests include travel, therapy, family, English literature, and culture.

Father: Francis, Ph.D. in Education. Francis is White/English; his father grew up in London, mother in Manchester. Francis's ancestry includes Irish and Scandinavian. Both parents have education degrees and taught all their adult lives; his father still does some teaching and curricular development. He was raised in a communal, Anabaptist (adult baptism, like the Amish) community, where both parents and four of his siblings still live. Francis is now an atheist. His hobbies include travel, photography, gardening, soccer, and writing.

Francis Wardle and family, including RaEsa Benjamin-Wardle (back left). Kealan is taking the photo.

RaEsa Benjamin-Wardle.

No Longer Invisible

Many young interracial and interethnic families must face the question of how to respond to their children's unique ethnic and racial identities. Francis and Ruth faced this dilemma when Maia, their oldest child, came home in tears after an argument with Carlos, another 4-year-old. They had a typical 4-year-old argument, but Carlos, a recent immigrant from Mexico, decided to use race as a tool in his argument, saying, "and you're Black anyway, and I'm not, so there!"

"How come I'm Black and he's not, when he is darker than me?" Maia asked through her tears. Francis and his wife had often discussed how they would raise their children—discipline, education, travel, etc. But they had never discussed race. Now they suddenly realized they would have to. They had to find a way to raise their children so that they would have a healthy identity and provide them with the tools to defend themselves from hurtful children (and, as they later discovered, hurtful adults). So, as good academics they researched the issue—looking for expert written advice and talking to people they respected. This was in 1982. The result of their research was:

- We don't know how to raise multiracial children. You will have to wait.
- You must raise your children as Black. While the children of Francis and Ruth are Black/White, parents with other racial and ethnic combinations are told to raise the child with the racial or ethnic identity of the parent

whose identity is the lowest in this country's racial hierarchy. Ruth and Francis were told that if they did not raise their children as Black, they will be confused, won't have the tools needed to deal with racism, and will develop a false sense of their worth and privilege—which will later be deflated when they discover the racism in this country.

None of these responses made any sense to them. They talked with each other, and to another interracial family they respected—a feisty, self-assured, opinionated Black mother and a German father who is decidedly more German than American. They also found a sympathetic psychologist who understood and supported their belief that multiethnic and multiracial children must be raised with a clear and affirmative sense of their total heritage and identity to withstand the single-race bias in this society.

But in 1982 much of the rest of the country was not ready for this approach, and many still are not. Since that early struggle, the couple have been accused by school principals of "being uptight about your child's identity," have been told their children must "select one identity," even though school forms explicitly require "an accurate identity," and have worked ceaselessly with their children to help them understand the blatant and subtle race-specific activities, expectations, and groups in their schools. They also found a variety of ways to expose their children to all sorts of racial, ethnic, national, linguistic, religious, and cultural diversity.

The experience of the two authors in raising their multiracial children—working carefully with their children's schools, teachers, counselors, coaches, and administrators—is shared by millions of other interracial and interethnic parents to lesser, or in many cases, greater, degrees. Many of these families of the turbulent 1960s and 1970s have raised multiethnic and multiracial children who are now articulate adults, and the multiethnic and multiracial community is no longer invisible—its members will no longer accept the official line that they must belong to the group of the minority parent or the lowest status parent if both parents are minority.

Diversity in the Classroom

School classrooms throughout this country are continually experiencing more and more diversity, with an increasing number of children whose first language is not English, more children of first-generation immigrants from non-Northern European countries, increased racial and ethnic diversity from within this country, and more children with a variety of special needs. Indicators of this increased diversity include:

- The mainstream White (non-Latino) population in this country is the slowest growing group (U.S. Census Bureau, 2001).
- Latin Americans are the fastest growing group, the youngest group, and the largest minority group in the country (U.S. Census Bureau, 2001).

- Native Americans are also a very rapidly growing group, increasing by 21 percent between 1980 and 1990 (Census Bureau, 1990).
- Asian American and Pacific Island Americans have increased 107 percent between 1980 and 1990 (U.S. Census Bureau, 1990).
- Immigrants from Eastern Russia, the Balkans, and new republics that used to be part of Russia have increased in recent years.
- The 2000 Census indicated that 6.8 million people selected more than one racial category for their identity. Many of these were small children (U.S. Census Bureau, 2001).

The 1980 and 1990 Censuses did not count multiracial births, so the increase of multiracial and multiethnic children we have discussed are included in these single-race numbers—usually with the racial or ethnic category of the parent of lowest status. Further, the term Asian American is a bit of a misnomer, because countries such as Canada, Mexico, Peru, Belize, Columbia, and Brazil have significant Asian populations, and these countries, of course, are part of the Americas. Thus, technically the Japanese who dominate the commercial and cultural life of Sao Paulo, Brazil, are themselves Asian Americans. And, in Brazil Native Americans are called Amerindians.

Multicultural Education

In addition to increased diversity in our classrooms, there has been a change in the way schools have responded to diversity. For example, before 1975, many children with special needs were systematically refused services in public schools; others were relegated to custodial care in self-contained classrooms. The **Individuals with Disabilities Education Act (IDEA)** changed this approach, and other laws were passed to require schools to meet the needs of all their students (see Chapter 3, Historical Developments). The increased diversity in our nation's schools has resulted in the movement known as **multicultural** or **anti-bias education,** which "involves transforming the schools in ways that promote educational equity and justice for all groups . . ." (Banks & Banks, 1997, p. xiii). The movement grew out of the ferment of the civil rights movement of the 1960s, with first ethnic and racial groups demanding that schools make changes to more accurately reflect the various groups that make up the student population; later, other groups joined the movement (Banks & Banks, 1997).

Today the purpose of multicultural education is to make sure all children experience equity in our schools—equal opportunity to experiences that will prepare them to succeed in society and the implementation of fair, just, and reasonable educational practices for all children. Multicultural education has been a powerful voice in advocating for the rights of minority students in our school, but we still have a long way to go. Minority students are disproportionately represented in special education programs, suspensions and other forms of discipline, and in the lower level classes, while mainstream White and Asian students are disproportionately represented in Gifted and Talented programs, Advanced Placement, and International Baccalaureate programs.

Multiethnic and multiracial children are students of color and experience all the harassment, prejudice, and discrimination students of color experience. Thus they fit squarely within multicultural education's purpose and mission. The multiethnic and multiracial children's **phenotypes** (physical appearance) complicate this issue; generally, the darker they are—or the more obvious traditional race-specific features they have—the more they experience prejudice from mainstream White people, while the lighter they are and the more their features approximate traditional European physiognomy, the more they experience distrust, prejudice, and **marginalization** from other minorities, including their own minority heritage. And, of course, the more their physical appearance does not match traditional racial and ethnic profiles, the more they are harassed, with the neverending and insulting, "Well, what are you, anyway?"

Additionally, according to Root (2003), they experience a variety of harassment from all single-race groups. Based on research, Maria Root has developed fifty of the most common comments and questions children of mixed heritage experience (2003). These include:

- You are told "You have to choose; you can't be both."
- You are accused of not acting or wanting to be Latino, Asian, Black. . . .
- You have repeatedly been the recipient of stares or longer than passing glances from strangers.
- Your choice of friends has been interpreted as your "selling out" or not being authentic.
- You have been accused of "acting or wanting to be White."
- You have been subjected to jokes about mixed-race people.
- You have been told "You think you're too good for your own kind."
- Your parents or relatives compete to "claim" you for their own racial or ethnic group.
- People assume you are confused about your racial identity or have a hard time figuring it out.
- People speak to you in foreign languages because of your physical appearance.
- You are told, "Society doesn't recognize mixed race."
- You have been told you must be full of self-loathing or hatred because of how you racially identify yourself.
- Your mother was assumed to be your nanny or maid.
- You enrolled in a Spanish class so you can say "yes" in Spanish to the question "So you speak the language?" to prove your authenticity.

The increasing number of multiethnic and multiracial children in our society, and the increasing advocacy of these students and their parents, challenges a concept called **essentialism** (Fish, 2002)—the notion that there is something essentially scientific about the minor biological characteristics that define membership to racial or ethnic groups in this country, that these groups are mutually exclusive, and that a person cannot belong to more than one group. Unfortunately, teachers and curriculum specialists tend to perpetuate this approach. Even lists of multicultural books and resources are categorized under these single-race labels, with few if any resources for multiethnic or multiracial children.

Francis Wardle teaches diversity to both undergraduate and graduate education students. At the onset of each class students are asked to define race and ethnicity and to discuss what they know about meeting the needs of children who don't neatly fit into any of the Census categories. Almost all the students believe that race is a biological construct—and none have any clue about how to meet the needs of multiethnic and multiracial children and their families.

One of the central tasks of multicultural education is to proactively advocate for students in our early childhood programs and schools who experience prejudice, marginalization, invisibility, and lack of equality, which includes multiethnic and multiracial children. Any view of diversity and multicultural education that limits itself to single racial and ethnic groups ignores children who are themselves truly multicultural—multiracial and multiethnic children (Thompson, 1999). Schools must learn to include these children and their families within the overall school's approach.

Chapter Feature
Bill of Rights for Racially Mixed People

I have the right

Not to justify my existence in this world.

Not to keep the races separate within me.

Not to be responsible for people's discomfort with my personal ambiguity.

Not to justify my ethnic legitimacy.

I have the right

To identify myself differently than strangers expect me to identify.

To identify myself differently from how my parents identify me.

To identify myself differently than my brothers and sisters.

To identify myself differently in different situations.

I have the right

To create a vocabulary to communicate about being multiracial.

To change my identity over my lifetime—and more than once.

To have loyalties and identify with more than one group of people.

To freely choose whom I befriend and love.

From Root (1996), p. 7.

Increasing Advocacy

The increasing number of interracial families and multiethnic and multiracial students are putting pressure on our schools to make significant changes. Additionally, a variety of national and international organizations are providing support for this growing population and advocating radical changes in institutions throughout the world (Olumide, 2002). The change on the 2000 Census is a direct result of this advocacy. Other examples are found in Internet sites and research.

Internet Sites.   The Internet has been a tremendous boon to the national and international multiethnic and multiracial movement (Wardle, 2001). Today there are a large variety of Internet sites dedicated to support and advocacy, including Interracial Voice, the Multiracial Activist, MAVIN, New People E-Magazine, and the Center for the Study of Biracial Children. Additionally, local interracial support groups have their own sites, and there are also a variety of sites dedicated to selling and distributing resources to multiethnic and multiracial families and professionals who work with this population. Internet sites have also been created in other countries, including Brazil, the United Kingdom, Germany, the Netherlands, and Australia.

Not only does the Internet provide resources and information to parents, young people, the media, and students doing research and school papers, but it bypasses traditional **gatekeepers** who insisted that any people who identified with more than one race or ethnicity were marginal and confused. These gatekeepers included journal, book, and newspaper editors; university professors; conference organizers; and advertisers.

Research.   Almost all research on multiethnic and multiracial children up and through the 1980s focused on proving these children to be marginal, pathological, and inadequate (Gibbs & Hines, 1992; Olumide, 2002; Wehrly, Kenney, & Kenney, 1999), a view still accepted by many psychologists, psychiatrists, and sociologists in the United States and England. For example, Gibbs developed an entire model focusing on conflicts of biracial adolescents (1987, 1989). The research used to develop these conclusions was conducted on children in jail, in juvenile delinquency caseloads, and/or in therapy. Obviously, children of mixed ethnicity and race in these settings were like all children in the same settings: dysfunctional compared to other children. But, because there was no true sense of the total number of multiethnic and multiracial children in this country, it was impossible to determine if the numbers were abnormal or not. Being a confused and pathological multiethnic or multiracial child became self-fulfilling: When they were in settings for the treatment of problems, professionals would identify them as multiethnic and multiracial; but when they were functioning well in schools, college, sports teams, and community groups, they were identified with the single race or ethnicity of one of their parents.

Treatment of multiethnic and multiracial children was based on the assumption that their problems were caused by confusion about their identity and that fully embracing their minority—or lowest status—heritage would eliminate this sense of confusion (Gibbs & Hines, 1992; McRoy & Freeman, 1986; Olumide, 2002).

In the 1980s a new group of students, products of the interethnic and interracial marriages of the 1960s, entered our universities. To their alarm and disgust, they discovered that they were supposedly marginal and dysfunctional; further, they realized there was almost no reliable and valid research on healthy multiethnic and multiracial children. Francis Wardle has worked with these students for over twenty years. The most common question from these college students is always "Where is all the research?" Because of a dearth of research, many of these students did their required college research projects on healthy multiracial and multiethnic children. The work of Marta Cruz-Janzen is a great example (Cruz-Janzen, 1997).

Interracial Parents

Like Marta Cruz-Janzen and Francis Wardle, other parents of multiethnic and multiracial children discovered that early childhood programs and schools are often the first place their child's full heritage is officially and systematically denied—largely because the school forms have no place for their children, often not even an "other" category (Wardle, 1999). Further, school personnel are often insensitive when collecting this information, not understanding why parents are so sensitive regarding this issue. Interracial parents also discovered that, at best, teachers do not know how to support their children's healthy identity development in the classroom and, at worst, forced them to identify with their parent of color, or parent of lowest status. Even some multicultural activities reinforce this approach (York, 1991). Finally, interracial parents also realized that their children are totally invisible in the schools' curricula: no stories, pictures, articles and reports, books, or textbook items that reflect their unique family experiences. (We discuss this issue at length in Chapters 7 and 8.)

With local **support groups** and national advocacy organizations, many interracial parents have become far more vocal (Brown & Douglass, 1996). Parents are refusing to select only one category on official school forms. They expect teachers, counselors, psychologists, and school social workers to understand the needs of their children and not to automatically assume that any school-based problems their children may have are caused by their unique racial identity (Wehrly, Kenney, & Kenney, 1999). These parents also challenge race-specific holidays, clubs, and hidden curricula. And interracial parents expect their children to see themselves and their families in classroom materials, curricular content, and school role models.

Needs of Multiethnic and Multiracial Children

Given the lack of good research on multiethnic and multiracial children and their families, determining their needs is, at best, tricky. Much of what we believe these children need is based on what the research tells us about the needs of single-race minority children (Aboud, 1987; Cross, 1987; Gibbs, 1987; McRoy & Freeman, 1986; Phinney & Rotheram, 1987). Furthermore, the limited research results suggest multiethnic and multiracial children have a more difficult task in developing a healthy identity than children of single-race background and that children whose physical characteristics seems to be less salient to their peers cause confusion among other children regarding their identity (Aboud, 1987; Gibbs & Hines, 1992; Phinney & Rotheram, 1987). Finally, as Root (2003) shows, these children receive harassment from all sides, including teachers and the school's professional staff.

As we discuss at length in Chapter 5, a child's age greatly impacts his or her view of the world and his or her needs from the world. And each child's social context is different. With this in mind, our tentative beliefs about the overall needs of these children—including but not limited to their early childhood and school experience and recognizing the already discussed tremendous diversity within this large group—include:

- Exposure to families like their own, peers like them, and multiethnic and multiracial heroes.
- A label to describe who they are and to answer children and adults (Brandell, 1988; Jacobs, 1992; Wardle, 1999). This is necessitated by the apparent need of people in this country to always know a person's ethnic or racial label.

Chapter Feature
Development of Racial and Ethnic Identity

Learning a sense of racial and ethnic identity is a complex developmental process. In this country, children progress through the following stages (Aboud, 1987):

- **Infancy:** Children can discriminate between dark and light stimuli, dark and light faces.
- **Ages 3 to 4:** Children can recognize Black and White children, but not their own racial or ethnic identity. Children are very interested in physical similarities and differences.
- **Ages 5 to 9:** Children learn to recognize their own racial identity label and develop beginning

awareness of group affiliation. Awareness of group belonging comes after learning group similarities

- **Age 7:** Recognition by White children of a Black child, Black children of a White child (racially).
- **Age 8:** Recognition by children of peers from other ethnic groups (Native American, Asian, Hispanic). Apparently, the salient features of these groups are less clear to children than those of White and Black children.
- **Ages 8 to 10:** Development of racial or ethnic constancy and a stronger sense of group belonging.

From Wardle (2003).

Chapter Feature
Student Profile

The conscientious teacher decided to have all her second-grade children involved in a Black History Month experience. She asked the Black children to develop a presentation about their families' backgrounds. A young girl eagerly started putting together a report on her grandfather, because her grandfather had been a leader of a small Caribbean country and because she was, understandably, very proud of him. Lots of newspaper clippings, magazine articles, and personal artifacts were available to create a wonderful, rich presentation, which she did with considerable care and deliberation. The teacher reviewed each child's offerings on the morning before the activity. After examining the presentation about the Caribbean leader the teacher told the child she could not present it to the class. The child was, of course, crushed.

The teacher rejected this child's effort because the child's grandfather was a multiracial Carib/White Canadian. The teacher had automatically assumed he would be Black, because the child was darker than the mainstream White children in her predominantly White classroom and because her mother was Black. The teacher did not see how she could use the presentation as part of a Black History Month celebration.

- Understanding staff who can help, support, and encourage students to explore their unique physical characteristics and know how to help them do so.
- Lots of opportunities to process their identity—books, mirrors, dress-ups, art activities, talking to others, studying racial and ethnic diversity, exploring family histories, studying the history of multiethnic and multiracial people and the history of racial categories, and deconstruction of our single-race language.
- Environments where they feel they belong—mixed-race social groups, curricular content, role models, pictures on the wall and in books, etc.
- Never having to choose one side of their heritage or hide, put down, or discredit one parent and one parent's family (Root, 1996; Wardle, 1999).
- The opportunity to be normal children without continually having to justify who they are, who their parents are, and why they are different to peers, other children's parents, teachers, administrators, counselors, etc. (Root, 1996).

Responsibility of the Schools

According to Carlos Cortes, ". . . educators who truly believe in freedom, individuality, and human dignity need to rid themselves of the unwarranted assumption of racial 'purity.' In the process they must disregard two oft-asked questions:

To what ethnic group (singular) do you belong? What race (singular) are you? For students of mixed backgrounds, such questions imply that they should reject or choose between parts of their heritage" (2000, p. 9). What does this mean for educators? At a minimum it means that ". . . they should support such students as they contemplate or assert their individual, often unique identities. At the same time, they should avoid the knee-jerk tendency of trying to cram racially-mixed students into inappropriate single-race categories" (Cortes, 2000, p. 9).

In later chapters we discuss in detail ways educators can respond to these children and their families, including finding ways to include them in curricular materials (written and visual) and providing opportunities for the children to explore their unique identities in positive and developmentally appropriate ways. Most of all, educators must

1. Understand that the old ways of categorizing students do not work, and are often destructive.
2. Learn all they can about the needs of these families.
3. Understand that in a society fixated on race and ethnicity, multiethnic and multiracial students have unique struggles that demand their support.
4. Recognize that these students require educators to be understanding and to support their ethnic and racial identity development—especially during the critical adolescent years.

Administrators, counselors, social workers, and psychologists also come into contact with these children and their families and should provide the support and nurturance they need. Like teachers, these professionals need adequate training in the unique characteristics of this population; further, because they often work with families under stress, they must know the latest information about working with multiethnic and multiracial families and intervention techniques that work (Wardle, 1999; Wehrly, Kenney, & Kenney, 1999). Of most importance, school psychologists, social workers, and special education teachers must rid themselves and their professions of the common assumption that people who cross racial and ethnic barriers to marry are somehow dysfunctional and that their children will have more social, academic, and psychological problems than their single-race peers (Wardle, 1999; Wehrly, Kenney, & Kenney, 1999).

School Forms.   As has already been discussed in this chapter, a major problem for multiethnic and multiracial families and their children are the federal forms almost all early childhood programs and schools are required to use and the **OMB categories** used on these foms. These forms come under the jurisdiction and enforcement of the federal Office of Management and Budget, OMB. Specifically, OMB directive #15 requires schools, "to provide standard classifications for record keeping, collection and presentation of data on race and ethnicity in program administrative reporting and statistical activities" (Root, 1996, p. 411). Directive #15 was developed to fulfill the requirements of various federal laws regarding equity and equality.

Chapter Feature
Supporting Multiethnic and Multiracial Children

To serve *all* children and families, our programs must be places in which

1. Multiracial and multiethnic children see themselves and their families in books, curricular content, materials, artwork, posters, and doll and people sets. They also need multiracial/multiethnic heroes.
2. Staff assist these children in integrating their diverse and complex heritage into a unified, healthy self-esteem and identity.
3. Activities and curricular approaches never require children to isolate part of their background over another part.
4. These children have a label (multiracial, biracial, mixed) to use to identify themselves and to respond to single-race children and adults.
5. A positive climate supports their parents' choice to cross societal barriers, and no one (staff, parent, child) is allowed to question parental motivation.
6. Staff provide support, accurate information, and resources to help multiracial/multiethnic parents raise their children (Wardle 1999).

From Wardle (2001a).

Horror stories abound about the processes some schools use to collect this data. One parent in Chicago was told her biracial child could not enter the public school until the parent selected a single racial category for her child. Teachers have been instructed by administrators to "sight" categorize the children in their classrooms, and parents are rarely told that providing racial information on their children is a voluntary process. Principals are sometimes told by the school district's central administration to select one category, usually based on either the child's physical appearance or confidential information in the child's files. Finally, some interracial parents have been told that not selecting the minority category for their child shortchanges critically needed funds for the school.

Usually, parents of early childhood and elementary students fill out the forms; in middle and high school, students fill them out themselves. Thus, just as multiethnic and multiracial children enter the adolescent years of identity crisis—including racial/ethnic identity—they discover that their school does not recognize their unique identity. They are required to reject or ignore the heritage of one of their parents and his or her family. While some school forms include an "other" category, one adolescent angrily proclaimed, "I am not an other, I am a somebody!" (Benjamin-Wardle, 1994). While the 2000 Census allowed people to select more than one racial or ethnic category, in aggregating the results, the federal government collapsed the data back into the original minority and

White categories of the old Census (Zack, 2002). Within two years of the Census, OMB is supposed to adapt federal school forms to the new Census approach—in this case, allowing people to select more than one racial/ethnic category. However, according to an official at the Colorado Department of Education, this will not occur until at least 2004, because OMB cannot agree on how to aggregate the results.

When the change is eventually made, there will be opposition, based largely on ignorance and lack of concern, since schools are not training staff on the new approach. Further, it is logical to assume the various groups that opposed the Census change will find ways to pressure local schools not to fully adopt the new process (Zack, 2002). Finally, as was done during the 2000 Census, some traditional civil rights activists may insist that families who choose more than one racial category for their child do not support civil rights and equality (Wardle, 2002c; Zack, 2002).

Educational Equity.   The multicultural education movement that grew out of the civil rights movement of the 1960s demands that schools respond to meet the unique needs of students from groups that have not been adequately served by the schools. The democratic ideal is that every child has the right to a free and appropriate education that maximizes his or her potential (Banks & Banks, 1997). This concept goes beyond equality, because it requires schools to be responsive to the unique factors that contribute to each child's school success—such as special education students who have IEPs (Individual Education Plans) that often differ substantially from the school's overall standards. Equity for multiethnic and multiracial children clearly requires schools to change radically. These changes will be discussed through the book, but include training of teachers and other professional staff, adopting a racial classification system based on the new Census approach, providing and using inclusive curricula and instructional materials, and conducting a careful examination of single-race activities, groups, celebrations, and programs.

Conclusion

The history of this nation is filled with people from all corners of the globe who have brought a richness of different religions, races, values, languages, and customs to this country. Institutions—including schools—have evolved in different ways to meet the needs of this rich tapestry of people. The multicultural education movement, begun as a result of the civil rights movement, has challenged schools to change to meet our increasingly diverse student population. Since multiethnic and multiracial children and their families are an ever-increasing part of our schools' diversity, meeting the needs of these children is simply the next step in this march to full equality and in making sure every child has equal opportunity to succeed in our schools. Multiethnic and multiracial children have unique needs that are not being met by our early childhood programs and schools. In the spirit of equity and working effectively with all families, schools—and teachers—must learn how to work effectively with this new and increasing population.

Questions/Projects

1. Find a multiracial or multiethnic family in your program or school and interview them. Determine the racial and ethnic makeup of the parents, the combined makeup of the student(s), and how the parents are raising the children.

2. Search the Internet for websites that cater to the needs of multiethnic and multiethnic children. Develop a resource list and share it with the class.

3. Find three or four contemporary college textbooks on multicultural education. Summarize what these books say about how the needs of multiracial and multiethnic children should be met. Do you feel their coverage is adequate and accurate?

4. Do you have a multiethnic or multiracial friend or colleague? If so, interview him or her and determine who raised him or her, how he or she views self-identity, and other views that person might have on this topic.

Resources

Book

Multiracial child resource book
MAVIN Foundation
600 First Avenue
Suite 600
Seattle, WA 98104
http://www.mavinfoundation.org

Websites

Association of Multi-Ethnic Americans (AMEA)
http://www.ameasite.org/

Center for the Study of Biracial Children, CSBC
http://www.csbc.cncfamily.com

Interracial Voice Online Magazine
http://www.Interracialvoice.com

National Advocacy for MultiethnicMultiracial People
http://www.namecentral.org/

New People E-Magazine
http://www.Newpeoplemagazine.com

People in Harmony
http://www.pih.org.uk

Project race
http://www.projectrace.com

You don't look Japanese
http//:www.angelfire.com/or/biracial/

2

Traditional Approaches

Multicultural education by the week, by the month, and definitively by the group—that's the approach far too many schools employ today. September 15 through October 15 is Hispanic Heritage Month, November is Native American Heritage Month, February is Black History Month, March is Women's History Month, and May is Asian/Pacific American Heritage Month. Even the Jewish population has been designated a time to celebrate: April 14 through 21 is Jewish Heritage Week. Early childhood programs and schools using this form of multicultural education claim that at least something is being done, which, they believe, is better than doing nothing. They believe this approach is a vast improvement from a totally mainstream White, male, **Eurocentric** curriculum, with nothing at all for students of groups of color in the curriculum, even in schools that have significant numbers of students of color.

The one-group approach to diversity results in a month studying the typical heroes of specific, isolated, ethnic and racial minority groups, while ignoring everyone else. African Americans, Asians, or Native Americans cannot be included in September and women are only discussed in March. Students decorate classrooms with images and artifacts deemed representative of the group such as Kente cloths for African Americans and piñatas and colorful crepe paper flowers for Latinos. It doesn't matter that not all African or Latino groups integrate these artifacts or cultural symbols or that Africa is a vast continent full of tremendous linguistic, religious, tribal, historical, artistic, and cultural diversity. Students learn songs, even in various languages, perform dances, eat traditional foods often at school assemblies, put on parades, and host numerous festivals. Once the celebration is over, all talk about the group ceases and students go on to study the next group.

This chapter examines traditional approaches to multicultural education in early childhood programs and kindergarten through twelfth grade (K–12) public schools in the United States today—both celebration-by-the-month approaches and more sophisticated and integrated solutions. We will examine some of the problems of these approaches to teaching authentic multicultural education both to mainstream White students and to students of color. Additionally, we will explore how the traditional inclusion of multicultural education in our schools is counterproductive for multiethnic and multiracial students, primarily by rendering them invalid members of all groups in their backgrounds and invisible members of society. We argue that an authentic approach to multicultural education must expand beyond single ethnic/race groups to include multiethnic and multiracial students, their families, and their unique experiences.

FOCUS QUESTIONS

1. Although the United States has historically been a nation of extensive interracial mixing, why has mainstream society, including PreK–12 teachers, failed to acknowledge and understand the lives of multiethnic and multiracial persons?

2. How does the school's completion of required OMB ethnicity/race forms reinforce the traditional approaches toward multicultural education?

3. What are the limitations to today's traditional approaches to multicultural education? What changes are needed to reform today's approaches to multicultural education?

4. What are the effects of the traditional approaches to multicultural education on the self-identity and self-concept of multiethnic and multiracial persons? What are the effects on mainstream Whites and students of color?

Single Race/Ethnicity Approach

The most popular approach of multicultural education in U.S. schools today is to study isolated and mutually exclusive groups during specific time periods. While studying a Native American unit, a biracial child wanted to include information about his African American heritage; another child wanted to include her mainstream White European heritage during Hispanic Heritage Month. In both instances, however, the teacher rejected the information because it did not "fit" the theme—and, she believed, including other races and ethnicities confused the message of group solidarity and differences. The students were told that other heritages would be studied during their respective times or units, but not together. One teacher even tried to justify his actions by stating that he did not want to make "full" members of the race or ethnic group feel that the celebration and their heritage were being watered down.

Unfortunately, one result of the single-group approach to multicultural education is that each group competes for the most time and attention in the school's calendar (Wardle, 1999). Another result is that multiethnic and multiracial persons are not considered legitimate members of any traditional racial or ethnic group. Rather than affirming their multiple ancestries and the existence of other persons like them, the teachers often make these students feel abnormal, isolated, rejected, and, as always, invisible. When Francis Wardle asked a Sesame Street

Chapter Feature
Avoid Diversity by Celebration

- To teach about Hispanic culture and history only at Cinco de Mayo and on September 15 shortchanges the important contributions of Hispanic people, histories, and culture to this society. Further, children with a Hispanic background need to see themselves in the program all the time.
- It's a "tourist" approach—communicating to children that diversity consists only of dance, food, and costumes, and that we can learn about diversity like tourists.
- It is not an integrated approach. Diversity should be woven richly throughout the entire curriculum, in every subject area, and throughout the entire year.
- It tends to segregate the program and its families—Hispanic families celebrate Cinco de Mayo, Black families Martin Luther King Day, and so on.
- It reinforces a group approach to culture, which teaches that everyone from the same group is the same. We need to stress diversity within groups, as much as diversity from group to group.
- Celebrations in early childhood programs and schools often focus on food and drink, as well as a high level of activity. Not only are the foods and drinks served usually inconsistent with good nutrition for children, but the atmosphere teaches children that the only way to have a good time is to drink and eat. Goals for many early childhood programs and schools include developing healthy nutritional food choices and eating habits, developing behaviors in children that resist substance abuse, and learning in low-stress, nurturing environments.

From Wardle (2003).

researcher, why the program's Race Project did not include multiethnic and multiracial children, she replied that this would simply be "too difficult to do" (Wardle, 1994).

Diversity within Traditional Racial Groups

But who or what are Hispanic? Hispanics/Latinos are not a race. Rather, they are a broadly diverse conglomerate of people who could be Asian, Black, White, Indian, or numerous overlapping combinations in between. Indigenous Indians originally inhabited Latin American nations and other nations in North and South America. It is believed that even indigenous populations were not isolated and encountered and mixed with other groups from various parts of the world. Once Spaniards, Portuguese, English, Dutch, French, and other European colonizers arrived and invaded Indian lands, they also mixed with the indigenous populations, creating extensive mestizo (White and Indigenous/Indian) off-spring. Indeed, the mestizo populations soon became the majority in many Latin American nations. Today, Mexico is recognized as a predominantly mestizo nation. Later, European colonizers brought African slaves, leading to extensive interracial mulatto (Black and White) and **zambo** or **cholo** (Black and Indigenous) populations. Brazil represents the nation with the largest Black/African, mulatto, and zambo population outside of Africa. Yet, it must not be forgotten that most Latino communities, whether in Latin America or the United States, are racially divided and stratified according to racial mixing and skin-color variations, with persons considered pure Whites at the top of the social ladder and pure Blacks and Indians at the bottom.

By the same token, who are **African Americans?** They are a racially mixed people who include persons from the African continent as well as their descendants from all over the world. The same could be said of Asians and Native Americans. Asians include groups of people with very distinct phenotypes such as Chinese, Asian Indians, and Malaysian. Just as North America is a racially mixed continent, most nations across the world have, throughout history, experienced racial mixing. There is no pure race anywhere in the world (Fish, 2002; Zack, 2002).

Even those people we refer to as **mainstream Whites** in this book contain an extensive level of diversity. Mainstream White(s) is the dominant White cultural group in the United States. This group, while having integrated other European Whites, developed from the original worldviews brought to North America by White Anglo Saxon Protestants (WASPs). Technically, **Anglo Saxon** refers to the Germanic peoples, such as the Angles, Saxons, and Jutes, who conquered England during the fifth and sixth centuries A.D. and are popularly believed to be the originators of the English language as well as the "traditions of political liberty and equality" (Springer, 2001). It also includes some level of Vikings, Romans, and others who conquered and left their mark on Great Britain. Like all world cultures, White Anglo culture has changed and evolved over generations through multiple **acculturations**, or the process of integrating cultural ideas and values from all the groups it has come in contact with. Clearly, these groups have been numerous, so that today's mainstream White culture does not resemble the founding Anglo Saxon culture or the White part of today's multiracial British culture. The mainstream represents the **macroculture** with other microcultures or subcultures subsumed within it. The mainstream White population in this country does not include Latino Whites or White Spaniards.

There is, as we have said, tremendous diversity within each of these single group categories—what we like to call **diversity of diversity**. And, of course, there are a lot of cultural, traditional, and historical conflicts and tensions between people from various groups within each of these categories. This includes the White category, where people from historical European enemy nations, such England and France, may well conflict, or people directly from Europe and Whites from South America have quite different cultural and historical experiences.

Chapter Feature
Student Profile: Tania Shifko

Tania Shifko is a fifth-grade student at a public school in a large western city. The school has a very diverse student population. The largest groups are mainstream Whites, Latinos, and African Americans. Tania's mother is Peruvian Quechua Indian and her father is White German. Along with many other Germans, his parents escaped the turmoil of World War II to settle in Peru. Tania's parents met as students at a university in Peru. Her father's parents longed to return to their homeland and moved back. After Tania's parents married, they decided to follow them to Germany. They then returned to Peru when Tania was 6, and she attended first, second, and third grades there. After returning to Germany for one year, the family finally came to the United States. Tania speaks Spanish, Quechua, and German. She was placed in a Spanish bilingual classroom where she is learning English. Tania's grandparents visited her family for the summer, and during that time she learned a lot about her German ancestry through German books with many pictures. Her grandparents helped her learn German and also learn about German culture and geography.

For a class activity Tania's teacher asked students to place a photo of themselves on a map of the world and link it with a string to their place of origin. Tania tied two strings, one to Peru and the other to Germany. During the first month of the school year the school also celebrates Hispanic Heritage Month. Tania's teacher asked parents and members of the community to come to the school and share stories of their heritage. She also asked the Latino children to bring something from their heritage to share during the Hispanic Heritage Month celebration. As a result, Tania asked her grandparents to participate and decided to wear a German native dress that her grandmother brought for her. Tania's teacher tells them that they cannot include her German heritage because it is not part of the Hispanic celebration theme. The teacher asks them to share her Peruvian background instead. Tania's grandparents become very offended and state that Tania is not Hispanic either but Quechua. They try to explain that the Quechua are still exploited and suffer in their own country because of colonization by the Hispanics and current oppression by the Hispanic ruling class of Peru. Besides, they emphasized to the teacher, Latin America is also made up of people from all over the world. Germans such as their own family, as well as Italians, other Europeans, and Asians, all moved to Latin America.

Race, Ethnicity, and Culture

As we have pointed out, a major goal of multicultural education is to reform P–12 schools to enable all students of diverse racial, ethnic, disability, gender, and social class to experience educational excellence (Banks, 2001, 2002; Davidman & Davidman, 1997; Diaz, 2001; Nieto, 1994; Ooka Pang, 2001). This is obviously a fair and egalitarian goal. However, to implement this goal, everyone involved must understand what it means and what it is we are talking about. Regular surveys of students in teacher education courses and of current P–12 classroom teachers indicate considerable confusion about what multicultural education is and is not (Cruz-Janzen, 2000). It is challenging, at best, to determine a course of action to reform schools when we are not all on the same page of understanding. One student expressed her frustration this way:

> Each class/professor gives me a different definition. Is a boys- or girls-only school diverse or multicultural? How is a school made up mostly of one racial or ethnic group diverse or multicultural, but a predominantly White school is not? Are Chicano and African American studies multicultural? I wish they would define these things clearly.

Marta Cruz-Janzen conducts needs assessment surveys at the beginning of each Introduction to Education and Introduction to Multicultural Education course she teaches. These courses are designed primarily for preservice teacher candidates, but also include some graduate students. Results of the surveys show that an alarming number of undergraduate and graduate students do not even understand the concept of diversity or believe that they themselves have any diversity. They lack an understanding of race and ethnicity and have received little information about multiethnic and multiracial people. These results reflect confusion regarding certain terminology, such as *diversity, culture, race,* and *ethnicity.* It is assumed that these terms are synonymous and/or interchangeable and that they refer exclusively to persons of color.

Understanding Race, Ethnicity, and Culture

It is not uncommon for mainstream White students to make comments such as: "I have no culture; I'm just White" and "We don't need multicultural education because we don't have any [students of color]." Most teachers in our public P–12 schools are mainstream White and middle class, while the student population in these schools is increasingly non-White and poor. Because mainstream Whites see themselves lacking culture and diversity, they tend to perceive that culture and multicultural education are about studying others and not themselves. Multicultural education curricular content that totally ignores the rich and diverse backgrounds that make up mainstream White cultures perpetuates this view. German spring festivals with traditional maypoles; Dutch bagpipe bands, tulip festivals, and clog dance festivals; English May Festivals with their Greetings of the May and Morris dance performances; St. Patrick's Day; Dutch St. Nicholas celebrations in December; Armistice Day remembrances in November; Guy Fawke's Day (celebrating an attempt to blow up the British Houses of Parliament); and other numerous European celebrations, customs, and traditions still celebrated by mainstream Whites do not seem to register as diversity or culture (except St. Patrick's Day). We don't even seem to acknowledge the tremendous language diversity of our mainstream White population. A college student who commented, "That's not cultural, that's just White!" brought forth the realization that mainstream Whites have normed their experiences and reality while unnorming everyone else's. Another mainstream White college student stated:

> I attended a mostly White school. We didn't have much diversity. I wish we had more multicultural students. I have never known a multicultural person.

Often educators with some awareness of culture and multiculturalism believe that the mainstream White culture doesn't need to be taught because it already permeates the curriculum and is taught during every day, week, and month of the year—what we call a Eurocentric curriculum. This approach fosters the sense that the mainstream White culture is normal, is the standard to which all other content is compared, and is in no need of any examination. It assumes that only the cultures of persons of color have to be examined, thus leading to the ingrained perception that they are not normal and perpetuating the idea that teaching other cultures is simply something added to the otherwise normal experiences.

Valid multicultural curricula must also focus on raising the cultural awareness of mainstream Whites. It must teach them that they, as everyone else, have cultures, ethnicities, and race. A mainstream White teacher puzzled, "How do you present multicultural lessons in a predominantly White school?" As Howard (1999) writes, many mainstream Whites have not learned, and have not needed to learn, to be "**multiculturally competent** people." The beginning of this process is to understand ones' own culture and diversity.

The Process of Assimilation

The **assimilation** process enthusiastically practiced for most of our history required all non-White Anglo Saxon citizens to become as White Anglo Saxon as possible. Assimilation entailed the process of shedding cultures rather than retaining them. Culture and ethnicity and non-English languages became taboo notions to be extricated from the vocabulary along with the traits they represent. They had to be eradicated from the consciousness of those wishing to become "American." White Europeans from non-Anglo Saxon countries had to shed or conceal their apparent ethnic characteristics and traits in order to assimilate into and be acceptable to mainstream White society.

Obviously, the process of assimilation was a process of Anglicization. Non-Anglo immigrants took on Anglo-sounding first names. Even last names were Anglicized: Gatsiapoulos became Gatchis, Rivera translated to River, among numerous examples. Polish names were systematically changed. Poles, Scandinavians, Germans and other non-English speaking immigrants were forbidden from using their native languages in public schools and other public places.

By the same token, minorities already in this country had to prove their American—Anglo Saxon—worth. Native American students were taken from their homes and placed in Christian mission boarding schools to learn English and become good Christians—a trait of Anglo Saxon Americans. They had to shed their "savage" and "uncivilized" ways to become "civilized." A Native American friend of Francis Wardle bemoaned what the federal government did to his Pueblo people when New Mexico became a state: "They made us wear trousers (instead of shawls), took away the siesta, and sent us to Santa Fe to learn useful trades, even though we had our own farms to care for." Obviously, this approach has literally destroyed many Native American languages because their oral traditions rely on each generation's learning the language and then passing it on to the next.

During World War I strong anti-German feelings led to movements to a ban on using the German language. Once de-ethnicized, immigrants learned to internalize the beliefs, values, and traditions of the dominant mainstream Whites. This process naturally prevented parents from passing on their heritage(s) to future generations. Then and only then would they become the new "true" Americans, and a new country could be born. While some mainstream Whites are aware of their diverse European ancestry, it is not uncommon for many others to say:

> I don't know what I am—just White. I don't know anything about my family. I don't know where they came from or when they came. As far as I know, they have always been just White. They don't talk about anything else.

Many mainstream Whites are not aware of the sacrifices their ancestors made for them to join the dominant White Anglo Saxon Protestant "image of the real American" (Howard, 1993). Some persons assimilated as mainstream Whites had to conceal their non-White progeny or risk being expelled from the dominant group:

> It's like he doesn't want to remember that . . . he was teased and really ridiculed. . . . He didn't want me to go through the same things when he immigrated here. He was different . . . and nobody liked him. He was kind of an outcast. So I think that's why he wanted me to be White.

As we have suggested, mainstream White culture in this country has changed and evolved over generations through the process of integrating cultural ideas and values from all the groups it has come in contact with through the decades. Today, mainstream White culture in this country reflects influences from each and all those groups, including other European peoples, Black/African Americans, Latinos, and Native Americans. Whites today are far more "American" than European; our macro-culture in fact appears to be closer to the culture of Australia than to present-day England.

What Is Race?

In this country there is much confusion between *genotype* and *phenotype*. Genotype is the genetic code each person carries in his or her chromosomes; phenotype is the physical characteristics an individual displays. However, two people with the same genotype may have very different phenotypes. Many believe that biological and genetic attributes correlate with physical appearance and that everyone in a group shares common, uniquely distinguishable, physical traits—called essentalism (Fish, 2002). Among the most prevalent physical traits are skin color; facial features, such as shape of lips, nose, and eyes; and hair color and texture. Comments such as "You don't look Latina" or "You don't look Black" are commonly directed at individuals who do not meet the fixed stereotypical "guidelines" for members of certain groups. A Black, Asian, Native American, or Latino person with straight blonde hair may be chastised as looking "too [mainstream] White," etc. Interestingly, these supposed "agreed upon" folk typologies for racial membership differ from country to country (Fish, 2002).

Obviously, this notion of physical traits defining group membership poses extreme problems for multiethnic and multiracial students who are often placed into the group that they most closely look like even when they have no biological connection to the group. Francis Wardle's children have routinely been labeled Latino, Native American, Asian Indian, Asian, Hawaiian, Vietnamese, Brazilian, and Samoan, even though they are Black/White. Multiethnic and multiracial children are often tossed about from group to group, accepted by none and rejected by all, and told: "You do not fit. You are not enough." The abuses multiethnic and multiracial children are subjected to are often excruciating. Marta Cruz-Janzen's daughter was excluded from a traditional African dance group because she didn't look "Black enough" and stood out "too much." She was asked, "How can we have a Black dance troupe with a White-looking—and blond—person in it?" In middle school the same child was teased by her Latino classmates about her blonde hair. Because it was so important for her to fit in with her Latino classmates, when she was 13 she dyed her hair black minutes before the family portrait was to be taken. She explained, "I want to look more like you"—her biracial, Latino Black and Latino White, mother than her mainstream White father. "In high school she was accepted into a cheerleading squad only to find out that she was the perfect way to "integrate" the team with a person of color, while still blending in with the other mainstream White cheerleaders.

What Is Culture?

It is common in this country to make a direct association between race and culture, as if the diverse human attributes of culture are somehow inherited at birth and are directly related to a person's racial or ethnic category and phenotype (Wilson, 1984). Children are seen as the product of the culture of their designated group, be it Asian, mainstream White, Native American, African American, or Latino (Wardle, 1996b). For example, casual mention is often made of "Black culture" as if all Blacks in the United States share the same worldviews by virtue of being dark-skinned. We stereotype all Black people as thinking and behaving the same, all Latinos of the same religion, family's practices, and so on. Then students from diverse groups of color are expected to be the experts in their group. During multicultural activities these students are expected to share cultural and historical information and conduct presentations about their group while everyone else is a passive audience. A Black student commented: "I was expected to know everything about slavery, as if my family or I was there." A college student said: "There were these group presentations and the students go through their own experiences."

Culture refers to the ways people view the world, acquired simultaneously as individuals and as members of various groups, and represents their orientation to all living things, their reality, and their worldview. It includes knowledge, values, beliefs, traditions, mores, and concepts of time from the past into the present and on to the future (King, Chipman, & Cruz-Janzen, 1994). And culture includes discipline methods used by parents on their children, educational goals and expectations, and gender role expectations. Culture represents both individual and multiple group membership because, for example, an individual with a disability such as blindness develops a unique worldview to accommodate his or her needs while also acquiring the worldviews needed to function within his or her racial or ethnic group. A Latino deaf and blind student explained: "I am Mexican American and love my culture, my people. But I also need to connect with other deaf-blind persons like myself in order to make complete sense of my world. I may not hear the music or see the steps, but I learned to dance in a school for the deaf and blind. I enjoy dancing [Mexican]." Another person of Irish ancestry and confined to a wheelchair also explained:

> As a [mainstream] White of Irish ancestry I participate fully in my cultural traditions and want to pass them on to my children. As a disabled person I also see the world from that perspective and advocate for the rights of disabled persons. Often things, even homes and sidewalks, are not built to accommodate our needs because abled persons do not see our world. Irish people love celebrations with lots of food. It means a lot to me to live in a home where I can reach the kitchen cabinets and am able to cook without assistance. I can participate equally in my culture.

Group Membership

So what is "Black culture"? How and where is this "Black culture" defined and shared equally by various groups collapsed within the Black/African American category? How do Blacks who have lived in this country for generations, Blacks recently immigrated from Africa, Blacks from the Caribbean, and Blacks from other parts of the world who now share our soil define "Black culture"? (Not to mention Blacks who live in other American countries such as Canada, Mexico, Brazil, and Belize.) A gathering of Latinos is irrefutable proof of the variation within "Latino culture." Meeting a person who somehow does not conform to the expectation that they will "act" Asian, Black, Latino, or White really confuses some people. This happens both within and between designated race and ethnic groups—and the mainstream White group.

James Banks calls this need to define group membership "in-groups" and "out-groups," often referred to as the "minimal group paradigm" (2001). Within each group exist definitions and expectations of in-group members as well as definitions and expectations of out-group members. This "sense of connectedness" often provides valuable support for individuals within groups, but also becomes manifested as "us" and "them" posturing, as defining and limiting behaviors, feelings, and perceptions. Everyone becomes an "expert" as to "who is good enough to belong to our group." Often this idea of group belonging is expressed as being a sellout to your group. Recently, BET TV (Black Entertainment Network) devoted an entire program segment to "Black sellouts." Even Francis Wardle, who is proudly British, was accused by other Brits of not "being English enough"!

Unfortunately, group membership definitions and the insistence on them to belong to the group can lead to stereotypes, prejudice, discrimination, and limitations of choices and freedoms. In other words, other group members may

A group membership approach to diversity can create an "us-versus-them" posturing.

see an Asian person's legitimate group membership with skepticism because the person does not look, sound, or behave Asian enough. Someone not of the person's race or ethnic group may also question the person's legitimacy as Asian. A Black person without musical rhythm and athletic dexterity sometimes raises astonished eyebrows, both among Blacks and persons of other backgrounds. Many Black students find themselves pushed toward athletics, as if they are all naturally gifted athletes, and away from academics. Many—including other Blacks—do not perceive that Blacks can achieve academically on a par with individuals from other groups, especially mainstream Whites and Asians. An Asian boy who is not adept at math and computers is somehow considered abnormal.

A Black woman with a British accent, say from any of the British African colonies or Caribbean countries, is often accused of sounding too White. A Native American student shared his frustration: "People don't believe I am Indian [Native American] because I don't wear beads or my hair in braids."

A mainstream White woman spoke up in a college course, and other students in the class, of all backgrounds, were noticeably surprised when she sounded like an African American. Later in the semester a student finally asked, "Are you Black?" She admitted that she self-identified as a "White Black woman." This led to a class discussion that resulted in the students' realization that societal expectations are clearly that a mainstream White person should act, sound, and think in certain ways; that phenotype should concur with an individual's identity; and that people's behaviors and ideas should parallel the racial and ethnic identity others ascribe to them, in addition to their phenotype.

> Most people don't know how to deal with me, Blacks or Whites. Blacks are uncomfortable because they say I look too White. Blacks first treat me like an [mainstream] Anglo White. Once they find out I'm not, they are like "cool." Still, they expect me to try to be as Black as possible. It's like "can you get rid of that straight blonde hair?" Whites are uncomfortable because I look White but am not. Whites first treat me nice, like I am one of them. The minute they find out I'm not White like them, they treat me as they always treat Black people—bad! For a while I used to try to change my appearance, but then I was not comfortable with myself. I'd try to talk real [mainstream] White. I even dyed my hair brown and permed it to make it curly. Why must I change my appearance to belong?

Interestingly, mainstream White students were mostly puzzled by their perceptions of this woman's lack of legitimacy based on speech patterns—her phenotype matched but not her language. In Chapter 5 we discuss that in some countries, such as Canada, language defines ethnic group membership. Many in this country believe that Latinos must speak Spanish. On the other hand, Black students were more concerned with her phenotype—the language matched but not the physical appearance. Students perceived and judged the same person through their own, unique cultural lenses that selectively filtered physical appearance, behaviors, linguistic patterns, and ideas. A student of Chinese parents agreed, stating that many persons expected him to "act Chinese" and even speak the language just because of the way he looks. Other Chinese reproached him for not being "Chinese enough," because he was always gregarious and outspoken. He was told that he didn't act "very Asian."

A similar situation occurred when a stranger rudely chastised Francis Wardle's daughter in a convenience store. The stranger was upset that the girl's parents had not taught her Spanish. Because this Black/White student "looked Hispanic," the stranger assumed the college student was a Latina and further judged that all good Latinas must speak Spanish.

Non-Whites

Further, a person with any minority heritage must identify with that racial or ethnic group. A person could appear mainstream White, but if he or she is part non-mainstream White, self-identity as a mainstream White is not allowed. Likewise, many persons today accepted as mainstream Whites look more non-White than some African American and Latinos—Arabs, Greeks, and other North Africa and Mediterranean peoples, as well as people from the Middle East. Most Pakistani and Asian Indians are darker than many African Americans. A racially mixed Latino child came home from school saying that Asian Hindu classmates, some of whom didn't look different than her, taunted her while referring to themselves as White/Caucasians. After the September 11, 2001 terrorist attacks that placed this country on edge, many persons from Latin America are misidentified as possible terrorists.

Clearly, many Latinos are phenotypically similar to people from the Middle East, due to extensive mixing with Arabs, Maghribs, and Moors by original Spanish settlers to the New World, along with extensive racial mixing within the Latin American context. Thus, phenotypically, it is very easy for North Africans and Mediterranean persons to blend in African American and Latino communities. People of Arabic descent who grew up in Latin America define themselves as either Latinos or compatriots of their nation—Colombian, Mexican, etc. For example, two well-known Latinas in the United States, Shakira (singer) and Salma Hayek (actor), self-identify, respectively, as Colombian and Mexican and are of Middle Eastern ancestry. And, of course, today's Brazilians include Italians, Germans, Japanese, people from the Middle East, and a mixture of all these groups with Native Brazilians and Black ancestry.

Group Acceptance and Multiethnic/Multiracial Identity

Sadly, even persons from the various racial and ethnic groups in this country internalize this limiting and oppressive belief system regarding group membership and racial/ethnic identity. They internalize the expectations and in turn use them to judge others within the group. A person who does not conform is then excluded from the group and/or punished by its members. For multiethnic and multiracial persons who live within simultaneous and overlapping worldviews and who are struggling to define their own identity, this is often profoundly painful. Persons of color tell them that they are ashamed of their true identity and want to elevate themselves from the group by claiming another heritage, including a multiethnic and/or multiracial one; they are accused by others of being racially impure, and, if they have partly mainstream White, they are further condemned as carrying the "blood of the enemy."

Being accepted by some groups becomes an emotional battle between competing sides of the students' background. Other persons encourage this deeply damaging tug-of-war, forcing multiethnic and/or multiracial students to "prove their true colors." A student of Latino White and mainstream White lineage shared how she denounced her mainstream White heritage in order to prove unequivocal and undivided identity and loyalty:

> I wasn't allowed to be White but I was also not allowed to be Latina. The White students teased me and called me names. The Latino students called me "Wonder Bread." I knew the White students would not let me be one of them so I tried to be Latina. But the Latino students expected me to prove just how much Latina I was. I was expected to be more Latina than them. I told really bad "whitey" jokes about my father. I feel so bad because now I realize how much I was telling bad jokes about myself.

She then continued,

> I feel so bad that I rejected my father, whom I love so much. I hurts that I rejected one of my parents. I still feel bad that I totally humiliated and degraded both of us to that level.

A person of Latino White and African American ancestry stated: "Blacks said I sounded too White and Latinos that I sounded too Black. I couldn't please anyone." Another student of African American and Native American heritage grew up primarily in a Navajo reservation. When he moved to a city where he was around Blacks, they mocked him, "They say I don't know how to act Black. When I tell them that I was raised as an Indian they say I should know how to act Black just because I am part Black."

Often, in attempts to prove adequate membership in the group of color represented by the minority parent, multiracial children acquire the stereotypic attitudes, behavior, and speech of the group of color: "I had to be Blacker than Black. I had to show it more." Many have reported that multiethnic and multiracial students who have not fully integrated all sides of their heritage spend lots of time and energy trying to prove they are truly Black, Latino, Native American, or whatever (Bowles, 1993; Wardle, 1999).

Getting on the Same Page

Diversity and Culture

Let's start with diversity, an umbrella term used extensively when discussing multicultural education in this country. Traditionally, the term has been used to discuss discrete racial, ethnic, gender, and disability groups. We must recognize that each person exists within overlapping layers of diversity that cannot and should not be separated from one another. **Diversity** is defined as human attributes that make us all individually and collectively unique as a variety of forms and conditions (Derman Sparks & Phillips, 1997). These attributes include age, gender, race, culture, ethnicity, socioeconomic status, abilities and disabilities, physical appearance, language, learning styles, national origin, forms of intelligence, levels of education, and religion. Clearly, then, everyone has diversity. Further, everyone has a combination of attributes: age, gender, race, culture, ethnicity, socioeconomic status, abilities, physical appearance, language, learning style(s), form(s) of intelligence, education, and so on. A true understanding of diversity requires that we view the whole person and the dynamic interplay of the diverse facets that comprises him or her and that we move away from the "box mentality" that limits our national thinking (Cortes, 2000; Cruz-Janzen, 1997).

Diversity acts and interacts in different ways to form a person's culture. Just as everyone has diversity, so does everyone have culture. Just as the worldview of a man will vary from that of a woman, so will the worldview of a mainstream White woman differ from that of a woman of color. The worldview of a Latina woman will differ from that of a Black woman. The worldview of a mainstream White abled woman will differ from the worldview of a mainstream White disabled one.

As social beings, all humans gravitate toward others they perceive to be like themselves. This is a natural phenomenon based on our comfort in being with other persons with whom we feel we have things in common, leading to the formation and solidification of groups. Yet, we must be clear that group membership is fluid, *self-chosen* by its individual members, and that no group is superior or inferior to any other group. We must recognize that everyone belongs to multiple, overlapping groups of equal status, with no one group membership—say gender or race—more important than another—say profession and language, occupation, or interests. Further, we must affirm that group membership must be individually selected, not dictated by others within or outside the group. Finally, because of the shifting, developing, and overlapping nature of social groups, we are all subject to competing social designations though our different group memberships (Olumide, 2002).

Historically in this country, we have promoted the concept of group membership, particularly for persons of color, to be rigid and immutable. While it is obvious that people who share various overlapping forms of diversity tend to develop common ways of interpreting and reacting to conditions in their environment, including survival and self-preservation, no two persons share 100 percent the same worldview. Even siblings within families will have variations. Additionally, culture is fluid and evolving. Marta learned this clearly from a student who was losing her eyesight and from a colleague who became disabled in a car accident. Their culture and worldview changed dramatically as they had to accommodate to their new environments. Maybe the most important fact about groups is to remember that there is more diversity within any kind of human group (race, culture, gender, values, ideas, expectation, education, etc.) than between members of different groups (Zack, 2002).

Race and Ethnicity

So what is **race?** What is **ethnicity?** In 1992, the United States and Canada organized an international conference on race and ethnicity. After many discussions and presentations, it was concluded that there is no international agreement on the meaning of either term (Allen, 2000). Further, it was determined that the entire concept of race and ethnicity is "false" and based on false assumptions. The conference concluded that race and ethnicity are both social and political constructs that vary from region to region, nation to nation, and time period to time period. Since this conference, genome studies that have coded all the genes in the human organism have categorically eliminated biology as a central determinant of race and ethnicity.

But, while the 2000 Census indicates that both race and ethnicity are sociopolitical constructs, the Census still leaves the door wide open for the superimposition of a biological or genetic interpretation. "The racial and ethnic categories set forth in the standards should not be interpreted as being primarily biological or genetic" (U.S. Bureau of the Census, 1997)—implying that they are "significantly" biological or genetic. While genes do transmit significant information from parents to offspring—the color of eyes, hair texture, skin color, etc.—a biological and genetic foundation for the establishment of distinct races does not exist (Fish, 2002; Zack, 2002). Because we have been taught throughout our education that race is a biological construct, the government knows that by discussing jointly biological and genetic interpretations and sociopolitical ones, the genetic view will predominate (Zack, 2002). According to Fish (2002), the federal government has actively adopted folk categories of race, which by definition are social, or popular, while intentionally adding the misleading "scientific" biological and genetic argument without further clarification. This approach clearly promotes misinformation, and thus public ignorance and fear.

According to Wardle (1992), today's "races" are really "social races" based on **physiognomy**, involving the practice of judging human character and abilities by observation of bodily hair and facial features. According to Banks (2001), ethnicity refers to membership, within a microculture, or subculture, of a larger macroculture. An example would be **Asians** as a microculture within the mainstream White macroculture of this country. He explains that ethnic groups share a common ancestry, culture, history, tradition, and sense of peoplehood. While Banks does agree that there is no consensus on a definition, the difficulty with this definition is that Latinos of Indigenous/Indian progeny have little in common, even today, with the colonizing European White Hispanics who continue to exploit them in their own lands—Mexico, Central America, and South America (except in Brazil where the ruling class is made up of people of direct Portuguese heritage). There is no common ancestry, tradition, or sense of peoplehood.

Similarly, persons grouped as Asians—for example, Japanese, Koreans, Cambodians, Hmongs, and Chinese—have long-standing animosities based on cruel histories of colonization, slavery, prostitution, and other atrocities that keep them very separate from each other. The commitment of the U.S. government to bring Hmongs to this country after the Vietnam War was a direct result of such animosity. The Japanese have always viewed Filipinos as very much inferior to their race (Spickard, 1989). Francis Wardle asked a Census Bureau official which group was most concerned about the Census category they were assigned to. She replied, "The nationalist Chinese—they are adamant that they do not belong in the same Census category (Asian) as the communist (mainland) Chinese!"

Ethnicity is then seen as related to the social and cultural adaptations of groups, which, while defined rather homogeneously, may remain internally clustered, differentiated, and layered, but which have been thrown together for convenience by our government. According to this explanation and based on a popular Latino refrain, Latinos remain linked at the hip by a lingering history of colonization, oppression, and hatred. However, some Latinos—particularly White-Latino Europeans in countries like Guatemala and Mexico—were and continue to be the oppressors. For example, the Mayan Indian majority in Guatemala are still very much social, political, and economic second-class citizens in their own land. Individuals from the Latino ruling classes who immigrated to the United States have little in common with the historically oppressed Latinos living in this country.

In 1976 our government recognized Hispanic as the only ethnic group for civil rights legislation. The label was changed to Spanish/Hispanic/Latino for the 2000 Census, discussed in detail in Chapter 4.

Approaches to Teaching Multicultural Education

James Banks has proposed two methods to use in implementing multicultural education in our early childhood programs and schools. There is overlap between his two methods, which are *Five Dimensions of Multicultural Education* (see Figure 2.1) and *Four Approaches to Multicultural Education* (see Figure 2.2 on page 40).

The Five Dimensions of Multicultural Education

These dimensions must work in unison and each is required for the effective development and implementation of multicultural education.

Content Integration.   The **Content Integration** dimension addresses the extent to which teachers include a variety of content, including key concepts, principles, and theories that are representative of various cultural groups in their lessons and programs. These groups include gender, racial and ethnic groups, socioeconomic status, and the numerous other forms of human diversity discussed

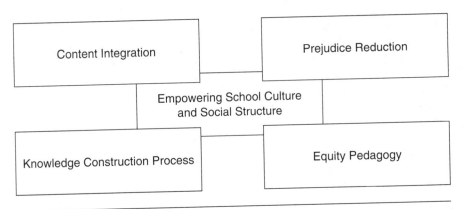

FIGURE 2.1   Banks's Dimensions of Multicultural Education

throughout this book. This is the method most often used by teachers today and, unfortunately, teachers tend to focus on integration of minute and isolated facts without integrating them into the overall lesson context. For example, heroes and "sheroes" of various race and ethnic groups are studied, yet not linked to the theme of the unit or lesson. Holidays such as Cinco de Mayo are celebrated without much connection to other activities and/or instruction occurring at the time. The events are usually viewed as significant only for the students from the same racial or ethnic group—and tend to reinforce group isolation and competition (Lewit & Baker, 1994; Spencer & Markstrom-Adams, 1990). These "factoids" are often presented during "appropriate" times of the year only and only in "appropriate" content lessons such as social history, language arts, and social studies.

Teachers express difficulty using this approach in areas such math and science. They believe math is math: It cannot be multicultural because it's universal. So they tend to isolate famous math and science people and events, while the lesson remains essentially intact. Children are not taught how diverse cultures have used and continue to use math and science to solve problems, define and shape their own environments and life experiences, and use these skills to survive and prosper. This approach tends to foster the study of groups as isolated and mutually exclusive entities.

During an activity that is typical of this approach, a multiracial student recalled that when the class read The *Count of Monte Cristo* and *The Three Musketeers* during Black Heritage Month, the author, Alexander Dumas, was described as Black. When the student tried to correct the information and discuss Dumas's biracial background, the teacher countered that Dumas was Black—only—because the class was studying the Black cultural group.

The Knowledge Construction Process.   The **Knowledge Construction Process** refers to teachers' helping students understand how individual and group views and histories determine how knowledge is shaped and defined—with the mainstream White, dominant society defining much of our current knowledge. This approach requires students be able to perceive and deconstruct various views and behaviors that people develop as they grow up within a culture, or multiple cultures, and to analyze their own sources for decisions, perception, and values.

The way each of us constructs knowledge develops our own unique biases, which all people use to process information, make life choices, and store data in long-term memory. Biases are developed from birth, can be negative and positive, and are reflected in individual attitudes and belief systems. Positive biases guide persons in making healthy life choices that support them individually and support others they come in contact with. A positive bias is the belief that humans are inherently socially gregarious and good, needing only the correct nurturance and guidance. Negative biases tend to isolate persons and judge people who are different as having lesser qualities. A negative bias is the belief that humans are inherently self-centered, causing them to engage in wrongdoing toward each other. Succinctly, biases help shape the learning process. According to Bruner, Goodnow, and Austin (1956) many basic learning processes are based on positive and negative processes—positive structures versus negative structures.

Equity Pedagogy.   The **Equity Pedagogy** dimension addresses ways teachers structure their teaching in order to ensure that all students, regardless of diverse backgrounds, experience an equitable environment that fosters academic achievement for all. Included in this method are a variety of teaching strategies that accommodate gender, learning styles, forms of intelligences, language, and socioeconomic status, as well as other differences. People develop different and preferred ways to learn and retain new information (Gardner, 1983). We know that this is true for boys and girls as well as for students of diverse cultural backgrounds. Some individuals are more independent learners while others learn better in group situations. Further, teachers need to know when and how to utilize competitive versus cooperative learning and when to use auditory, kinesthetic, spatial, and other forms of teaching to capitalize on the numerous learning styles of students in the classroom (Gardner, 1983).

Prejudice Reduction.   The **Prejudice Reduction** dimension helps students analyze and become aware of their own biases, particularly toward others of different diverse racial, ethnic, gender, or disability background(s). Teachers must first explore their own perceptions and understand their own views of culture, race, ethnicity, and other diversity attributes. They must know how they feel about their own diversity, especially their gender, race, and ethnicity, and must explore these aspects of themselves and their heritage. Otherwise, mainstream White teacher assume that only persons of color have those attributes and therefore approach multicultural education from an "other" perspective.

Some mainstream White teachers acknowledge their multiple European heritage, and some of Native American background are often surprised to discover that they are not truly White, but persons of color, according to our current rigid classification system. This often helps open their eyes to other persons of multiracial and multiethnic heritage they never recognized before or saw as being different from them. It also helps them understand the unscientific, subjective, and folk nature of our racial and ethnic categories. A teacher participant in a college class expressed,

> We have some Indian [Native American] but I never saw myself as racially mixed because I look White and my family has always been White. We always talked about the Irish but I know my grandmother was very dark—Indian. I have pictures of her. We never saw ourselves as anything else other than just White. Now I know why. They had to suppress that and we could pass. I always saw biracial as Black and White. Other biracial people cannot pass. Now I know.

Minority teachers who investigate their own background also come to acknowledge their multiethnic and multiracial heritage and are then more able to support their multiethnic and multiracial students.

Teachers use this self-understanding to guide students in developing healthier, more positive attitudes toward themselves and each other. Prejudice clearly is a developmental process that can be addressed by effective teachers. Banks (2001) believes that children in elementary school are very receptive to instruction geared toward prejudice reduction. Manning (1999/2000) identifies early adolescence as a crucial psychological and cognitive developmental stage in prejudice education, an "optimal time" for effective multicultural education, because he believes that at this age a child's prejudices are not fully crystallized. We believe, as we discuss in detail in Chapter 5, that a healthy sense of racial, ethnic, and other diversity understanding is a truly developmental process, where children can benefit from the appropriate instruction at each **developmental age,** starting in early childhood.

An Empowering School Culture and Social Structure.   The **Empowering School Culture and Social Structure** dimension requires radically reforming school beliefs and practices that currently provide inequitable educational opportunities for diverse populations of students. The current structure of our public schools provides academic tracking of students according to their perceived academic potential and uses assessments to sort students into gifted and special education programs. As a result of this approach, nationwide more children of color, and especially African American males, are placed in special education programs while gifted programs are predominantly representative of mainstream Whites, especially girls and Asians, and more mainstream Whites and Asians are in advanced academic tracks. More children of Latino heritage are placed in special education language programs (Banks, 2001). Education policymakers need to analyze these practices and the belief systems that underlie them.

This phenomenon is also true of programs such as Head Start, which is focused on empowering low-income children—especially minorities—to succeed in schools. Head Start's special educational population is overwhelmingly minority and male (Wardle, 1991), and many of these students automatically become part of the K–12 special needs population.

Students who study this approach would develop and implement ways to shift the paradigm: more minority students in gifted programs, fewer minorities in special education; maybe less emphasis on athletics in minority schools, etc.

Approaches to Multicultural Education

James Banks (2001) also proposes four approaches to multicultural education: Contributions, Ethnic Additive, Transformative, and Decision Making and Social Action (Figure 2.2). These approaches are hierarchical, starting with the Contributions approach, and represent increasing levels of critical analysis and problem solving, in addition to commitment to end social injustices.

Contributions Approach.   The **Contributions Approach** is similar to the Content Integration dimension already discussed. This is the heroes and holidays method, often called the *Restaurant Approach* or the *Tourist Approach*. Content dealing with diverse populations is isolated, limited to specific times of the year and units of instruction. This approach marginalizes and trivializes the significant contributions of non-mainstream Whites to the advancement and culture of this society. Further, when students who were invisible are suddenly thrust into the limelight, they find themselves within a "three-ring circus act" and the focus of attention, often leading to competition between minority groups for the most

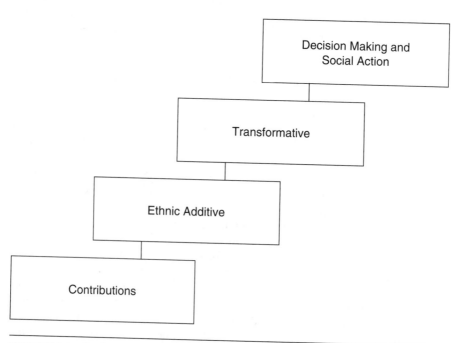

FIGURE 2.2   Banks's Approaches to Multicultural Education

The contributions approach to multicultural education can lead to a tourist approach—studying costumes, food, and dance.

time and the best exposure in school—resulting in extremely negative and stereo-typical behaviors (Programs for Educational Opportunity, 1996).

Examples abound: One high school decided to serve ethnic food during the Martin Luther King, Jr. commemoration, so they served fried chicken, collard greens, and watermelon! For a Hispanic Heritage Month celebration another school served burritos and refried beans (and mainstream White teachers with Hispanic last names were presumed to know how to prepare them). They asked Marta Cruz-Janzen, who is Puerto Rican, to judge the Mexican food. While the students and school faculty, including administrators, thought they were doing a great job, the parents were, rightfully, infuriated and offended. To celebrate Thanksgiving, a group of students at an elementary school sang *Ten Little Indians* while dressed as Indians, including feathered headdresses, burning incense, and fanning the smoke with an "eagle" feather. Clearly this approach reinforces and perpetuates stereotypes and group differences.

Another result of this approach is that minority students are expected to know and represent the entire group to which they belong. Marta Cruz-Janzen (a Latino/Black multiracial person from Puerto Rico) recalls being asked during an assembly presentation, "What was it like to grow up in a poor neighborhood [ghetto] with lots of criminals? Weren't you scared? How did you succeed in getting out of there to get an education?" It was appalling! Marta was a middle-class student tracked into the college-bound classes.

Ethnic Additive Approach.   The **Ethnic Additive Approach** adds more extended content, concepts, themes, and perspectives within curricular content without making significant philosophical and structural changes. A classic example discussed by Banks is the study of the westward movement in our history. Traditionally, the westward movement is presented from a Eurocentric male perspective and does not address the Native Americans moving southward, westward, and northward; Spaniards and Mexicans or any other group simultaneously moving within the continent; and the Asian railroad builders and gold miners moving to this country, etc. It merely focuses on the movement of mainstream White people fulfilling their Manifest Destiny, while displacing existing populations and belittling different religions and cultures. The ethnic additive approach to westward movement would include perspectives from these different points of view (discussed in more detail in Chapter 7).

Transformative Approach.   The **Transformative Approach** begins to unravel the traditional Eurocentric male perspective by examining the points of views of other groups, including women of all backgrounds. Students begin to learn about women who made signification contributions within each and all groups—Native American women who helped in explorations; mainstream White women who homesteaded and led groups moving west; Indigenous women who fought against the encroaching Europeans, Spaniards, and mainstream Whites alike. Katz writes about Mary Fields, a six-foot-tall, 200-pound Black woman who delivered the U.S. mail and drove a stagecoach in Montana (2002). As well, this approach examines the Westward Movement from the point of view of others encountered along the way.

For multiethnic and multiracial students, students involved with the transformative approach would examine examples of people from different racial, ethnic, national, and linguistic backgrounds who married and then became successful, along with multiethnic and multiracial individuals who used their membership in several groups to bring people together and solve problems. Studying the history of the Black and Indian experience in this country is just one example (Katz, 1996).

Decision-Making and Social Action Approach.   The **Decision-Making and Social Action Approach** comes out of Paulo Freire's critical pedagogy analysis (1970). It empowers students to systematically problem-solve issues of inequity and injustices in their schools and communities while also gaining an education. At their developmentally appropriate level students learn how to take action, whether it's cleaning an area of the school grounds or community, writing letters to legislators, or making speeches. For example, students decide what action they can take to reduce prejudice and discrimination within their schools, communities, and society at large. Multiethnic and multiracial children might insist their school's approach to collecting racial and ethnic data include a multiracial category, and engage in an effort to lobby their legislators to create a legitimate multiracial category on the next Census.

Reforming Multicultural Education

The Problems with Traditional Approaches

"For female students and students of color, it is not just what they are taught but what they are not taught that hurts them" (Cruz-Janzen, 1997–98, p. 227). This is, of course, true for all children. Female students—and to some extent, male students—and students of color are taught the limiting stereotypic roles they are expected to assume rather than the potential and choices they possess. They are not taught about the wonderful contributions members of their group have made to our nation and all humanity. Likewise, mainstream White children are not taught about the contributions of others; they are taught that only persons like them have made contributions. This leads to misinformation, inaccurate assumptions, anger, and resentment. As a mainstream White college student in one of Marta Cruz-Janzen's classes put it,

> It affects your opinion. If these people [of color] have never contributed anything and all they have done is take from what others have contributed, why would we want them in our country? Why would we want them in our neighborhoods and schools? Why would anyone want them? If you don't know these things, you assume these people are worthless.

We have already discussed the problems inherent within a multicultural approach that focuses exclusively on group membership—an approach particularly problematic for multiethnic and multiracial students. For these students, the question always is: Which group do I belong to? We are somehow unable to talk about people who are simultaneously individuals and members of various fluid groups. The traditional multicultural approach is always about groups, one group at a time, and with some groups having more relevance than others; further, it assumes that race and ethnic groupings supersede other identities, such as gender, socioeconomic status, and so on. A person is above all African American, then male or female, followed by economic status, and other attributes. Marta is constantly being assaulted with: "You are above all Black" or "You are above all Latina," and "You may be all that [female, educated, middle class, a professor, married, parent, daughter, etc.] but don't forget who you really are [Black/Latina]." This group approach to diversity is damaging to all children, but particularly to children who do not fit the neat Census boxes or people's preconceived phenotypes of those boxes.

The traditional approach to multicultural education would not support these multiracial children's studying their White/British heritage.

For multiethnic and multiracial children to develop a healthy identity in a society so fixated on single-race/ethnic categories, forcing everyone to fit into one of these categories, and assuming those who can't or won't are somehow abnormal and dysfunctional (Fish, 2002; Olumide, 2002; Zack, 2002), they must have lots and lots of opportunities throughout their school experience to integrate their full identity and to know for themselves what they truly are (Cruz-Janzen, 1997).

> You feel like you are faceless. I didn't know who I was. My whole life it was my quest to understand.

❈ ❈ ❈

> I didn't learn about anyone who was like me. I always wondered about other people's heritage and if they were like me. I wanted to talk to them and find out more about their growing up. It's important to have someone who is just like you.

Learning about themselves would help multiethnic and multiracial students see themselves as legitimate, real members of humanity and society. Further, since the limited focus and knowledge about interracial and interethnic persons in this country and Europe has been narrowly defined as between mainstream Whites and Black/African Americans, people of other racial and ethnic combinations feel further invalidated. As a Japanese American and African American person said, "It would have helped me knowing that I was not the only one, that there are more people like me." Many students are torn and anxious. "I remember for a while in middle school I wanted to be Hispanic but when I saw how Hispanic students were treated, I thought I better be White. I couldn't let them know about the other because I would be ostracized somehow."

Multicultural Education That's Truly Multicultural

Multiethnic and multiracial children in our schools are often hurting and living in fear. They fear the constant harassment, hostility, and insensitivity—not to mention feeling invisible. No educational model that proclaims to combat social inequities and injustices can allow this to continue. By not having accurate information about multiethnic and multiracial children in our schools, by not supporting the inclusion of all their unique racial and ethnic combinations in official school statistics, and by not including them in our schools' curricula at all grade levels and subject areas, we condone their continued abuse; we promote our ignorance and allow the stereotypes and fears to prevail.

Multiethnic and multiracial children must learn that having multiple heritages is an asset in an increasingly diverse nation and world. Further, knowing and feeling positive about one's heritage and having real and affirming role models is critical to academic achievement and general well-being and success. By being rendered abnormal, illegitimate, and invisible, multiethnic and multiracial persons are placed in hostile school environments that promote harassment by other children and adults. Invisibility creates lack of existence and humanity (Cruz-Janzen, 1997–98). Lack of humanity condones oppression, and multiethnic and multiracial students in our P–12 schools often find themselves harassed and rejected both by the mainstream White society and by representatives of all the single-race groups in their background.

Most of the antagonism and abuse against these children occurs at the hands of adults, including teachers, and other students in or near the early childhood programs and schools (Cruz-Janzen, 1997; Wardle, 1993). Multiethnic and multiracial children are often antagonized and pressured to turn against their own siblings and family members by their school peers and society in general: "That's your sister? She's Indian! You are a half-breed!" They are pitted against each other according to physical appearance: "I always resented my brother [White-looking]. It's like he got everything and all I had was the leftovers." The single-race approach to multicultural education encourages isolation and discrimination against multiple ethnic and race persons. It also fosters the creation in children's cognitive development of inaccurate and false schemas, or mental categories. All children need to develop complex and sophisticated constructs of individual differences, not simple mutually exclusive ones. Traditional multicultural approaches encourage put-downs of other races to elevate solidarity within the group. This is the biggest problem with the single, isolated group approach to multicultural education.

What is urgently needed are truly inclusive multicultural curricula that are also humane; multicultural education that recognizes, respects, and integrates all individuals and groups that comprise society, including persons of multiple racial and ethnic backgrounds. We need multicultural educational approaches that always start with the concept of individual, independent human beings who experience and construct their world in unique ways (Wardle, 2001b; West, 2001). We must legitimatize these various personal constructions and contexts to prepare each one of us to be able to be cultural bridges and empowered members of the world. These approaches are discussed in future chapters of the book.

Conclusion

Proponents of multicultural education state that their goal is not just to include issues of race, ethnicity, social class, gender, and other exceptionalities in schools, but also to transform education to provide an accurate view of our society. Further, multicultural education is designed to empower every child to maximize his or her own unique potential. The fundamental goal must be that all children can choose to be anything they wish and that the schools will help them manifest this goal. With increasing numbers of multiethnic and multiracial students, multicultural education must expand, grow, and shift to embrace this emerging population.

Questions/Projects

1. Develop a multicultural curriculum for the age student you teach in a specific subject/content area including all students.

2. Explore multicultural/diversity resources in your community. How many address the needs of multiracial/multiethnic students?

3. Interview the person in charge of multicultural education in your school. Based on the interview, determine the kind of approach (see Banks) used by your school.

Does the approach include multiracial/multiethnic students?

4. Develop an extensive family history. What kind of diversity can you find—racial, ethnic, religious, political, language, etc.?

5. Some argue that learning about the contributions of all people to this country's success is divisive and will cause the country to disintegrate. What is your opinion, and why?

Resources

Books

Lumpkin, B., & Strong, D. (1995). *Multicultural science and math connections*. Portland, ME: J. Weston Walch.

The multicultural math classroom: Bringing in the world. Portsmouth, NH: Heinenann, 1996.

Zaslavsky, C. (1994). *Multicultural math: Hands-on math activities from around the world*. Jefferson City, MO: Scholastic Books.

Website

Black Indians and InterTribal Native American Association

http://www.blackindians.com

Journal

Multicultural Perspectives. Official Journal of the National Association for Multicultural Education.

Organization

Black American West Museum and Heritage Center
3091 California Avenue
Denver, CO 80205
(303) 292-2566

3

Historical Developments

Radical democratic theories of government formulated in the 1700s and crystal-lized in our Declaration of Independence rest on the assumption that all humans are equal and that environment and self-advancement rather than heredity and privilege are the crucial factors determining human success. This idea was a rev-olutionary concept foreign to the European view of divine rulers and state reli-gions. The original colonists claimed to seek a new and different society from the Europe they left behind. Yet the same men who wrote the eloquent words about equality, liberty, and justice for all did not view all fellow humans, includ-ing women, in the same light and were slave owners and even fathers of slave children. These children, though carrying their very own European lineage, were still seen as inferior, as not human; indeed, they were seen as beasts. Their main-stream White heritage didn't make them White or Whiter; their Black blood—even one drop—made them Black and slaves for life. They were chattel to be sold and traded. These same founding fathers saw Native Americans as a prob-lem standing in their way to progress and as subhuman heathen savages to be saved or eliminated. To White Anglo Saxons equality meant only other White, male Anglo Saxons in Europe (Grant, 1916)—and their descendants in the New World. Thus the new colonists—and later the leaders of the new nation—adopted Europe's historical and social preoccupation with the superiority of the wealthy, White, Anglo Saxon man.

As a result of this elitist view, the United States of America developed a long-standing preoccupation with the racial composition of its population, probably more so than any other country in the modern world, except maybe Japan.

This chapter examines significant developments in the construction of race and racism in this country and the quest to expand the White race to create a White-dominated world. We examine the policies of this country designed to control the racial composition of its population through immigration and the institutionalization of racist beliefs in public institutions, including the schools. Results of this examination show why persons of multiethnic and multiracial heritage are still not viewed as normal, are not fully accepted within our society, and must struggle against both a single-race mythology and a racist history (Zack, 2002).

FOCUS QUESTIONS

1. What is the historical development of the racial classification system in this country? Why does this system present a "moral dilemma" for the nation?

2. How has this country's racial classification system impacted persons of multiethnic and multiracial heritage? Why are multiethnic and multiracial persons considered a threat both to mainstream Whites and to minority groups?

3. How does the current system represent the nation's obsession with racial purity, resulting in the rejection of multiethnic and multiracial people?

4. How and why does the designation of Spanish/Hispanic/Latino as the only ethnic category invalidate the entire concept of race? Why has the nation refused to abandon the concept of race and replace it with ethnicity for all groups?

Chapter Feature
Student Profile: Deidra McAllister

Deidra MacAllister's mother is Asian American (Japanese) and her father is mainstream White. She has sandy brown hair, medium brown eyes, and the physical appearance of a U.S. mainstream White. She considers herself biracial but never identified as "different than anyone else or even a minority" until high school when a counselor told her that he had seen her cumulative record from elementary and middle schools and found out that she was Asian. He told her that now she had to check *Asian* instead of *Other* because she was a minority. Deidra said, "He had this smile on his face as he said it like he was making fun of me. I don't know why, but I felt like he was making fun of me." He told Deidra, "Well, I didn't know you were Chinese. I didn't know you were a minority. You had us fooled." Deidra was offended: "Fooled! I never tried to fool anyone. My mom is not even Chinese. She's Japanese. My parents always checked 'Other' because I am not one. I am BOTH."

Deidra recalls that the counselor told some students and suddenly, "My friends started teasing me and telling me that if I was Chinese I had to have 'fuzzy dice' on my windows because all Chinese have fuzzy dice on their windows. The label changed me, going against me and making me an outcast. I was no longer like everybody else. The Japanese students said I was not Japanese because I was half and called me 'gaijin' which in Japan means foreigner but here they mean that I'm an outcast. The other Asian students wouldn't talk to me. They called me 'wonder bread' and 'white girl.' The White students called me 'chink,' 'yum yum,' and 'Jap.' When I was categorized or labeled, I didn't feel totally comfortable being different and I never thought of myself as different." Deidra described her high school experience as frustrating and lonely. "No matter what I did somebody was always angry with me."

Development of a Racial System

Colonialists

Most colonizers of what became the United States left Europe to escape political repression; to leave overcrowding, disease, hunger, and misery; to breathe freedom from tyrannical monarchies that had no room for social mobility or basic human rights; and to rid themselves of absolute religions that allowed no choice and persecuted nonbelievers. Others left seeking adventure and wealth. Still others were slaves and indentured servants whose preferred choice was to come to the New World rather than go to jail.

Initially, these new citizens intermingled and created a new, egalitarian society made up of free Blacks, poor Whites, and people from all over the world—developing the first melting pot myth. "People of all sorts were to come to America, contribute their part, intermarry, create a new mixed people, and enjoy the unprecedented liberty of life in this place" (Spickard, 1989, p. 4). Men often traveled alone and mixed freely with Native American women. Indeed, most original newcomers socialized and mated with people who were not like them—in race, religion, or national origin (Spickard, 1992). Part of the vision of a new nation was a racially mixed panacea where everyone was free and equal and where people came from all over the world in search of freedom and opportunities. For a short while these mixed people were viewed as the "New Americans" (Spickard, 1989).

However, English colonists brought feelings and beliefs of racial purity and superiority to North America during the seventeenth and eighteenth centuries. They believed that their Protestant religion, English language, and British culture of laws, education, music, literature, and so on, were superior and destined to become dominant in North America, an idea mirrored by the Portuguese in their conquest of Brazil, and the Spanish and other European nations' colonial pursuits.

Preoccupation with Race

> In the United States if you are part White and part something else, you are something else. No matter how much White you have in you, you are definitively not White. (Cruz-Janzen, 1997)

These are the comments of two multiracial people. Angela's parents are White, one mainstream White, and the other Latino White. She looks mainstream White with very light complexion, blonde hair, and blue eyes. David's father is mainstream White and his mother is half Japanese; David also looks mainstream White. Angela and David represent many persons in this country—and much of the world—today. While many mainstream White people have other mixtures in their background, the nation appears in complete denial of the interethnic and interracial past of its White citizens. Because of trade, movement of whole groups of people, and wars, European Whites are mixed with a variety of other "racial" groups; further mixing occurred after Europeans came to this continent, including the extensive racial mixing that occurred during slavery.

Nora's mother is a native of Sierra Leone, her father, a native of France. She lives in Paris and speaks French, yet we view Nora as Black or African.

Many believe that there are no pure White Americans in the country today: Millions of mainstream White Americans today have African American ancestors, millions more have Native American heritage, and many have both. Further, most Black/African Americans have some mainstream White lineage (Haizlip, 1994; Root, 1992; Scales-Trent, 1995; Williams, 1995). Thousands, perhaps millions, of White-looking Blacks—or Whites with some Black heritage—have "passed" to the White side across the generations. The fact that the descendants of Thomas Jefferson and Sally Hemings are divided into two camps—those who consider themselves Black and those who see themselves as White—is a result of this phenomenon.

Our obsession with race and racial categories is largely because we want to be known as a White country to the rest of the world. We want to pretend that little racial mixing occurred and that a clearly distinguishable, pure White group continues to exist. The notion of distinct and separate racial groups that never mix is obviously absurd, since contact between human groups always results in mixing—through marriage and less formal relationships. And, as we create more and more equality and mobility between different groups, the incidents of intermarriage will naturally increase (Zack, 2002).

While our fixation on race developed from the sense of superiority of White Anglo Saxon Protestants, it became crystallized through our history of slavery and our need to justify slavery by viewing slaves as nonhuman. To maintain White superiority we also engaged in racist practices toward other groups of color, including Japanese and Filipinos, Chinese, people from Mexico, and Native Americans. On one side stand only those persons deemed acceptable as Whites, or mainstream Whites, excluding, as we have said, Latino Whites and other Latinos; on the other side is everyone else, including all the other racial groups and everyone in between. Thus, anyone with any amount of racial mixing is part of the non-White.

Racial Boundaries

In a society obsessed with race and racial demarcations, it is crucial to be able to discern who belongs to which group and to keep the groups apart. The institution of slavery in our history led to the need to establish who was slave and who was master. While it is often not mentioned, some White Europeans were brought to the colonies as slaves. White slaves were sold and traded along with other Black slaves. It was also not unheard of that White children were captured and sold as Black slaves (Loren Katz, 1968). But in a society obsessed with race and racial demarcations, it became crucial to be able to discern who belonged to what group and keep the groups apart. Since early in the colonial period, states began to enact stringent rules to establish clear racial lines. In 1664 Maryland established that all Black/Africans within its boundaries, then or in the future, would be slaves "**durante vita.**" Prior to this time Black slaves had the opportunity, though limited, for eventual freedom. Other colonies followed suit as it became apparent that to maintain the institution of slavery, rules prohibiting the mixing of the races had to be enforced. Slavery became equated with Blackness and lack of humanity. Whites who intermarried with these "inferior beings"—not even human but beasts—lowered the status and morality of White persons as well as the offspring of such unions. The eugenics movement, discussed later, was an attempt to rid the White race of these impurities. By the mid eighteenth century six of the thirteen colonies had **anti-miscegenation** and cohabitation **laws** (Knepper, 1995). Other new world countries that imported and enslaved Africans followed different approaches to keeping Whites and slaves apart. For example, Brazil allowed slaves to buy their freedom—which many of them did; Brazil also passed legislation proclaiming children of slaves, including mixed race children, to be free.

Because laws were also passed to limit the rights and freedoms of other non-White immigrants, states began establishing generally narrower definitions of who was White with accompanying broad definitions of who was Black. In the 1854 legal case *People* v. *Hall*, the California Supreme Court ruled that the term White excluded "black, yellow, and all other colors" and Black included everyone who is not of White blood (Knepper, 1995). After the emancipation of Black slaves, it became even more critical to keep Blacks and Whites not only distinct but also separate. The *Plessy* v. *Ferguson* case of 1896 challenged the definition of White and Black. Plessy argued that he was only one-eighth Black and no longer discernible as a person of color, entitling him to the same rights as a White person. The Supreme Court disagreed, acknowledging the variability between states' definitions of White and Black, but establishing that each state had the right to create its own definitions. In this case the Supreme Court ruled in favor of states' rights—which it tended to do at that time—and not in favor of any view of race. (The *Plessy* v. *Ferguson* case was used to press another legal argument, discussed in Chapter 4).

Much confusion and litigation resulted from these decisions, particularly because many Whites were mistaken for and treated as Blacks in public facilities. The increasing lawsuits led to ever more stringent definitions and measures across the nation—separate public facilities including schools, more severe anti-miscegenation and cohabitation laws, and lots of other racially discriminatory legislation. In general, state after state upheld the **one-drop rule**, declaring any person with any amount of Black or "Negro blood whatever" and their descendants as Black only. A White person must have no trace whatsoever of any blood other than mainstream White blood. The laws provided no limitations of time and/or family generation (Knepper, 1995). Furthermore, the courts generally maintained that the burden of proof rested with the person(s) being accused of being Black, not with the courts.

Immigration Acts and Court Rulings

The nation's highest court upheld many state definitions of White through rulings impacting many areas, including education, citizenship, and immigration laws. As early as 1790, naturalization laws (Naturalization Act of 1790) limited U.S. citizenship to White Europeans. In 1909 Takao Ozawa was denied citizenship because he was not sufficiently White. Takao had a mainstream White father (English) and a half-Japanese mother (Knepper, 1995). In 1927 (*Rice* v. *Gong Lum*) the Court ruled that the White race meant exclusively pure Caucasians (Knepper, 1995), supporting the White versus "other" notion and the fact that states did not have to provide schools for non-Whites.

Further, in 1922, the Court ruled that although Hindus had been classified "scientifically" as members of the Caucasian race, they were not considered White by understanding of the common man and therefore, not entitled to naturalization, writing that, "It may be true that the blond Scandinavian and the brown Hindu have a common ancestor in the dim reaches of antiquity, but the average man knows perfectly well that there are unmistakable and profound differences between them today" (Knepper, 1995, p. 20). This decision led the way for the folk-nature basis of racial categories in this country (Fish, 2002).

Several immigration laws were enacted to prevent the flow of "inferior races" into the country: The Immigration Act of 1917 excluded Asians and Pacific Islanders, and other acts were designed to promote increased immigration from White/European nations, particularly those of Anglo Saxons. Indeed, most immigration acts before 1965 were very racist and designed to keep "inferior" Whites from Southern and Eastern Europe as well as all other non-Whites from entering the country (Banks, 2001; Knepper, 1995).

In 1970 Louisiana defined as Black anyone with more than one-thirty-second Black ancestry, yet established in 1983 that a person needed to provide a preponderance of evidence to change his or her racial designation. In 1983 Susie

Phipps attempted to change her racial designation from Black to White. Her family had lived for generations—over a hundred years—as mainstream Whites. All her siblings looked mainstream White, with some having blonde hair and blue eyes. She had twice married as a mainstream White. On her birth certificate she had been designated "colored" based on the testimony of the midwife who delivered her and supposedly knew the family history—a Black great-great-great-great-grandfather. The district court ruled that Mrs. Phipps was Black. This case was appealed to the Supreme Court, which refused to hear it, thus maintaining the one-drop rule as still the law of the land in 1983, a rule that also still applies to Asians and Latinos with significant mainstream White heritage (Spickard, 1989).

False Equality

The ideal of the founding fathers of a nation of equals, with liberty and justice for all, while more advanced than the European countries immigrants came from, did not include women, other people from European groups, or Whites without property. Belief in the racial purity and superiority of White Europeans was used to justify aggressive and inhumane genocide of Native Americans and the takeover of their lands and resources, along with a rationale used to turn Africans into permanent "natural slaves"—especially in the New World, where native peoples were considered unsuitable for the extreme physical labor. While the original draft of the U.S. Declaration of Independence included a section on "the horrors of the slave trade" (131), Southern colonies caused it to be deleted (McCullaugh, 2001).

In colonial times many individuals, including noted public figures such as Benjamin Franklin, openly worried that Whites, particularly Anglo Saxons, represented a numerical minority in the world population and that undesirable Whites from Central, Eastern, and Southern Europe and non-Europeans were increasing in North America. Many openly declared that colonization and expansion represented the opportunity to increase the Anglo White race outside of Europe, to civilize the whole world (Grant, 1916; Springer, 2001). Andrew Jackson worried that pure Anglo Protestant blood was becoming contaminated with inferior White and non-White blood through immigration and racial mixing. Significantly, the vast racial mixing within the Black population in the South, particularly in places like New Orleans—after it became part of the United States—alarmed them. Much of the ruling class envisioned the United States of America as a land inhabited primarily by White Anglo Saxon Protestants.

Origins of U.S. Racism

According to Grant (1916) and other White supremacists of the early part of the nineteenth century, racial prejudice is a "natural antipathy" that serves to maintain "purity of type" and is "deeply rooted" in the "everyday consciousness" of Anglo Saxons. Initially, European colonists justified their behavior toward Native Americans and Africans by declaring them to lack souls and to be inferior forms of life. However, in 1537 Pope Paul II ended this view by declaring that all people were created in the image of God and therefore had souls and were equal (Smedley, 2002). Thus Europeans had to find different reasons to justify capturing and exploiting other humans. North Americans and Europeans began to develop ideologies capitalizing on the perceived racial differences and the so-called innate superiority of some races over others to further support colonialism. To this end, scientists, who often support society's prejudices (Fish, 2002), began searching for and developing "conclusive" proof that Anglo Saxons and Nordic Europeans were the superior race and therefore selected by nature to hold power over other races. By the nineteenth century, ideas about the inherited and immutable characteristics of the races had become well established within the European and U.S. social and scientific doctrines.

Racial Hierarchies

According to Spickard (1992), the view of race originally developed by White Europeans defined four discrete races that included White/Europeans, Black/Africans, Red/Indians, and Yellow/Asians. Within a White supremacist framework, these races were arranged hierarchically based on skin color, with Whites at the top, followed by Asians, then Indians, and finally Africans—a ranking that represented both their perceived moral qualities and mental and physical abilities. In any mixtures between the races it was believed the "power" of the lower race always trumped that of the superior race (a device clearly designed to shame people into not mixing). Europeans' system of racial classification divided the races into subunits. For example, the White race was divided into Nordic or Teutonic, Alpine and Mediterranean, with Nordic being the highest type and Mediterranean the lowest (Banks, 1995; Spickard, 1992; Wells, 1961). The Nordic people represented persons from Scandinavia, Northern Germany, and the British Isles. Alpines were other Europeans such as the Bretons, Basques, and Walloons, and included Northern French, Southern Germans, Northern Italians, Swiss, Caucasians, and Russians.

Mediterraneans were the "Southern Dark Whites" (Wells, 1961) and included Iberians, Southern French, Southern Italians, Northern Africans, Hindus, Persians (Iranians), and many Middle Easterners. Among Mediterraneans the Iberians were particularly perceived as backward (Wells, 1961). White supremacists believed that the Alpines and Caucasians were more Asian in nature, but Mediterranean Whites were closer to Africans (Grant, 1916). The hierarchy was based on White racial purity manifest through lighter skin and eye and hair coloration. The superior Nordics were tall with very light skin and light-colored hair and eyes. The Alpines were brown-eyed brunettes and the Mediterraneans additionally had "swarthy" skin complexions (Grant, 1916).

Proving Racial Superiority

In the early 1900s scientists set out to prove the scientific differentiation and superiority of some races. They began to look at the size and shape of the human skull, and established the classification of cranial shapes, long and round, and "cranial indices" (Grant, 1916). This **cephalic index** was used to subdivide the European races. The Nordic White race was described as long-skulled, very tall, with blonde or light brown hair and light-colored eyes. According to White supremacists, the ideal White man par excellence had an absolutely fair skin and represented the Aryan languages and culture. The Alpine subspecies remained in the mountains and high plateaus of Asia. They were round-skulled and of medium height. They were described as having dark hair and eyes, although some light-colored eyes are found among them. The Mediterraneans were long-skulled but with a smaller cranium than the Nordics. Their eyes and hair are very dark with "more or less" swarthy skin coloration.

In this racial grading system, it was believed that eye coloration was more important in determining race than any other trait, as all blue, gray, and green eyes in the world were believed to come from the same source. Light-colored eyes represented a specialization exclusive to White Nordic Europeans. Grant (1916), a White supremacist, stated that dark-colored eyes are "all but universal" among wild animals and "entirely among primates." As such, he believed, all dark-eyed humans are members of older, more primitive—less specialized— races (Grant, 1916). Blonde hair, ranging from flaxen to red to chestnut to light brown, was attributed exclusively to Nordics. The darker shades of blonde were believed to indicate some racial crossing. Black-haired Whites indicated racial mixing with inferior darker races (Grant, 1916). According to Grant, all darker-skinned humans have always been envious of the fair-skinned Nordics.

It was strongly believed that brain power and moral traits were related to the physical distinctions between the races and that certain races had special aptitudes for certain things (Grant, 1916). Nordics all over the world were described as a race of aristocrats, rulers, and organizers who further distinguished themselves as natural adventurers, explorers, soldiers, and sailors. Mediterraneans were more emotional and "natural," thus excelling in the arts.

Irish Americans

The original White population in the U.S. colonies was from White Nordic and Anglo Saxon backgrounds and viewed immigration by people from the Mediter-ranean as a threat to racial purity. This fear included Irish immigrants. Before American colonization, the English invaded Ireland, claiming to subdue the Catholic population. When Irish immigrants began coming to the United States in the 1820s, the White Anglo-Saxon Protestants addressed them as *Irish niggers* and *mongrel mass of ignorants* (Carnes, 1995). In some cities, anti-Catholic and anti-Irish feelings flared into violence. Signs that read, "No dogs or Irish" were common.

The terms "Irish niggers" and **Black Irish** have a long history as well. One version of this term dates back to 1588 when the Spanish Felicima Armada, on its retreat from attempting to invade England, shipwrecked on the coast of Ireland and Scotland, where popular legend tells the story of the survivors inter-marrying with the locals to create a new interracial (Hibernian-Iberian) strain of progeny whose "dark hair and soft brown Southern skin testifies to its remote Spanish ancestry" (Kunesh, 1984). Other legends suggest a strong religious, polit-ical, and social bond between Ireland and Spain since the sixth century or even biblical times. While these stories have been debated and denied, they are accepted as popular folklore. Since all racial categories are based on folklore (Fish, 2002), this is not unusual.

Today's Racism

The Nazi ideology was a direct outgrowth of European racist thinking. The Nazis, of course, believed non-Aryans, Jews, Gypsies, homosexuals, and people with disabilities were inferior and thus to be eliminated. Race and racism have been and remains very much a part of our psyche. Today, beliefs in White racial superiority, particularly Anglo Saxon racial superiority, are expressed by extreme separatist groups, such as the Ku Klux Klan, that call for reunification with the British Commonwealth—ironic since much of the commonwealth is Black and Indian, and Britain itself is numerically and socially multiracial—and White supremacists who continue to proclaim the racial superiority of Anglo Saxons around the world (Springer, 2001).

One of the ways all racial and ethnic groups use to maintain their member-ship and loyalty is to declare themselves superior to other races. Some of the most persistent racists are people who at one time were considered part of an inferior race. Thus, after the Irish became accepted into the mainstream White dominant group, they in turn began to view nonaccepted groups, including some Europeans, as inferior. The controversy over the inferiority and superiority of some races con-tinues today, with some scientists still believing that intelligence tests prove that African Americans are intellectually inferior to European Americans. *The Bell Curve* (Herrnstein & Murray, 1994) resurrects the old idea that Blacks throughout the world are genetically inferior to Whites.

Rejection of Racial Mixing

Anti-miscegenation laws have existed in this country since 1661 and mainly tar-geted groups not allowed to marry acceptable, or mainstream, Whites. This pro-hibition included Blacks, Jews, Italians, Chinese, Filipinos, Japanese, and people from Mexico, Spain, and Portugal. This prohibition produced considerable intermarriage between people of these "unacceptable" groups. This is particu-larly true for Japanese, Chinese, and Filipino men who were brought here to help build the railroad and mine gold, but initially were not permitted to bring their wives (Spickard, 1989).

In 1815, Thomas Jefferson tried to nail down the science of racial categorization. He devised an intricate algebraic equation to show that "one-fourth Negro blood mixed with any portion of White constitutes the mulatto." To guarantee that mixed-race children of slaveholders would be included in the slave population, the "one-drop rule" was promoted in the antebellum South. . . . It got slaveholders out of having to recognize that many of their enslaved progeny were basically White. (Steel, 1995, p. 47)

Beliefs in **racial purity** and superiority have further fueled rancor toward persons of multiethnic and multiracial heritage. The rejection of mixed heritage has been so strong that even our language is permeated with vocabulary against it. Among them "mixed" connotes abnormality, and the term "mulatto" has been rejected because it is a Spanish derivative of mule, an animal that cannot reproduce, implying that Black and White biracial people are not only illegitimate but biologically abnormal too. This comparison "makes clear that people from Africa and people from Europe are two different animal species, species that should lead separate lives, species that cannot be family. It also emphasizes the notion of hierarchy, for it seems obvious that our culture values horses more than donkeys" (Scales-Trent, 1995, p. 101). Today academics who study interracial and interethnic marriage use the term *out marriage* (close to "outcast") to describe people who choose to marry someone from another racial or ethnic group.

The prevailing academic opinion of multiethnic and multiracial people during the nineteenth and twentieth centuries was that they were biologically, morally, sexually, and intellectually inferior (Olumide, 2002; Sickels, 1972)—a view held by many professionals to this day. With few exceptions, such as Brazil, Mexico, and other Latin American nations where the majority population is of mixed racial background, interracial people are separate racial minorities in most other countries around the world. Multiracial persons are perceived as intruders and outsiders. They have been the target of public condemnation and ridicule, labeled abnormal, immoral, and uncivilized (Nakashima, 1992). They also challenge the powerful in-group orthodoxy detailed by Banks and Banks (1997), Tatum (1999), and others. There is extreme discrimination against Amerasians by fellow Vietnamese both in Vietnam and in this country (Valverde, 1992); Japanese or Chinese of interracial ancestry are still considered impure and not fully accepted by their own Asian communities (Spickard, 1992), and Asian groups generally look down on dark skin and associate it with lower socioeconomic status (Valverde, 1992). Perceived as racially impure, multiethnic and multiracial persons are seen as a threat to the world's White racial purity—and their domination—and a threat to the political power of single-race minority groups in this country (Zack, 2002).

Negative Influences

Around the turn of the nineteenth century, anti-immigration feelings also arose against Jews, Italians, Poles, and other ethnic groups. In 1836, Samuel F. B. Morse (who invented the telegraph) wrote:

The question is now placed . . . before the whole American people, whether it is or is not expedient that the naturalization laws be so altered as to put a stop to evils under which our democratic institutions are suffering, and to guard against dangers with which they are threatened from the influx of a vicious, ignorant foreign population, danger enhanced by the combinations of these foreigners throughout the country. (Carnes, 1995, p. 42)

In the nineteenth century, **Nativists** (Anglo Saxon Protestants born in this country) and scientific racists were deeply concerned about the negative influences these predominantly non-Anglo Saxon and Catholic immigrants would have on the development of civilization and democracy in the United States; they were also concerned about the negative effects, through interracial marriage, on the development of the Anglo Saxon race (Banks, 1995). Even President John F. Kennedy had his loyalties questioned because of his Irish ancestry and Catholic beliefs (Carnes, 1995). It was popularly believed that Kennedy would not be elected president because of the strong anti-Irish and anti-Catholic views of many voters. Universities such as Brandeis (Jewish) and Notre Dame (Catholic) were created, in part, because of anti-Catholic and anti-Jewish sentiment on the part of the traditional Ivy League schools.

One result of this anti-immigrant and anti-miscegenation movement was the development and popularity of the **eugenics movement**. This movement took hold as White Anglo Saxons believed it their duty to rid the human race of undesirable persons, those with undesirable traits that could be passed on. One example of this movement occurred in the town of Shutesbury, Massachusetts. Without telling the residents of the town what they were doing, eugenicists spent many months collecting information about the residents of the town and charting genetic information that detailed what might happen when "good pioneer stock is mixed with bad immigrant stock." More frightening was the forced sterilization of twenty-six teenage boys in Philadelphia for things such as kleptomania and masturbation, justified by a doctor as "an effective means of race preservation" (Barry, 2002, p. 62A). In Virginia 7,450 people were sterilized from 1924 through 1979 under the eugenics thinking (Barry, 2002).

Japanese Racial Purity

Anglo Saxon Protestants are not the only people with a history of believing in their own racial superiority: The Japanese also have a pervasive sense of racial purity and superiority. They see themselves as a pure race that developed separately from other races because of the geographic and cultural isolation of the islands. They view other races—including Whites—as polluted and hereditarily strained. Further, because of their political and past military power in Asia, most Japanese believe they are superior to other Asian groups (Spickard, 1989).

A critical component of this sense of racial superiority is their view about skin color. From very early times the Japanese liked white skin, associating it with spiritual and cultural refinement and high social states; they disliked black or dark skin, which they associate with being primitive (Spickard, 1989). For example, their porcelain is highly regarded for its delicacy and whiteness. Japanese saw themselves as being white-skinned, Okinawans as Black (dark-skinned).

However, based on other preferred physical characteristics, the Japanese did not like Europeans or Africans. Shortly after the first Europeans came to Japan, they were excluded and put to death. Japan deported all children of Iberian men and Japanese women; however, they accepted unions—and children—from other Asian/Japanese combinations. When Japanese first came to this country in the 1860s their racial hierarchy of acceptance was first Japanese (pure race), then other Asians, except Filipinos, whom they seem to universally despise, Europeans next, and then Africans. Even in the 1960s most Japanese in Japan viewed Europeans and White Americans as different, inferior, more hairy, and "animal-like" (Spickard, 1989). Japanese anti-Black sentiment has been well documented.

Latinos

The 1848 **Treaty of Guadalupe Hidalgo** ending the Mexican War forced Mexico to relinquish more than half of its national territory to this country, which became California, Nevada, Utah, and parts of Colorado, Arizona, New Mexico, and Wyoming. Thus a significant number of current U.S. citizens were Natives with a colonial Spanish tradition. The treaty established many agreements, most of which were flagrantly violated and/or stricken out by official acts of Congress—much as treaties between this country and Native American tribes were systematically ignored. Mexico insisted that former Mexican citizens be integrated into the dominant society with full rights as U.S. citizens. Since citizenship at the time was limited to Whites only, this meant integration of Mexicans into the mainstream society as members of the dominant White group.

Mexican Whites quickly moved to ingratiate themselves with mainstream Whites by shedding their association with Mexico's racially mixed mestizo and mulatto populations. As we have discussed, Mexico has a history of racial mixing—first Indians and Spanish (White), then Indians, Spanish, and Blacks (from Mexican slaves). Today many Latinos either insist on their pure Spanish heritage or are proud of their mestizo background; few, however, acknowledge any Black heritage. Mexican Whites from the Southwest claim geographic distance from Mexico and regional isolation has kept them pure descendants of the conquering White Spaniards. The mountainous area between Santa Fe and Taos, where the movie *The Milagro Bean Field War* was filmed, is such an area.

The Term "Hispanic"

The term **"Hispano"** was first introduced around the turn of the nineteenth century by "los ricos" (wealthy) descendants of Spaniards to establish their direct lineage to Spain (España or Hispania) and alliance with mainstream Whites (Oboler, 1995), thus signifying their distinction from Mexicans and Mexico.

While the United States formally accepted Mexicans' classification as Whites, wealthy former citizens of Mexico found themselves ostracized and discriminated against, and particularly poor and apparently racially mixed former Mexicans were subjected to mainstream White supremacist views and treated as the Blacks in the West and Southwest. As a racial group, Mexicans were equated with Blacks for discrimination and segregation purposes.

In 1965 the Justice Department declared that Mexican Americans and Puerto Ricans would be treated as racial groups (Allen, 2000). As the government moved to formalize the classification of Mexican Americans as a racial group, Hispanic leaders fought even harder to avoid the racial stigma of belonging to a non-White, and thus lower status, racial group. However, with the rise of Black Power during the Civil Rights movement, Mexican Americans became identified as an ethnic group that was neither mainstream White nor non-White but a unique category in between (maybe to avoid further racial dislocation). This new ethnic category mirrored the traditional classification system of Latin American countries that recognizes Whites at the top, pure non-Whites at the bottom, and various mixed categories in between—a system that allows for *social Whites*— persons who appear White and are publicly accepted as White, even if they had some racial mixing.

Chapter Feature
Student Profile: Alysyn McKinley

Alysyn McKinley is biethnic. Her mother is Latina Black (Puerto Rican) and her father is Black/African American. Although both parents are Black, they belong to two different ethnic groups: Latino and non-Latino. Alysyn has been raised within both cultures and speaks Spanish fluently. She often visits her mother's family in Puerto Rico and her father's family in North Carolina. The issue of self-identity has been very difficult and painful for Alysyn. Her parents tell her that she belongs to both groups equally. They affirm both cultures at home. Some of Alysyn's Latino friends tell her that she is Black because her father is Black/African American. Others tell her that she is better off being Latina because Blacks are perceived as lower than Latinos.

Her African American friends tease her, telling her that she is trying to better herself by being Latina. They say that she is more African American than Latina and laugh when she speaks Spanish. Many Blacks tell her that society will see and treat her as Black. They also say that Puerto Ricans are "nothing but Black folks in hiding."

In school Alysyn is told that she has to choose one over the other on official school forms—she cannot be both. Alysyn is proud of both of her parents and heritages. Why can't she be proud of both? Why must she choose between them? She used to select "Other" but always felt uncomfortable with that label. What is an "Other"? Are "Others" less human? Then she found out that the school counselors changed the category she chose to Black/African American.

In the 1990 Census the "Hispanic" option was given as one of the racial choices, but was greatly criticized because Hispanic is a label that is exclusive to White European Spaniards and to Spanish-speakers (Cruz-Janzen, 2001). When many Latinos chose "Other Race" rather than the Hispanic option, they were reclassified. However, the debate surrounding the identity of multiethnic and multiracial persons had begun and this automatic reclassification was challenged from two ends. Many Latinos—who are of various racial mixtures—felt the government was forcing them to identify with White Spaniards; yet White Latinos who claim direct, genetic lineage to Spain, identify with mainstream Whites, and still desire full inclusion under the White category. As a result, the 2000 Census changed the category to "Spanish/Hispanic/Latino" and presents the question of ethnic origin before the question of race—asking Latinos their origin in the question on ethnicity first and separately from the question on race.

Mexican American leaders—most of whom were from the White group—successfully argued that the Hispanic ethnic category would protect all Mexican Americans, especially those who were White. Further, it would protect the group's insistence that they not shed their language or culture to assimilate. While many Mexican Americans from the Four Corners Area—Colorado, New Mexico, Arizona, and Utah—call themselves "Hispano," they refuse to accept the English translation, "Hispanic." Simultaneously, Latino White elites hoped to maintain their distance from non-White Latinos while continuing their quest to eventually join the mainstream White elite.

Immigration

When slavery ended, many of the newly colonized nations were very keen to attract immigrants from the old world to provide needed labor and to help develop the emerging countries. However, several of these countries, including the United States and Australia, went to great lengths to only allow immigration of White people and to restrict immigration of "inferior races" (Knepper, 1995, p. 19).

> Feelings of antipathy toward non-White people have been reflected in statutes making immigration and naturalization eligibility contingent upon geographical location and/or racial heritage. Because of the nature of these immigration policies, spouses of citizens were until recently among the few non-Europeans eligible for entry to U.S. shores. . . . In fact, much of this legislation has focused on keeping non-Europeans out of the U.S., and, for most of U.S. history, has affected most directly the presence of Asians in this country. (Thornton, 1992, p. 65)

While Brazil encouraged racial mixing of its immigrants, first with Indians and later Africans, and encouraged immigration of Italians, various Asian groups, and people from the Middle East, other nations with a history of extensive racial mix-

A typical Brazilian child. The Brazilian government uses one of many mixed-race labels to categorize children like him.

ing, such as Mexico, promoted immigration of White Europeans as a way to whiten its population. Mexico realized that denial of its extensive mestizo population would be quite futile and useless and openly proclaimed itself as a mestizo nation. Over time, Blacks and Indians in Mexico, Brazil, and other Latin American countries assimilated through interracial unions (Cruz-Janzen, 2001). Countries previously ruled by the Spanish then instituted a whitening policy, called *blanqueamiento*—a commonly known, if not officially acknowledged, policy throughout most Latin American nations.

Thus, throughout most of Spanish Latin America, the one-drop rule applied in a very different way from its application in this country. Anyone with any amount of White heritage becomes Whiter and no longer a member of an unmixed group; mestizos and mulattoes are not considered Indian or Black. This is also known as *mejorando la raza* (improving the race) and is clearly designed to reduce or conceal physical evidence of racial mixing, promoting racial mixing to transform Blacks into mulattoes and Indians into mestizos, and eventually into Whites. Foremost, the policies of *blanqueamiento* call for extensive infusion of pure White "genes" into the population through increased European immigration (Andrews, 1980; Muhammad, 1995). At the extreme, these policies also call for the complete extermination of non-Whites. Massacres of Black people have been recorded throughout Latin America: In 1912 several thousand Blacks were killed in Cuba (McGarrity & Cardenas, 1995), and it is known that Blacks have disappeared in Uruguay, Chile, and Argentina due to racial genocide (Comas-Diaz, 1996). The genocide of Native Americans in almost all the New World colonies is well documented.

Japanese American Immigrants

The first official record of Japanese coming to America is 1861; by the 1880s the flow of Japanese laborers to work in Hawaiian cornfields and on the West coast increased, with 200 in 1880, 2,800 in 1890s, and 225,000 in the first two and a half decades of the twentieth century (Spickard, 1989). These Japanese immigrants were men who came to the United States to earn enough money to eventually return home and reestablish their lives after losses of their land due to crop failures and new laws. They left their wives and families at home. Only 6 percent of Japanese who came to this country before 1906 were women.

The immigration of Japanese to this country is similar to the immigration of other groups to Canada, Mexico, the Caribbean, and Central and South America, for example. It usually resulted from economic hardships at home (e.g., the famous Irish Potato Famine) and political persecution, combined with opportunities in the new world. This story is illustrated here by the Japanese experience and differs markedly from people who were already in the new world (Natives) and people forced to come here (slaves)(Ogbu, 1978).

The first Japanese men were part of what Spickard calls the frontier period. According to Spickard, Japanese American history can be divided into five periods: (1) the frontier period; (2) the era when Japanese women came and created families and stable communities; (3) the youth of these families, or second-generation Japanese; (4) the incarceration of Japanese Americans during WWII; and (5) the postwar period, where Japanese Americans moved ever more closely to fully joining the American mainstream (1989).

Anti-Japanese Sentiment.   In 1882 the U.S. Congress voted to exclude all Chinese laborers because they were considered a threat to White laborers. As a result, many Chinese returned home or retreated into ethnic slums. The initial Japanese male workers, known as **Issei** took the place of the Chinese in Western industry and agriculture, but racists simply replaced the Chinese with Japanese as their favorite targets of hatred. Added to this anti-Japanese feeling was the emerging military power of the nation of Japan in Asia, including a victory against Russia, a European power. This challenged the deep-seated belief of White Americans that White power would always reign supreme in the world (Spickard, 1989). As a result, the *San Francisco Chronicle* started an anti-Japanese campaign, including the accusation that Japanese men were a menace to White American women. While politicians tried, unsuccessfully, to add Japanese to the list of barred people, the San Francisco School Board took Japanese and Korean students out of the regular schools and placed them with Chinese students in segregated schools. This produced an outcry from the Japanese government. As a result of this outcry the U.S. and Japanese governments signed a *Gentleman's Agreement* that forced California to rescind anti-Japanese legislation, while Japan promised to prevent the immigration of any more laborers.

Settling Down.   At about this same time—1910—some of the original Japanese laborers decided their stay in this country would have to be longer than originally expected; others decided they liked it here and stayed (much as the Portuguese did in Brazil). These Japanese men began to think about settling down and having families. Since the Gentleman's Agreement between Japan and the United States said nothing about women, some of these men went to Japan to marry and then returned with their brides; others recruited women from Japan and married them here. In 1900 there were 5 Japanese men to 1 Japanese woman; in 1920 the ratio was 1.6 men to 1 woman (Kitano, 1976).

The arrival of Japanese women produced a radical shift in the lives of Japanese Americans: changing from transient farm laborers to settling down to raise families and create Japanese communities. They became small businessmen, and Japanese associations and Buddhist and Christian churches flourished, primarily in California and other Western states. Additionally, many of these families lived in mixed neighborhoods. By 1920 there were Japanese Americans in every state of the Union.

According to 1924–1925 marriage records in Los Angeles, Issei had fewer marriages to people of other ethnic/racial groups than any other racial/ethnic groups—Blacks, Chinese, and Filipinos. During the Frontier Period more Isseis married non-Japanese than during the period after Japanese women became available. The emerging Japanese American communities enforced marriage within the group.

However, anti-Japanese sentiment continued, and in 1913 California passed the Alien Land Law, denying the right to own real property to Japanese and Chinese. Because Japan supported the United States against Germany in WWI, there was a short-lived lull to the antagonism, which renewed itself with the height of the Nativist movement in the 1920s. In 1924 Congress passed a law strictly limiting immigration in general and stopping Japanese immigration altogether.

The Nisei.   Because of the cutoff of immigrants from Japan, the second generation Japanese Americans, called **Nisei**, differed from their parents, rejecting their parents' backgrounds and questioning their own Japaneseness (Spickard, 1989). Most Nisei went to school with mainstream Whites and tried to conform to the White norm. They experienced the inner conflict of wanting to be American, knowing they were still Japanese, and being rejected by White Americans. The internment of all Japanese of the Pacific Coast during World War II was further proof of their unacceptance as White Americans.

Many Nisei thus developed a form of self-hatred, as they desperately tried to assimilate into middle-class mainstream White U.S. society. The children who had White peers in elementary schools, and often in their neighborhood, discovered in high school and college that when it came to dating they were not fully accepted. Further, they were often shut out of social interactions, so they established all-Nisei social groups—associations, dances, sports teams, and so on. While these groups were totally isolated from other groups, including Whites, they still aspired to the White, middle-class view of American success.

Since the Issei's own marriage partners had been chosen for them by their families, they expected to do the same for their own children. Very few Nisei married before World War II and, since nearly all came of age while living in the camps, they had little choice regarding spouses from other groups. While living in the camps, it was considered totally unacceptable to socialize with the White staff; the White staff themselves despised consorting with the inmates. The few mixed-race Japanese families that did exist at this time were also included in the camps.

After the war the Nisei still strove to prove their loyalty to the United States and focused on assimilation and upward mobility (Spickard, 1989). Even those Nisei who married after they left the camps married other Japanese Americans. They returned to rebuild their lives, but settled in the suburbs, where they raised their families and their children attended integrated schools. They also pursued education as the vehicle to success. "The decade of the 1950s witnessed a stunning rise in occupational and educational status, so that by 1960 Japanese Americans had the highest average amount of schooling and highest average occupational status level of any American ethnic group, including white Protestants" (Spickard, 1989, p. 56).

Part of the Nisei ambition was the wish to become acculturated as White Americans, but the other impetus was a direct result of the war: to prove they were good Americans who should never again be questioned regarding their loyalties.

Sansei.   Children of the upwardly mobile Nisei, the **Sansei,** were mainly born after the war. Many of these third-generation Japanese Americans followed their parents' example of education and middle-class careers, emerging in the later 1970s and 1980s as ambitious and career oriented—and with a high probability of out marriage.

The Sansei grew up in predominantly integrated—Asian-White—communities, attended integrated schools, and enrolled in integrated colleges. The Sansei were raised in non-Japanese neighborhoods and had non-Japanese friends. Most dated non-Japanese Americans. An ever-increasing number of Sansei also began to marry non-Japanese Americans. By 1970, nationwide, 42 percent of Sansei men and 46 percent of Sansei women were married to non-Japanese (Spickard, 1989). These numbers reflect the normal progression of generations among American immigrant groups: low out marriage in the first generation, higher in the second, and very high in the third. These changing rates for Japanese Americans reflect not only their acculturation into America's middle class society, but a gradual erosion of opposition to interracial marriage—both from Japanese themselves, who initially were totally opposed to it, and from Whites and other Americans. While much of this opposition has disappeared, there is still opposition from some Whites and socially/politically active Japanese Americans—and there is still considerable opposition among Japanese Americans to marrying African Americans.

Opposition to Non-White Immigrants

The original colonists were, of course, English, and the English and other Northern Europeans became established as the dominant social, economic, and political group. As persons from other parts of Europe, perceived as inferior races, began arriving, it became necessary to limit their entry. The 1790 Immigration and Naturalization Act restricted immigration and citizenship to Europeans; later immigration from Southern, Central, and Eastern Europe was restricted, largely to halt the incoming flow of Catholics.

The same climate that led to these laws also created several secretive organizations designed to prevent new immigrants from becoming part of mainstream U.S. society. Between 1849 and 1860 the **Know-Nothing Party** emerged as a secret political organization to discriminate against immigrants and Catholics (Carnes, 1995). The name was derived from its practice of secrecy; a member questioned about the party always answered, "I don't know." Their chief aim was to prevent foreign-born citizens from holding political office. In the late nineteenth century a movement called Nativism attempted to establish Protestants as the only legitimate Americans. They believed that they were the only rightful inhabitants of North America and that the new immigrants presented a threat to civilization and democracy. Primarily, they were committed to preserve national racial purity.

In 1882 Congress passed the Chinese Exclusion Act, suspending further entry of most Chinese immigrants into the country. The Geary Acts of 1892 and 1902 further limited Chinese immigration. Other Asians were recruited to build railroads, mine gold, and farm the West. These immigrants were mostly males, who were not permitted to marry interracially, ensuring that these undesirable laborers did not increase in numbers through birth or their genes filter into the mainstream White population. Later acts were passed to reduce the entry of Japanese, through the Gentleman's Agreement already discussed.

The Immigration Act of 1917 was also designed to halt the immigration of Southern, Central, and Eastern Europeans and Asians and Pacific Islanders, by requiring an English reading test in order to enter the country. When this act failed to reduce immigration from these nations sufficiently, the Immigration Act of 1924 was established, specifically limiting the number of immigrants from all countries except Northern and Western Europe. As a result, immigrants from Great Britain and Germany were assigned generous quotas, resulting in what Northern Europeans caustically called the "Great Brain Drain." Eastern European nations received smaller allotments. Quotas for countries such as Russia, the source of most Jewish immigrants and some Asians, was also cut back; practically all Asians were barred (Cruz-Janzen, 1997).

Puerto Ricans and Filipinos

Under the Treaty of Paris, Spain ceded the Philippines and Puerto Rico to this country, giving the population unlimited access to the mainland. Immediately, the racial composition of Puerto Ricans began to raise concerns. The 1846 Census by the Spanish colonial government reported 51.24 percent of the Puerto Rican population as African or Negro, but in 1959 the count dropped to 23 percent. North American congressmen wondered how there could be so many Whites in a Black man's country and, fearing a large migratory flow of non-Anglo Saxons to our large cities, decided that it was "the duty of the United States to impose a strict color line on Puerto Rican society" (Toplin, 1976, p. 305).

In 1935 and 1939, the United States passed legislation promising to pay passage to any Filipino returning to the Philippines. The 1943 Act repealed the Exclusion Act, raised the Chinese quota to 105, and made the Chinese eligible for naturalization. However, this new Chinese quota covered Chinese immigration from any country, including Latin America. In 1946 a new quota included persons from India and all Filipinos. Following World War II, immigration of persons of color, especially foreign spouses of U.S. service persons, increased dramatically, which created a catalyst for drastic changes in the way race and ethnicity were defined and perceived (Nakashima, 1992). Legal restrictions blocked substantial migration from many other regions, including Mexicans, who were allotted a very small quota.

Civil Rights Movement

The civil rights movement of the 1960s resulted from centuries of civil rights violations against the non-[mainstream] White population and the moral dilemma that brought the nation face-to-face with the hypocrisy of its founding creed. One result was that Congress abandoned its open policies of maintaining a primarily all-White nation dominated by Anglo beliefs and culture. The Immigration Reform Act of 1965 abolished national-origin quotas and established an annual limit of 170,000 visas for immigrants from countries in the Eastern Hemisphere, with 20,000 immigrants per country, and an annual admission of 120,000 persons from the Western Hemisphere with visas available on a first-come, first-served basis. Preference was given to close relatives of citizens and preferential status was also assigned to individuals who possessed job skills in short supply. The act exempted family members of citizens' spouses and certain categories of special immigrants from the numerical limits.

Congress anticipated a new wave of European immigrants as a result of these reforms, but within ten years the majority of immigrants arrived from Asian and Latin American nations, such as the Philippines, Korea, China, and Mexico. During the Vietnam War, our government made secret pacts with the Hmong, who lived in the mountains of Laos and Cambodia, in order to recruit them as allies, promising them protection and asylum if the United States lost the war. Additionally, others who supported the United States in Southeast Asia came to this country as refugees at the war's end.

New Restrictions

Because of these increased numbers of non-European immigrants, the government responded to pressure from various groups, passing an amendment to the Immigration Reform Act of 1965 in 1978 abolishing separate quotas for each hemisphere and instituting an annual quota of 290,000 immigrants worldwide, with a maximum of 20,000 for any one country. The Refugee Act of 1980 further reduced the quota for all immigrants to 270,000 persons, excluding refugees—which it estimated at about 50,000 people annually. New measures established household income levels to be met by sponsors of immigrants and limited benefits, such as social security and government subsidies, including food stamps, for new immigrants. Wealthy foreigners able to invest over $1 million in business ventures in the United States received preferential immigration treatment. The 1990 Immigration Act granted increased quotas to countries that had sent few immigrants in recent years, such as Ireland.

A major result of the shift to immigrants from Asia and Latin America, along with immigrants from Russia and the former Soviet Union, combined with decreased numbers of immigration from Europe and a low birthrate among native-born Whites, has reduced the percentage of the mainstream White population. And, of course, because of the still existing one-drop rule, any person with any non-White heritage is added to the non-White group. However, despite this rule, more than 2 percent of the mainstream White population self-identifies as members of more than one race.

Racism and Segregation

The assassination of President Abraham Lincoln in 1865 brought Andrew Johnson, a Southern sympathizer, to the presidency. Johnson blamed a few rich aristocrats for the Confederate rebellion and decided to be lenient on the former rebels. According to Frederick Douglass, he was wholly incompetent in many other ways (Douglass, 1994/1845/1855/1893). Knowledge of a supporter in the presidency motivated Southern states to blatantly restore a society that withheld the newly gained rights of Blacks. Once Reconstruction ended in 1877, Southern states moved to reverse all the progress Blacks had made. The establishment of the Black Codes greatly restricted the rights of freed Blacks, including property rights and employment Blacks could hold. It provided that "vagrant" Blacks, or Blacks viewed as unemployed, could be "bound" to White employers and/or incarcerated with forced labor. Despite freeing the slaves, the South created a two-tier society—Black and White—very similar to the former slaveholding society.

Over the next seventy-five years, segregation expanded rapidly, establishing separate facilities for Whites-only in schools, hotels, transportation, and public parks. Facilities for non-Whites were poorly funded and very inferior. Southern states prevented Blacks from voting by requiring them to read and write, own property, and pay poll taxes. Since most Blacks were uneducated, unable to acquire property, and could not afford the taxes, these requirements were very successful. As a result, Blacks were unable to halt the creation of laws that further segregated the South and kept them second-class citizens.

Legal Segregation

In 1891 a group of New Orleans mulattoes of mixed Black and mainstream White ancestry formed the *Citizens Committee to Test the Constitutionality of the Separate Car Law*. In June 1892, Homer A. Plessy purchased a first-class ticket on the East Louisiana Railroad and sat in a car reserved for mainstream White customers. A conductor immediately challenged his right to sit in the "White" car. When Plessy refused to move, he was arrested and arraigned before a judge. Plessy complained that having to sit in separate cars while traveling through his native state of Louisiana violated the equal protection guaranteed to him by the Fourteenth Amendment of the Constitution and the Thirteenth Amendment's prohibition of involuntary servitude. Eventually, the Supreme Court upheld segregation, ruling *that separate but equal* facilities were acceptable (Davis, 1998).

Within a few years of the *Plessy* ruling almost every institution or facility in the South was segregated. Added to the list of segregated places were sports arenas, telephone booths, movie theaters, and elevators. In some states Blacks and Whites could not fish on the same lakes, play baseball together, or shoot pool at the same establishment. The Black wife of Francis Wardle can vividly remember not being allowed to swim in the Kansas City public pools on sweltering summer days and only being allowed to usher in White theaters after she promised "not to raise your eyes and watch the movie." One result of this segregation was that little money was allocated for the education of Black children.

World War II

World War II saw many citizens, including persons of color, travel across the world to fight for a free country against a fascist enemy, despite calls by some minority leaders not to fight. In 1948 President Truman ordered the desegregation of all branches of the armed forces. Returning soldiers of color were ill-prepared to return to the segregated and oppressive status quo. Some of these soldiers returned with European and Asian brides, only to find their marriages declared illegal in their home state (Spickard, 1989). The war also created job opportunities in northern cities, prompting many African Americans and mainstream Whites to leave the South in search of better opportunities, resulting in racial conflict as groups, particularly African Americans, Latinos, and lower class mainstream Whites, competed for jobs and housing. The most destructive racial riot occurred in Detroit in 1943, rocking the nation and propelling national action to increase economic, educational, and political opportunities for disenfranchised groups. Schools began offering ethnic studies courses to reduce racial and ethnic prejudice and increase interracial understanding.

Changes and Improvements in Education

Desegregation

With the 1954 Supreme Court case of *Brown* v. *Board of Education of Topeka* (Kansas), African American parents sought to have their children admitted into any public schools in their community, regardless of race. The Court ruled that separate educational facilities were "inherently unequal." Even if the physical facilities and other aspects of the educational system appeared equal, the Court ruled racial segregation has a negative psychological and educational impact on the children, thus rendering the education unequal. The Court left it up to the states to establish their own desegregation plans. Not surprising, ten years after this ruling, almost all African American children in the South remained in racially segregated, poorly funded schools. Additionally, most school districts that did integrate provided separate tracks for White and Black students. Whites were tracked for college while Blacks were tracked for vocational occupations and menial work.

By the late 1950s and early 1960s racial tensions between African Americans and mainstream Whites escalated. It became clear that assimilation did not include African Americans. Discrimination in employment, housing, and education, combined with rising expectations, forced African Americans to lead an unprecedented fight for their rights. Racial tensions escalated and intensified during the 1960s with more race riots, resulting in a civil rights movement that brought global attention to the plight of many disenfranchised Americans, including African Americans. One result of this movement was federal acts that directly impacted education, including the 1964 Civil Rights Act, which gave the government power to force desegregation of schools (Title IV) and Title VI, which prohibited the distribution of federal funds to schools with racially discriminatory facilities and programs.

Language Proficiency and the Rights of Disabled Students

The 1968 Bilingual Education Act encouraged school districts to provide bilingual education to **Limited English Proficient** (LEP) students, better known as **English Language Learners** (ELL). This act created much controversy as it failed to establish concrete recommendations for program development and implementation—as is the case with most federal laws. Also, it was not forceful enough, and many school districts either failed to respond adequately or established a wide array of programs of varying quality.

In the 1970s Kinney Lau and thousands of other Chinese students from the San Francisco area were failing due to their lack of English proficiency. Their parents sued the school system because it did not provide their children with any remedial instruction to learn enough English to be able to take advantage of their education. In 1974 the Supreme Court determined that teaching students in a language they did not understand was not appropriate and that sometimes equal educational opportunity requires special educational programs for students. Under Title VI of the Civil Rights Act, any school district receiving federal funds is obligated to provide special instruction for language minority students. The Equal Educational Opportunities Act (EEOA) required school districts to take steps to provide equal education for language minority students.

In 1972, Title IX of the Education Amendment Acts prohibited any form of gender discrimination in public education—thus legislating equal financial support—in school admissions, counseling and guidance, competitive athletics, student rules and regulations, and access to programs and courses, including vocational and physical education. Title IX also covers sex discrimination in employment practices, including interviewing and recruitment, hiring and promotion, compensation, job assignment, and benefits.

Brown v. *Board of Education* led to further legislation in support of other disenfranchised Americans. As a result of the *Pennsylvania Association for Retarded Children* v. *Commonwealth* and the *Mill* v. *Washington DC Board of Education* cases, public schools were mandated to provide free and appropriate education for all children with disabilities within their districts. The principle of "zero reject" established that no child with disabilities could be denied a free, appropriate education, because excluding children with disabilities from public schools violated the Supreme Court's decision in *Brown* v. *Board of Education*. Again, it was left up to individual districts to implement the decision.

In 1975 Public Law 94-142, also known as the Education for All Handicapped Children Act, was passed. This act, which later became the Individuals with Disabilities Education Act (IDEA), mandated coverage for all disabled learners from birth to 21 years old, established specific legal protocols, and provided some financial support to local school districts.

Multiracial and Multiethnic Children in Schools

In 1967 the Supreme Count determined, in the *Loving* v. *State of Virginia* case, that all state laws prohibiting interracial marriage were unconstitutional. This decision, along with desegregation in schools and more equality in society, led to an increase in interracial and interethnic marriages—and multiethnic and multiracial children. Unfortunately, schools have not responded to the needs of this new population. Further, the research on multiethnic and multiracial students in schools is still very recent and scanty. There are significant gaps in the literature, particularly in areas related to academic achievement and the role of socialization in shaping the ethnic and racial identity and self-concept of these students in a society fixated on single race and ethnic identity. While the little research we have focuses on children from African American and mainstream

White unions (Funderburg, 1994; Rosenblatt, Karis, & Powell, 1995; Winn & Priest, 1993), the nation is facing a rapidly growing population from combinations of ethnic and racial unions (Thornton, 1992). This bias in research, according to Root, is because unions between people of color have not been perceived as posing as direct a threat to the White versus non-White dichotomy (Root, 1992). Further, some believe children of other unions, such as Asian and mainstream White, or Spanish/Latino and mainstream White, receive more acceptance by the mainstream culture because of their more *ambiguous* physical appearance (Bradshaw, 1992). The racial mixing that causes most popular and professional concern in this country is between groups that are perceived to be most culturally and socially different—Blacks and Whites and Japanese and Blacks. Exacerbating this dilemma is in fact that Asians and Whites are the two groups most wedded to preserving the purity of their races (Root, 1992).

However, most multiracial Black/White children are continually misidentified with the racial label from other groups, and "multiracial people are racial minorities in most countries, and have been labeled as immoral and uncivilized in the same way that racial and ethnic minorities are often characterized by the dominant racial and ethnic group" (Nakashima, 1992, p. 168). Furthermore,

Marny (the baby) has a Pueblo Indian father and a mother who is White and Latino. We have very little research to help us understand children like Marny.

people who come to this country bring their racial prejudices with them, such as the discrimination against Amerasians by fellow Vietnamese both in Vietnam and in this country (Valverde, 1992).

Multicultural Education

> Why is it that everyone has rights, except us? Persons who speak other languages, women, handicapped, Blacks, gays, lesbians. Everyone except us. What we want is quite simple, we want to be who were really are. We are not one identity or the other. I don't want to be told who or what I am. I have the right to identify myself and not be reclassified by any government agency according to what they think I should or could be. That's not so much to ask. (Personal communication, 1998, student paper)

Finding ways to make the dream of the Declaration of Independence a true reality has been the focus of much of our history. Disillusionment with the "American Dream" and a long history of civil rights abuses exploded into a struggle for humanity and fair access to opportunities for all. This struggle shed light on two vastly different "Americas," one for mainstream Whites and people fully assimilated into mainstream America and a lesser one for everyone else. The 1960s and 1970s were marked by swift court actions to force the end of segregation, including ending legal racial segregation in schools and racism in education practices. African Americans demanded recognition of African American culture and heritage in the public schools; Native Americans, Mexican Americans and other Latino groups, and other disenfranchised groups followed by demanding preservation of their cultures and the teaching of their languages; and women demanded equal access to education and success.

These demands created the impetus for the New Pluralism and Multicultural Education Movements of the 1980s and 1990s. New Pluralism advocates for the rights of all groups, including bisexual and transgendered, disabled persons, the elderly—in brief, everyone disenfranchised by the nations' institutions. Many mainstream Whites began to reaffirm their own ethnic cultures and heritages. They too realized that they had been the victims of an oppressive system that forced them to shed their ancestry and began to ask for inclusion of White ethnic groups in the schools' curricula.

The last remaining frontier of this long, hard fought journey is at hand—the support, recognition, and full inclusion of multiethnic and multiracial students, adults, and their families.

Conclusion

This nation was founded on the concept of equality for all. Our history has been a slow, often painful progression toward that lofty goal. This history has involved restrictive immigration laws, specific Supreme Court decisions, the Civil War, and various liberation movements. It has experienced giant steps forward, followed by slowly receding activities and attitudes. While we still do not have full equality for all—including full educational equality—progress continues to be made. Further, we have come to the logical place in our country's progress where the full rights of multiethnic and multiracial children and people can no longer be ignored.

Questions/Projects

1. Find someone who came to this country within the last year, someone who came twenty years ago, and someone whose parents immigrated. Interview each person, then present a class discussion comparing and contrasting their experiences.

2. Select one different "new" country—say, Canada, Australia, New Zealand, Brazil. Study the country's efforts to attract new immi-

grants and keep certain people out. Pay special attention to the role of race and color.

3. Study a country where mixed-race people are the norm (Brazil, Mexico, Cuba, Costa Rica). What enabled this country to follow this approach?

4. Why, in your opinion, did it take so long to provide full legal equality for every citizen in this country?

Resources

Books

Katz, W.L. (1997). *Black Indians: A hidden heritage.* New York: Simon and Schuster.
Littlefield, D.F. (1977). *African Seminoles: From removal to emancipation.* Westport, CT: Greenwood Publishing Group.

Websites

William Loren Katz: Black Indians
http://www.williamlkatz.com

Eurasian Nation. Mixed European/Asians
http://www.eurasiannation.com

Mixed racial heritage/Frontline/PBS
Historical people of mixed ancestry—royalty, aristocracy in Europe and United States
http://www.pbs.org/wgbh/pages/frontline/shows/secret/famous

4

Categorizing People

Since the 1967 *Loving* v. *Virginia Supreme Court* decision striking down anti-miscegenation laws across the country, the nation has faced swelling numbers of interethnic and interracial marriages (Stephan, 1992). Interracial unions increased from 500,000 in 1970 to 2 million in 1990 (U.S. Bureau of the Census, 1990), and schools are seeing increasing numbers of children from these unions. According to Morrison and Bordere (2001), over 2 million children of interracial parentage attend our P–12 schools; the 2000 Census shows that nearly 7 million people identify as multiracial, many young children (Schmitt, 2001; U.S. Bureau of the Census, 2001). However, since many multiethnic and multiracial persons still identify with one racial or ethnic group, these numbers are most likely quite low. The increasing numbers reflect the result of increased immigration and interethnic and interracial unions in the country. Since 1964 more immigrants came here from Asia and Latin American than from Europe, as well as more from Russia and former Soviet Union satellites.

The four most common interethnic and/or interracial categories reported in the 2000 Census are mainstream White and Black/African American, mainstream White and Asian, mainstream White and Native American Indian/Alaskan Native, and mainstream White with some *other race*. While 6 percent of all Latinos declared themselves as interethnic and/or interracial, the *other race* category was most selected by Latinos, apparently unable or unwilling to fit within any government prescribed choice (U.S. Bureau of the Census, 2001). But, of course, there are all sorts of multiracial and multiethnic combinations not counted by the Census, within broad Census categories, such as Korean and Japanese or Chickasaw and Sioux.

In this chapter we present information and research on the controversy that challenges the traditional, widely accepted, "racial" categorization in this and other societies. Race has been constructed in different ways at different times and places to reflect local social, economic, folk, and political realities of the times throughout the world. The current racial categories in this country do not further inter- or intragroup understanding, tolerance, and racial harmony; indeed, they aggravate centuries-old angers, distrusts, fears, and misunderstandings, par-

76

ticularly for individuals who self-identify in ways that openly challenge the established categories.

Ethnic and racial identity begins in the preschool years, with adolescence being another critical period for its development. Children's behavioral, psychological, and academic development is impaired when they do not achieve a

Chapter Feature
Student Profile: Kevin Santiago

Kevin Santiago is very critical of the United States for focusing mostly on a "lot of separation" and making everything revolve around race. "Who's labeling us? It's not ourselves. When did you label yourself 'Latino'? Who decided that? The government decided that. Government is made up of how many White members? It's the majority! So who's the interested party in labeling here?" Kevin has a Latino White Mexican father and a mainstream White American mother. The physical differences between his parents, or himself and other people, are not apparent because both sides of the family "Have a lot of White in them." Yet, he knew the differences. "American schools and society tend to push you to one side, always being the minority side." He is often mistaken for a mainstream White until people see his last name. That's when the discrimination begins, and it is constant.

As a young child, Kevin grew up between Mexico and the United States. In Mexico being "pocho" (multiethnic/multiracial) was "no big deal." He came to the United States permanently in middle school, and "it was here in the United States that everything blew out of proportion." He is convinced it happens everywhere in the United States and especially the schools, from administration to students. "They reject you for being different; they treat you differently for being different. It's all in a put down way." Being biethnic and deciding what or who he was created difficulties that affected his learning because the struggle was constant and he spent a lot of time thinking about it.

Kevin asks, "What is White? Who is White? What is Anglo? What is Caucasian? What is Hispanic, Latino? I'm not White if I'm from Spain? What are all these things?" He is adamant that any country that places such strong emphasis on race labeling and separation should spend equal emphasis explaining this in the schools. Even though it is there constantly, the schools act as though the issue does not exist and expect students and parents to know all these things. "In history class we are learning about nationalities, we're not learning about races." Yet, people are required to fill out official government and school forms. They are expected to know and understand all the background history and significance of all those categories but are never taught. "How do these races or categories come about? They teach about the English, that's a country. They teach about Mexico, that's a country. It's not fair that they force you to put a category on a form when they don't teach you what that category is or where that category comes from."

strong sense of self-identity that is inclusive of gender, class, and ethnic and/or racial identity (Morrison & Bordere, 2001). Clearly, a single-race approach to racial labeling denies a multiethnic or multicultural child or adult a full identity that is legitimized, validated, and—foremost—affirmed.

Focus Questions

1. How does the historical development of racial classification systems reflect social, economic, and political realities of the times throughout the world? How do notions of racial purity and racial superiority permeate this development? How have these approaches worked to punish and prevent interracial mixing?

2. How is the White racial category constructed differently and more narrowly than the other categories? What does this say about how we view and feel about White racial purity and superiority?

3. How and why does the Hispanic category represent formal acceptance of multiethnic and multiracial identity in the 2000 Census?

4. How has the traditional single-race classification system led to both internal and external group competition and conflict? How would a multiethnic/multiracial category be a threat to the White group and minority groups?

5. How did the civil rights movement open the door to recognition of multiethnic and multiracial persons?

Understanding Race, Racism, and Categorizing People

Historically and legally, Anglos, Aryans, and Caucasians have been considered exclusively White; Asians, Latinos, Native Americans, Hindus, and mixed-race persons were decidedly not (Knepper, 1995). Further, as we already discussed, our history and institutions are grounded in Anglo Saxon culture and our cultural roots remain Anglo Saxon, especially as they manifest themselves in our schools.

Many of the ruling classes of European nations—including Britain—were believed to descend from Nordic ancestry. The notion of having "blue blood," or royal blood, is seen as a remnant of a not-so-distant past ruled by blue-eyed Nordics (Grant, 1916). European monarchies were based on this "blue-blood" lineage. The male nobility of Spain are known as **hidalgos** (meaning "son of the Goth" [Grant, 1916] or blue-eyed Nordics) and are believed to be descendants of Nordic Whites. While the English monarchy publicly distanced themselves from their Nordic heritage before World War I and World War II (to avoid accusations of German sympathies), it is still much of the folk belief in England.

These aristocrats of noble birth were viewed by all as superior to others, but especially superior to Gypsies and Jews. Gypsies across Eurasia have suffered centuries of oppression and victimization due to their perceived racial impurity. A nomadic people said to originate in India, gypsies have a history of intermarriage with different racial groups and are darker than most national populations—especially in Europe. Hitler saw Gypsies and Jews, along with gays and "cripples," as separate and inferior races of people. Jews have a rich history with origins in the African continent (Wells, 1961) and a long history of discrimination in Europe. In the Balkan states, Albanians, many of whom are Orthodox Christians and Roman Catholics, have a historical animosity toward Islamic Muslims, whom they see as remnants of the Turks. Turks are descendants of nomadic Asiatic invaders, known to intermarry with the various groups they conquered, including Armenians, Arabs, Greeks, Kurds, Jews, and various northern Africans. Turks are not perceived as White in many parts of the world, even today (Davis, 1998; Grant, 1916)—a fact that caused much of the debate regarding the racial status of Arabs in the United States (see Chapter Feature "Not Quite White: The Arab American Experience" on page 84).

Slavery

The word *slave* comes from Slav, a European people. In a world once controlled by dark-skinned peoples, light-skinned people made natural slaves, and slavery was an accepted feature of most ancient civilizations. Slaves provided armies, and wars provided captives, who became slaves for the conquerors. Slaves performed hard labor such as agriculture and construction of buildings and roads. Slavery settled disputes, provided transport to distant places, and provided income and shelter. People sold themselves or family members into slavery to later buy their freedom back. Slavery was also practiced among Native People of the New World, both in North and South America.

Colonizing Europeans took slavery to a new level. The coastal exploration of Africa and the invasion of North and South America by Europeans provided impetus for the "new" Black slave trade. As Europeans took control of the world, they turned slavery into a lifelong, cross-generational nightmare. Not only was a person declared a slave, but so were his or her future generations in perpetuity (as we discussed earlier, Brazil eventually passed laws freeing all future children of slaves, including mixed-race children). The economic value of Black slaves superseded their human worth. Throughout the conquered "New World"—the Caribbean, British North America, Spanish Mexico, Central and South America, and Portuguese Brazil—permanent enslavement and lack of humanity became undistinguishable from Black Africans.

However, these colonizing European powers, blinded by greed, power, and a belief in their superior religious and cultural superiority, needed an ideology to justify the permanent enslavement and exploitation of people in the conquered territories. When the Catholic Church would not provide one, they adopted the concept of the natural—or *scientific*—inequality of people, based on racial group membership (Smedley, 2002). And, of course, once you have decided people are unequal, a method must be developed to keep those unequal people apart: racial categories.

Categorizing People

The practice of categorizing people by *race* evolves as nations develop and become powerful. While many of today's conflicts across the world appear as the result of economic, national, and religious discords, there is often an underlying racial reason. The Catholic Irish, popularly associated with the dark-skinned inferior Mediterranean Whites and the Black Irish, are still struggling against the Protestant Irish associated with Nordic Whites. (England, of course, has a long history of Protestant versus Catholic religious antagonism.) The Iberian Catalonians of Nordic decent maintain a centuries-old discord with the dark-skinned "native" **Iberians**, descendants of Arabs, Moors, and African Maghribs. Ensuing distrusts and rancor between Spain and Portugal and other European nations have a long history dating back centuries, illustrated by the contemporary expression "Africa begins in the Pyrenees" (Cruz-Janzen, 2001).

As we examine the racial classifications used in our society, a society where racial lines and racism are reinforced by all institutions, including the public schools, it is obvious that racial categories were originally created to be used to support the controlling powers in a society, and in many cases they continue that purpose today. In fact, the ACLU petitioned the Census Bureau to eliminate the race question from the 1960 survey due to its racist origins (Samhan, 1997). James Banks (2001) defines *race* as socially constructed by groups in power to maintain their privilege while marginalizing others. Thus, races are obviously socially and politically invented categories. However, today, particularly in the United States, many single-race minority groups and their official representatives are the most vocal advocates of maintaining this system of control (Sullivan, 1998; Zack, 2002). The National Association for the Advancement of Colored People (NAACP), the National Council of La Raza, and several Asian civil rights groups fought hard against the attempt by multiracial groups to place a multiracial category on the 2000 Census. According to Hilary Shelton, deputy director of the NAACP's Washington, DC office, the purpose of the existing, single-race categories is to assure "how resources are going to be distributed, how the Voting Rights Act is being enforced, and (political) reapportionment" (Sullivan, 1998, p. 35). Some believe this reasoning is why the OMB has not, to date, adopted the 2000 Census rules for official school racial/ethnic collection forms (Zack, 2002).

Shifting Identities

In this country racial classifications have shifted over the decades with persons finding themselves classified differently across time. These classifications, while uniquely "American," are aligned with traditional racial categories developed in Europe that arranged the people of the world hierarchically based on skin color, with Whites at the top, followed by Asians, then Indians, and finally Africans—with mixed races scattered throughout. The perceived mental abilities and moral qualities of each group justified these rankings (Grant, 1916). In this country we adopted this racial hierarchy, with one twist: We divided all people into essentially two opposing groups, White and non-White. We defined Blackness in such a way that it would ensure all children born to Blacks would remain slaves, and later second-class citizens, even if they had any amount of White progeny. As a result, many slaves soon included White ancestry, and it was not uncommon for slaves to be physically undistinguishable from the masters, posing an obvious dilemma. Frederick Douglass, the famous slave who gained his freedom and became a powerful abolitionist, was, of course, the son of a Black slave and White slave owner.

In 1808 the United States agreed, along with England and other European nations, to end the slave trade. Ending the trade forced the states to maintain and/or breed their own slave populations. In 1787 the U.S. Constitution had been approved, establishing a representative form of government, with the number of seats in the House of Representatives based on a state's population. This caused great debate, as Southern states wanted slaves to be included to increase their political power, while the Northern states obviously did not. Native Americans were not included in this count at all—only becoming full citizens much later. The result of this debate was termed "The Great Compromise"—the First Clause of the Constitution, which counted slaves as three-fifths of a person. The Constitution also established the Census Bureau to count the population every ten years, making sure they knew who were slaves and who were not.

Our strict racial hierarchy depended on the ability to keep the groups apart, particularly the White superior race. Laws of the land and interpretations of those laws by the Supreme Court buttressed this system, as did other policies of European domination, such as decisions supporting the removal of Native Americans from their ancestral homelands. While many Europeans were originally categorized as non-White, today Southern and Eastern Europeans, Irish, and even Jews, are integrated into "Whiteness" and the dominant group, as are Arabs (Davis, 1998).

Boundaries between other Census groups have also shifted over time and remain extremely fuzzy. For example, people from the Middle East, while geographically Asian, are not currently in the Asian category. Over half of Russia is geographically in Asia, yet Russians are considered White. According to the 2000 Census, northern Africans are not Black but Caucasian, and very dark people from Pakistan are not considered Black either. A very dark-skinned person from Tunisia who looks more Negroid than an African American is considered White, while a light-skinned African American who looks more mainstream White than Black cannot be accepted as White. This further illustrates that race is not a logical concept but a sociopolitical construct.

Foreigners who visit this country are extremely confused by our fixation on racial categories. A Brazilian college student of typically Brazilian mixed heritage was continually accosted by peers and professors at his Louisiana school. They wanted to know if he was Black, Native American, Latino, or from the Middle East. He kept saying, "I'm Brazilian."

Justifying Racial Labels

While the labels may change, the underlying ideology remains intact. The 1950 **U.S. Census categories** included White, Black, and Other. In 1976 the government imposed the label "Hispanic." In 1980 the Census included White, Black, Hispanic, Japanese, Chinese, Filipino, Korean, Vietnamese, American Indian, Asian Indian, Hawaiian, Guamanian, Samoan, Eskimo, Aleut, and Other. In 1990 it sorted people into four racial groupings: White; Black, African American, or Negro; American Indian or Alaskan Native; Asian and Pacific Islander; and two ethnic groups: Hispanic and non-Hispanic. This was the first time the Census openly used an ethnic category—a group protected as a "language minority" group (Allen, 2000).

While the other Census groups are technically considered races, they are more accurately defined as ethnic groups as well (Zack, 2002). For example, there is a great deal of cultural, language, historical, and phenotype diversity between groups classified as Asian. If Whites are persons from Europe, the Middle East, and Northern Africa, we can see an ethnic definition rather than a racial one. Other racial categories are defined broadly and linked to place of origin—Black or African American, American Indian or Alaska Native, and Asian. The only category that is narrowly defined is White. Broadly defined, like the other categories, it should be "White or European American." But, because race rather than place of origin is the critical criteria for power, the categories must protect the pure White race. This can only be accomplished if unequivocal parameters can be established for who is White and who is not.

Current Racial Categories

Our obsession with race continues to this day. The 2000 Census racial categories are "White," "Black or African American," "American Indian or Alaska Native," "Asian," and "Native Hawaiian or Other Pacific Islander." A sixth racial category is "Some Other Race." Finally, the Census Bureau specifies that ethnic origin is a separate concept from race, with two minimum categories for ethnicity: "Hispanic or Latino" and "Not Hispanic or Latino." The 2000 Census also allows persons to choose more than one racial category with 63 possible combinations, which, combined with ethnicity, creates 126 possibilities (Zack, 2002). According to the 2000 Census, a White person is someone "having origins in any of the original people of Europe, the Middle East, or North Africa. It includes people who indicate their race as 'White' or report entries such as Irish, German, Italian, Lebanese, Arab, or Polish" (U.S. Bureau of the Census, 2000). The Census defines as Black or African American, a person "having origins in any of the Black racial groups of Africa. It includes people who indicate their races as 'Black, African American, or Negro,' or provides written entries such as African American, Afro American, Kenyan, Nigerian, or Haitian" (U.S. Bureau of the Census, 2000). Asia is defined by the Census as self-identification of one of 17 categories: Asian Indian, Bangladeshi, Cambodian, Chinese—except Taiwanese—

Filipino, Hmong, Indonesian, Japanese, Korean, Laotian, Malaysian, Pakistani, Sri Lankan, Taiwanese, Thai, Vietnamese, and other Asian.

" 'Some Other Race,' includes all other respondents not included in the 'White,' 'Black or African American,' 'American Indian or Alaska Native,' 'Asian,' and 'Native Hawaiian or Other Pacific Islander' race categories. Respondents providing write-in entries such as multiracial, mixed, interracial, Wesort, or a Hispanic/Latino group (for example, Mexican, Puerto Rican, or Cuban) in the 'some other race' category are included here" (U.S. Bureau of the Census, 2000).

Arabs have struggled with their racial classification, moving in and out of the White label (see Chapter Feature "Not Quite White: The Arab American Experience" on page 84). As we have pointed out, they are now back in the White-elite category, either because, as some speculate, we do not want to offend an important ally who provides us with our needed daily supply of oil or because of the political power of Arab American groups, or both. Clearly, Arabs themselves do not see themselves as White but—as defined by religion— Moslem. In fact, in today's world, many peoples see themselves in nonracial terms with wealth/poverty, developing nations, and religion being three important categories. A poster for the First International School Health Conference in the United Arab Emirates is illustrated with a group of decidedly brown, non-European-looking children.

Arab children are White, according to U.S. Census categories. These children are in Abu Dhabi, United Arab Emirates.

Chapter Feature
Not Quite White: The Arab American Experience

During the over 100 years that Arabs have immigrated to this country, there has been tension regarding how they fit into our polarized racial categories. At all times, Arabs have been considered not quite White. The two issues affecting Arab identity were and are the immigration laws and the Census labels—which often contradicted each other. Immigration laws were designed to keep non-Northern Europeans out of the country; the Census laws were driven by the three-fifths designation of Blacks for representational purposes.

A 1870 statute defined Syrians as White, but the wave of immigrants from Syria, Mount Lebanon, and Palestine just before World War I were classified as originating from Turkey in Asia. After 1899 they were classified as Syrians, and in 1909 the courts began questioning whether Syrians were really White, or rather Asian—critical because of the strong anti-Asian sentiment in the country. In 1917 a judge declared that while Syrians might be "free Whites," they were not free Whites to whom the Congress had assigned the privilege of citizenship (in 1790, only to Northern Europeans). A judge then ruled that, while they were mixed-race, they were mixed-race Caucasians.

The Census was established in 1790 to designate Blacks from Whites. At the turn of the nineteenth century, Mexicans, Jews, Hindus, and Syrians were all categorized as different races; in 1910 people from the Middle East were categorized as Asiatic by the Census. From 1920 to 1940 Asian Indians were classified as Hindus; from 1950–1970 as White; in 1978 people from the Indian subcontinent became classified as Asian.

Immediately after World War II, the ACLU led an effort to eliminate the Census categories, due to their racist origins. However, the civil rights laws reinvigorated the system, with five overall categories (four races, one ethnicity) adopted by OMB in 1978: American Indian/Alaskan Native; Asian or Pacific Islander; Black; White (including Middle Eastern and North African), and Hispanic. "The new impetus for racial classification as a civil rights check transformed dramatically the role of the Census, which acquired a political importance that it never had in the past" (Samhan, 1997, p. 7).

In 1980 and 1990 the Census also decided to ask a question on ancestry, which allowed politicians and researchers to further break down the broad racial and ethnic categories—for example, tracking Arabs as part of the overall White category. As a result of the civil rights legislation that celebrated and polarized ethnic groups, the Arab group has become situated outside of the White race. This has caused considerable confusion—for example, in one study, 15 percent of Arab children were misidentified by their schools as Asians. Many Arabs have become accustomed to the perennial "other" status—straddling the technical White category with an affinity for people of color. Arab students and scholars have advocated Arab, Muslim, and Middle East issues in school and college multicultural efforts. In universities there are Middle East Studies departments and Arab student groups. Some in the Arab community argue that Arabs should be recognized as a disadvantaged minority by the government; others want to keep their White status.

Chapter Feature **Continued**

As part of the reexamination of the Census categories before the 2000 Census, the Arab American Institute (AAI) presented the Census with a proposal to classify people of Middle Eastern and North African backgrounds as a unique ethnic group within the overall White racial category. Also, the American Arab Anti-discrimination Committee (ADC) proposed an ethnic regional category based on a linguistic identifier (much like the Hispanic/Latino category). The Census Bureau rejected both these proposals; however, Arab advocacy groups were able to assure the ancestry question (place of origin) remained.

Based on an article by Helen Hatab Samhan (1997). Georgetown University, Washington, DC.

The Ethnic Category: Latino

Historically, **Latinos** have resisted being identified by race, but the current Census approach forces the Latino group into the traditional racial groups, including White, Black or African American, American Indian or Alaska Native, Asian, or Native Hawaiian or Other Pacific Islander—since after selecting the ethnic category, they are then required to select a racial group. The implications of this new approach by the Bureau of the Census must still be explored. Some Latinos view the move as an insidious plan to rupture the group, which, as a united entity, is the largest minority group in the country. The 2000 Census reports that nearly half of all Latinos respondents still selected "Some Other Race" rather than one of the "official" race categories (Allen, 2000).

Being classified as the *only* ethnic group under the Census enabled Latinos, first, to not be classified as a racial group, which would require them to be viewed as non-White, and second, it provided them with benefits and protection—a protected class—against discrimination (Allen, 2000). If mainstream Whites or others became defined as ethnic groups, they would benefit from civil rights legislation (affirmative action, protected class, etc.) and Latinos would lose. Allen (2000) believes that the motivation to create the ethnic Census category was, on the one hand, to keep Mexican Americans segregated from mainstream Whites, while on the other hand, to prevent an alliance between Blacks and other disenfranchised racial groups in opposition to ruling mainstream Whites, which occurred during the civil rights movement. Thus, according to Allen, separating Latinos, most of whom are racially mixed, from other minority groups draws a divisive line through the ranks of people of color (2000), fueling the rancor that has evolved between the groups and is continually fostered by the single-race categorizing system.

Maybe, however, a better explanation is simply that an arbitrary, artificial system devised to keep people separate and maintain power in the hands of

Whites could no longer bend and morph in light of an ever more contentious population, marking a need for total abandonment: The system no longer "works."

Today, Hispanics, even White ones, are seen as one group—an inferior group, inferior to mainstream Whites in this country. In fact, South Americans discuss the Latino category as "invented by the Americans" (Pena, personal communication, 2003). In South America, however, wealthy Latinos and other Europeans are socially and politically the same. In reality, the Latino ethnic Census category has become as clearly defined as the racial categories in the United States, especially in relationship to the mainstream White category (Zack, 2002). Marriage between mainstream Whites and Latinos is still considered by many on both sides as unfavorable, and progeny from these unions are still considered Latino, inferior, and confused, because of the one-drop rule and theory of **hybrid degeneracy**.

The Hispanic category is a misnomer. Indeed, most persons labeled Hispanic are not White but Asian, Black, Indigenous, and racially mixed. When the label was created in 1976, it incorrectly classified many non-Spanish speakers as Hispanics, including Brazilian Portuguese speakers and non–Spaniard-related indigenous groups, such as the Mayan Indians of Central America and the Quechua of South America. Yet, as we discussed earlier, even members of the Hispanic group reject the label (Gonzalez & Rodriguez, 2002). This disagreement resulted in a class action suit in 1979 (*Rodriguez X* v. *U.S. Census Bureau*) by several Mexican American and Puerto Rican citizens who claimed the label was not only inaccurate but also discriminatory because it assumes that most persons in the category are White and, on the basis of his Indigenous ancestry, Rodriguez believed that the category excluded him. While there has been no ruling on this lawsuit, its very existence illustrates the problem with the label.

While Mayan Indians are oppressed by the Latino ruling class in Guatemala, the U.S. Census mislabels them as Hispanic/Latino in this country.

While the 2000 Census allows people to select more than one category, when calculating Census figures, all people who checked at least one minority will be allocated to the minority group (Holmes, 2000; Zack, 2002). Clearly, for whatever political reasons, the 2000 Census created the illusion of flexibility while maintaining the system of racial segregation, stratification, and inferiority, even for people who fit the Latino ethnic group. The 2000 Census clearly establishes that anyone claiming more than one racial or ethnic category is definitively not White. The Census Bureau admits that for "civil rights enforcement," a person of mainstream White ancestry and some other "minority" race will still be allocated to the minority race. A person of two or more "minority" races would be designated to the group allegedly discriminated against most (Associated Press, 2000)—a practice that aligns totally with the one-drop rule and rule of **hypodescent**. Many believe that if the OMB ever provides schools with racial classification forms that allow more than one choice, this data will be "analyzed" in the same way (Zack, 2002).

The Race Myth

While it might be argued that racial mixing has occurred throughout human history, the reality, according to Zack (2002), is that since race as a biological concept has been totally discredited, the notion of racial mixing must also be dismissed. In other words, all people are such a mixture that distinct racial grouping based on biology cannot be created—that essentalism is no longer viable—and racial mixing cannot be seen as something "out of the norm." For example, in this country, mixing of socially constructed racial groupings has been widely practiced—openly and clandestinely—over the centuries, dating back to the days of colonization and slavery. During the seventeenth and eighteenth centuries, there was "more sex and marriage between Whites and Blacks than at any other time in the country's history. . . . Many of those mixed couples were indentured servants or a free Black and an indentured White . . . (and) . . . . Jews in New Orleans frequently married Black women in the nineteenth century" (Haizlip, 1994, p. 39).

The Theory of Hybrid Degeneracy

While anti-miscegenation laws failed to keep the races apart, two other strategies were developed to maintain well-defined and separate categories. The first was the theory of hybrid degeneracy (Nakashima, 1992), under which intermarriage was seen as lowering the biological superiority of the mainstream White race and labeling multiracial people as mentally, morally, emotionally, intellectually, and physically weaker than and inferior to each parent's race. Interracial marriages and multiracial people were considered immoral and promiscuous. The second strategy was simply to deny the existence of interracial marriages and multiracial people (Nakashima, 1992). The one-drop rule, the rules of hypodescent, and the rules of hybrid degeneracy were designed to "impose a broad definition of 'Black' and a correspondingly narrow definition of 'White' " (Knepper, 1995) to enable mainstream Whites to maintain their superiority, survival, and growth and ensure that they remain as pure as possible (Ogbu, 1991; Spickard, 1992). Ironically, despite the rules of hybrid degeneracy, many believed that White ancestry improves the intellectual capacity of single races. Lighter-skinned persons of multiple racial heritages found that mainstream Whites considered them more acceptable than darker-skinned Blacks and afforded them more status and privileges than darker African Americans.

It is estimated 75 to 95 percent of African Americans today could define themselves otherwise because of multiple heritage (Haizlip, 1994; Steel, 1995), and between 30 and 70 percent have Native American ancestry (Wilson, 1992). Traditional Brazilian racial groups are even more mixed (Alves-Silva et al., 2000). The rules of hypodescent were also supported in Europe and led to the establishment of racial purity laws in Germany and Apartheid in South Africa (a Dutch colony). The Nuremberg Laws of 1935, as they were known, upheld the innate superiority of Aryans and the inferiority of all other races, including Gypsies and Jews. According to Madison Grant (1916), the children of mixed marriages between contrasting races therefore belong with the lower type, and only pure Whites could develop the higher forms of culture—religion, writing, art, music. Mixing with "inferior" races would cause their superior "specializations" to disappear—an evil idea that Hitler gladly embellished.

The Problem with Race

Historically, in this country a person must be considered Black or African American even if he or she has mainstream White progeny, but it is not acceptable to be mainstream White and have any Black ancestry—although, as we have said, many do (Zack, 2002). We confuse race and ethnicity, as they are both social rather than biological constructs relying on social rather than biological criteria, making it appropriate for most persons to accurately claim a multiracial heritage (Johnson, 1992; Knepper, 1995). Indeed, even some "White" colonizers were not pure mainstream White at all. Since the notion of race has been totally discredited, the notion of mainstream White (or any other category) is no longer tenable.

Additionally, 10,000 "light-skinned" African Americans who look more White than Black "cross the invisible color line and become 'Whites' each year" (Haizlip, 1994, p. 15). They are said to "pass" into the mainstream White world. "Multiply these instances many times over and the footprints of those who have crossed—or pushed—the color line become infinite and untrackable" (Haizlip, 1994, p. 34). The phenomenon of crossing group boundaries is true, of course, with people of all different backgrounds—linguistic, national, ethnic, racial, and religious—what Root calls the new racial frontier (1996).

Passing as White

Passing has often been seen as a strategy of resistance, challenging the one-drop rule, and a necessity of survival. Many believe that, regardless of how light-skinned an African American, "once White Americans understand that you are

Black, they construct your racial identity the way they always do—by treating you badly because of your race" (Scales-Trent, 1995, p. 9). Sometimes African Americans who could pass did so to gain opportunities and then returned to their communities at the end of the day or for periodic visits (Haizlip, 1994; Scales-Trent, 1995). At other times passers left their families and communities forever or created new communities.

Although it is believed that many knowingly prefer to downplay their African American background or directly challenge the absurdity of the one-drop rule, some are no longer aware of their African American background. Numerous cases of people who thought themselves mainstream White Americans, then found otherwise, have occurred, particularly as a result of the popularity of cultural and ethnic revitalization and tracing one's genealogy. Others, of course, never fully accepted the premise of the one-drop rule and believed that, if they could function in a White world, they were White for all *practical* purposes. And if Fish (2002) is right in his belief that racial categories are **folk categories**, then the folk can obviously change those categories! The Phipps case discussed earlier, where a person who was legally Black lived for many generations as White, demonstrates this view (Zack, 2002). It must be pointed out here that many Latinos and Native Americans also deny Black heritage, thus "passing" for non-Black status within their own groups.

Today, of course, the multiracial movement is challenging the very idea of the one-drop rule and the embarrassment of passing, claiming that people have the right to self-identify and to associate with whichever group(s) they choose (Root, 1992b). Further, the multiracial movement is founded on the premise that it is positive and affirming to acknowledge and celebrate one's entire racial and ethnic identity, including White and non-White (Wardle, 1999).

People of all backgrounds have grown increasingly interested in searching their family roots. Many "Whites," particularly, wish to become un-"generic Americans" and search for their cultural and ethnic origins. For example, many from Eastern Europe who changed their names on entering this country have resurrected their original last names. Some mainstream Whites are finding their ethnic and racial origins in the Black/African American history pages.

Multiethnic and Multiracial Native Americans

Multiracial or multiethnic persons with indigenous Native American ancestry "usually referred to pejoratively as 'half-breeds' were often excoriated as social and psychological misfits, caught between two cultures, and frequently betrayers of their Indian heritage" (Wilson, 1992, p. 122). It was further assumed that "White persons who adopted Indian ways 'lost their civilization' living among the savages and producing degenerate, 'mongrelized' offspring" (Wilson, 1992, p. 122). Many Native American tribes institutionalized Black slavery, captured Black slaves on raids of White settlements to resell them, and participated on runaway slave hunts. Yet, others, such as the Seminoles, protected runaway slaves by allowing them to become members of their tribal bands.

Unions between Native Americans and African Americans became common (Wilson, 1992). Though Native Americans did not originally accept the racial categories constructed by American mainstream Whites, identifying mainly through communal tribes, they became increasingly influenced by the mainstream culture to the extent that Native American **blood quantums** (degree of Native American ancestry expressed in fractions such as one-half or one-fourth), and "Identity Cards" are now considered an important part of their life (Wilson, 1992). Persons of partial Native American heritage are still viewed with skepticism by *full-blooded* Indians; their physical appearance, lesser blood quantum, lack of culture, and "dubious motivation" are often referred to in denying them full membership within the group or tribe. Some "mixed-blood" Native Americans succumb to this pressure and accept the higher status of "full-bloods." Some African Americans have "sufficient" Native American Indian heritage to become classified as Indigenous; some have chosen to do so and see themselves as Native Americans exclusively.

Supporting the One-Drop Rule

Physical evidence such as skin color, hair texture, and shape of nose and lips, along with knowledge or any suspicion of any Black ancestry, was used to establish African American identity (Funderburg, 1994; Scales-Trent, 1995), assuring that African Americans did not also become identified as mainstream White, thus limiting access to social, economic, and political power to mainstream Whites exclusively (Miller, 1992; Scales-Trent, 1995). However, one of the many ironies of our race saga is that today many African Americans are as equally insistent on maintaining the one-drop rule as Whites. "Blacks are just as anxious as Whites to instruct the young and the deviant about how the rule works and how important it is to follow it" (Davis, 1998, p. 137). According to Zack (2002), minority groups steadfastly adhere to this concept to maintain their political, social, and protective status in society. In fact, today the rule appears to be supported more by members of minority groups than mainstream Whites (Rasberry, 2002). Many multiracial and multiethnic students report far more opposition to embracing their full multiracial identity from minority students and staff than from White students and staff.

The one-drop approach to the identity of mixed-race progeny was a departure from English law, which determined racial status by the status of the father—a rule the British continued in India, where mixed children of British fatherhood were claimed and supported by their fathers, and in the Caribbean. It differed also from the approach used by the Portuguese in Brazil, who saw mixed race people as the new Brazilians—an amalgamation of the New and Old World.

Today, however, most African Americans are not so concerned with phenotype as they are with genotype (Davis, 1998)—any amount of it. Marriage outside the group is frowned upon, racial disloyalty is ridiculed, and adoption of Black children by non-Blacks, particularly mainstream Whites, is sharply criticized by groups such as the National Association of Black Social Workers and most state social workers, both in the United States and in Britain. In Britain, mixed race children are viewed by the system as Black or the identity of the parent of color, if not Black (Olumide, 2002). Many African Americans and British Africans object to mainstream White parents adopting or being foster parents to Black and mixed-race children, because they believe mainstream White parents will destroy the Black culture in the children.

After the Civil War

Light-skinned African Americans recognized that they were not fully accepted by mainstream White society, irrespective of the lightness of their skin (Bradshaw, 1992) or how far removed their African or Black "taint" was (Funderburg, 1994; Haizlip, 1994; Scales-Trent, 1995). Yet these people were often seen as superior and having greater potential than unmixed Blacks (Nakashima, 1992). Biracial persons such as Booker T. Washington, Frederick Douglass, and George Washington Carver were believed to have greater ability and potential than pure African Americans because of their European mainstream White lineage (Spickard, 1992). They were seen and promoted as more capable leaders and models for their own people and were often placed in positions of power and prestige by their own people. Mixed-race Native Americans were also highly regarded, particularly because it was believed they could help negotiate agreements between tribes and local White folk (Wilson, 1992).

Dark-skinned Blacks and other groups of color accepted and internalized this view. They accepted the idea that lighter-skinned members of the group were superior and preferable. "There is strong evidence that light-skinned Blacks still receive preferential treatment in White and Black America" (Haizlip, 1994, p. 34), as well as in parts of Africa colonized by Blacks from this country—such as Liberia, Sierra Leone, and the Ivory Coast. The wife of Francis Wardle, a very dark-skinned Black, was continually harassed by her Black peers for being too dark and was told on many occasions that she was inferior because she was a field slave (thus darker), and they were house slaves. This apparent contradiction between the "preferred" multiracial person and the "messed up," degenerate, marginal person of mixed heritage illustrates just how ludicrous this whole issue has become!

Because of the preferential treatment received from European Whites, racially mixed Blacks, particularly lighter-skinned ones, emerged as an elite unto themselves. They gained access to trades, skills, and education that allowed them to become better off financially, even wealthy. These elite Blacks shunned dark-skinned Blacks and in many instances became more oppressive toward dark Blacks than Whites were (Graham, 2000; Russell, Wilson, & Hall, 1992).

Attempts to Classify Blacks Differently

From 1850 through 1920, the Census separated African Americans into Black or Mulatto; in 1890 it included categories for Mulatto, **Quadroon**, and **Octoroon**.

These categories gave more status to multiracial persons according to amount of mainstream White ancestry and segregated them from the masses of African Americans. These multiracials often served as American mainstream Whites' allies against the Black majority, contributing to the persistent distrust between dark- and light-skinned African Americans. Even social clubs and colleges—such as Howard University—were created for these light-skinned Blacks.

While most Blacks were suffering from the brutal **Jim Crow system** of the South and blatant discrimination throughout the North, elite—mixed-race—Blacks existed in a world that, while isolated from upper-class Whites, ran parallel to it. They concerned themselves with prestigious social events and organizations, country clubs and vacations homes, yachts, and all other signs of wealth and social privilege. They also focused on their looks—not too dark or too Black and with nose shape, hair length, and texture. They cared about who had a summer home in Martha's Vineyard and other exclusive elite enclaves, who belonged to which prestigious—exclusive—organization such as the Links, and who was being presented at the cotillions. Indeed, they looked down on poor, dark-skinned Blacks and did not consider them "our kind of people," much as White Hispanics looked down on mixed-race Latinos. Further, these elite Blacks did not become involved in the civil rights movement until they began experiencing direct discrimination and their privileged world was threatened by racist Whites and dominant White institutions (Graham, 2000).

The historical antagonism between multiracials and Blacks still exists, particularly in groups of color themselves, leading to the accusation that persons of multiple racial heritage and their families are not Black enough, that proud multiethnic and multiracial people and their families have "dubious political and social loyalties," and that "people of color who marry Whites are trying to 'raise' themselves economically, socially, and racially" (Nakashima, 1992, p. 165). At the same time there are vestiges of **colorism** within the Black community, where light-skinned persons are still preferred. "In the end, a fair skin emitted mixed signals. It became a badge of prestige or a mark of disdain" (Haizlip, 1994. p. 56).

Hardening of the Lines

Over time, however, U.S. society polarized into Black and White, and most of the nineteenth-century labels fell out of use. It was just too difficult to measure and track how much Black and White "blood" was flowing and in what direction, so some form of the one-drop rule was adopted in most states (Haizlip, 1994). Being a light-skinned multiracial and being able to pass as mainstream White became a dangerous threat to mainstream Whites who, needing to maintain their racial purity and power, could not allow African Americans to move in and out of their world. Mainstream Whites also began to view light-skinned African Americans with suspicion (Miller, 1992) and no longer as trustworthy allies. Mainstream Whites began to withdraw privileges from African Americans, including the light-skinned ones, while they in turn began to seek alliances with the masses of dark African Americans.

"**Marginal**" **Whites**—Italians, Irish, Jews, Polish, etc.—who were gaining entry into White America and establishing their Whiteness, perpetuated much of the anti-Black attitude. The Jim Crow era emerged as a way to keep the races apart and prevent further miscegenation. Unable to track who had what amount of mainstream White and/or Black ancestry, White supremacists declared that any amount of Black ancestry made the person Black, even if that person visibly appeared mainstream White. During the Jim Crow era, White supremacists enacted a bewildering variety of laws requiring racial separations in public life, and racial categories acquired their modern rigidity.

Mainstream Whites

As we have detailed, the mainstream White Protestant view of Whites has morphed over the history of this country, widening to accept other immigrant groups from Europe, and also acculturating immigrants from parts of Europe not originally considered British or Nordic. Others believe the newly freed Blacks posed a threat to Whites that caused them to coalesce as one dominant White group. In some parts of the country, there are still some vestiges of discrimination against darker Whites, such as Greeks, Italians, Jews, and Poles; lighter skin, blonde hair, and blue eyes are still sometimes preferred, and marriage between the two may cause problems. However, today there is also opposition to marriage between rich and poor, original Daughters of the American Revolution and newcomers to the country, and educated professionals and "hicks" from the country.

Categorizing People in Other Nations

Our country's approach to race and racial labels comes both from European racial superiority that was brought with the colonialists and various attitudes and approaches to race and categorizing people brought by immigrants from all over the world. Thus, it is befitting that we briefly view ways other countries approach this issue; further, this examination reinforces our belief that race, racial categories, and racial restriction are sociopolitical entities—differing from country to country and society to society.

South Africa

In South Africa persons can change their racial classification openly and legally: A White-looking Coloured may reclassify him- or herself as White. Persons may reclassify themselves several times. They are required to prove that in addition to being able to pass for White, they are accepted as such by other Whites. Additionally, they must prove that they "act" White by having the right education, profession, and belonging to the right organizations, such as the church. "Coloured" persons are acknowledged as a separate category not subsumed under any other classification. South African **Coloureds** are considered neither Black nor Asian. Although predominantly mulattoes, Coloureds may include

Black-Asian and White-Asian offspring rather than just Black-White and Black-Coloured. Other groups brought in as laborers, such as Arabs, Chinese, and Muslims, are also included among the Coloured category. Racial classification in South Africa is therefore affected by religion (Davis, 1998).

Latin America and the Caribbean

Across Latin America, colonizing European men often came alone, mixing freely with the indigenous populations they encountered and producing a large mestizo population in Brazil, Mexico, and most of Latin America. Later, as slaves from Africa were introduced, Europeans intermarried with Africans, creating a mulatto population. In many places, such as Brazil, intermarriages were encouraged by the European colonizing monarchies as a way to quickly populate the nation—a huge area for such as small European power to conquer and control. This led to a racial transformation as light-skinned mulattoes or mestizos were no longer considered Blacks or Indians. Throughout most of Latin America, the racially mixed population soon outnumbered both the pure Whites and the pure Blacks and Indians. Today Mexico is recognized primarily as a nation of mestizos; a majority in Brazil is of various mixed races; Haiti, Jamaica, Belize, and the West Indies are known as Black nations, even though most nations in the Caribbean basin are nations of mulattoes.

Depending on the variations of racial mixing, some countries such as Brazil may have as many as forty different labels for various racial types. Emancipation was frequent and freed mestizos and mulattoes often received education and special privileges. Strategically, they became a much-valued working class buffer between the ruling Whites and slaves.

Brazil officially recognizes the many gradations between Blacks and Whites, Blacks and Indians, and Indians and Whites in its population. A person categorized as Black in this country could be considered coloured in Jamaica or even mulatto in Puerto Rico. In fact, this same Black person, depending on skin coloration and physical attributes, could be considered White in Puerto Rico, Cuba, and many other parts of Latin America. Fish (2002) reports how his biracial daughter changed her race by simply leaving New York as Black and flying to Brazil where she became **morena**.

Generally speaking, skin coloration and physical appearance have been the key factors in facilitating social mobility across all Latin American nations. Social class ranking is closely tied to several factors, including family heritage and position, education, income, and physical appearance. In many nations racial mixing and skin coloration affect social class just as education and social class sometimes affect racial classification. Depending on coloration, racially mixed persons may—and often do—cross over to become White. Parents and siblings within the same family may not be classified equally: It all depends on each individual's circumstance of education, income, and appearance. One sibling may be considered White, while another is mulatto or Black.

Two typical Brazilian young women reflect the racial and ethnic mixtures in Brazilians.

Additionally, as a person's economic and social status changes, so may his or her racial designation. The expression "money whitens" refers to this practice of upward mobility. A Brazilian soccer player who expressed, "When I was Black," illustrates this concept. Many upper- and middle-class Whites across Latin America are of known or assumed racial mixture partly because original Spanish and Portuguese were themselves mixed, and darker than Northern Europeans. A trigueña/o (wheat-colored) is a light-skinned person who may be mulatto or mestizo. Ironically, this term is also used in connection with persons from Spain. As well, *moreno* (Moor) means dark-skinned and may equally refer to brunette Iberians or dark-skinned mulattoes. Generally, it is accepted as the darkest a person can be and still be White. In Brazil a moreno "has brown or black hair, that is wavy or curly but not that curly, tan skin, a nose that is not narrow, and lips that are not thin" (Fish, 2002, p. 121).

The upper class in British, Dutch, and French Caribbean islands is composed of many apparent mulattoes and mestizos. Across Latin America, though, unmixed Africans tend to remain Black regardless of education and/or socioeconomic status. Brazil, Jamaica, Haiti, and other known Latin American nations with apparent Black lineage appear to be the only countries that accept unmixed Africans into their elite upper class, and the new Brazilian constitution provides them equal protection under the law. Yet, throughout Latin America, even in the Black nations, the multiracial population is treated more favorably.

Spaniards and Portuguese and their direct descendants remain the upper-most stratum and ruling elite throughout all of Latin America, although in Brazil the significant Asian population is very powerful, dominating the most powerful state of Sao Paulo. And, of course many Latin American countries have significant Northern European immigrants, such as Germans, English, and Welsh, who have become part of the ruling elite. Many Latin Americans of European heritage see themselves as White and recoil at the thought of being grouped with their mixed and non-White, particularly Black, compatriots.

The Legacy of Slaves and Slave Owners

The interracial children of Black slaves and mainstream White masters had to be accepted by the Black slave community because they were legally slaves and were not accepted by mainstream White society of the times. To some contemporary Blacks, Blacks with White heritage symbolize centuries of enslavement, domination, the exploitation of Black people, the rape of Black women, and the destruction of the African American community and family, both in Africa and in America, by mainstream Whites (Funderburg, 1994; Steel, 1995). The term "high-yeller" emerged and became a sign of illegitimacy and disdain (and is still used today as a derogatory term for multiracial children, mostly by Black peers). This history is not far removed, as many African Americans today can still name direct family descendants of slaves. While many of today's multiracial and multiethnic persons openly proclaim and affirm their multiple heritages, some remain enraged by and resentful of the brutality their relatives were subjected to. They are not so eager or willing to open up those pages in history.

At a conference where Marta Cruz-Janzen spoke about the need to validate persons of multiethnic and multiracial heritage, an African American proclaimed,

> Look at me. I am your color and I am not biracial like you. I am Black. Just as you are Black—like me. My momma is Black and my poppa is Black. They are different colors, mixed too. We have Black and White and some Indian. All my brothers and sisters are different colors. I have a sister who could pass for White and a brown brother with blue eyes. I don't know how my children are going to come out. Do you hear me? Whose blue eyes are those? Whose hair is this on my head? Whose hair is on my sister's head? Whose brown skin is this? Why so many different brown shades? Where did they come from?
>
> This is not about one race reaching out to another. This is not about creating a bridge between the races. I'll tell you where this is all from. This color is about the abuse my ancestors had to suffer. This is about the pain we still have to endure every day, [the reminder] day in and day out for the rest of our lives and our children's lives. Not knowing who you are. Not knowing whose blood you carry. This is a living reminder of what they did to us. This color means the rape of our mothers and the emasculation of our men. This color still means that we are less, that these White folks still see us as less. Each time they see one of us, they laugh inside, knowing that they did this to us. That they still have the power to do this to us. Look at the prisons. Look at our streets. They still think they can do whatever they want to us, because they still think they own us. They had us before and they have us now. They

are still killing and raping us. This [pointing at her body] is never going away. For-ever we are going to have to live with this.

You biracial people need to accept that. They don't see you as any part of them. They don't want you! They'll never let you forget that either. Biracial? Sister, you are Black! So the sooner you come to your senses the better for you and your children.

Clearly, this is a reminder of a painful part of our history—and the history of all countries who kept people in bondage—and those that still do. However, throughout the history of this country, starting before slavery, there were many legitimate and consensual interracial and interethnic relationships that produced offspring. Results of new mitochondrial DNA research of current populations in North and South America are beginning to tell us the exact percentage of White male–minority female and white female–minority male mating (Alves-Silva et al., 2000). However, our history regarding slavery and abuse of minorities cannot—and should not—in any way prevent people from proudly embracing their total racial identity and be a reason to prevent us from achieving the final elimination of racial, ethnic, and other barriers that exist to separate and divide people.

Maintaining the Color Line

Maintaining the color line truly translates to maintaining the power line. Main-taining that line demands knowing unequivocally where it is located. Thus, multiracial and multiethnic persons are feared by all single-race/ethnic groups precisely because they represent the blurring of the line. Multiethnic and mul-tiracial people can appear to look very White—even with white skin, blond hair, and blue eyes, along with all other racial "types." Without the color line there would be no way to separate the power; in today's world there would also be no way to isolate protected groups. As Zack (2002) suggests, "anything that disturbs the ontological premises underlying the racial status quo, no matter how liberat-ing it may be in principle, will at this time be perceived as a threat to the gains justly secured by non-Whites on the group-based pluralistic model" (p. 8).

Hawaii has historically recognized persons of multiple racial heritages with-out stigma and has developed extensive vocabulary to define the varieties; but as it did with Puerto Rico, the U.S. government felt it necessary to impose strict racial codes on Hawaii when it became a state. Much like Native Americans, indigenous Hawaiians must now prove "blood quantums" or family lineage in order to be classified as Native Hawaiians. Blood purity ideologies, rules, and practices pose a true—and painful—quandary for our society, particularly for disenfranchised groups of color. There is lingering fear among Native Americans and Native Hawaiians of losing what little remains of their tribes and rights as their legal claim to valuable lands and resources is eroded through out-of-group marriages. Many feel that the "blood quantum" laws and practices established supposedly to protect their rights have really ensured their decimation and continued the robbery of their assets. Thus, many Indian tribes try to control membership and limit out-marriage. Zack (2002) calls this need for group preservation a group-based model of pluralism, as opposed to our traditional view of individual liberty (2002).

Group Solidarity

Many minority groups in this country insist on maintaining and representing their rights as a group. They believe that when mainstream Whites are interested in a group's valuable possessions, particularly productive land and minerals, they establish rules that regulate and ultimately diminish the group size. Once the group ceases to exist, according to legal requirements, their assets revert back to the federal government. Thus, members of oppressed groups fight for numbers: They cannot afford to let anyone out of the group because they need numbers to maintain power, to fight against the institutional structure designed to perpetuate their dehumanization and oppression. And they also fight against other minority groups for the perceived limited resources tossed to them by the mainstream White society.

This view, of course, is one of the strongest arguments used against allowing multiracial and multiethnic people to have their own classification on the Census—and why the powerful minority organizations officially opposed a multiracial classification on the 2000 Census. Often people of color, who have internalized the country's belief in a racialized society, accuse racially mixed persons of upsetting the racial boundaries and perceive multiethnic and multiracial people not only as a threat to mainstream White purity but also as a threat to minority groups of color who believe they will reduce their political power.

The Census racial classification system promotes this argument. Mainstream Whites have devised a system designed to decrease the chances of a coalition among all groups of color. Below them, groups of color see themselves as isolated units in opposition to each other. Furthermore, through selective association, the dominant group has recruited the support of certain ethnic and racial groups. Although not assimilated into the dominant group, these selective groups are elevated socially, economically, and politically from the masses below them. They, in turn, then join forces with the dominant group against other groups below. Members of minority groups then enforce certain encoded, even though oppressive, patterns to maintain their progress and better increase their own individual membership, rather than create coalitions across oppressed groups. It should be emphasized that not all groups that lack power are minority groups—the largest one, of course, is the poor, which includes millions of poor Whites.

Many participants in interethnic and interracial unions are mainstream Whites; further, through organizations, conferences, writings, and polemics, these Whites have been at the forefront of insisting that multiethnic and multiracial children not be placed with the group of their parent of lowest status. Francis Wardle presented at a conference where Black participants insisted the only reason the multiracial movement exists is because White women refuse to label their children Black. These participants did not see this as a good thing. Clearly, raising mixed-race children as multiracial will blur the borders of the powerful and powerless (Root, 1996).

True affirmation of multiracial and multiethnic people in this society requires full acceptance of the equality of everyone and the total destruction of racial labels that are used to control, limit, and separate people. Ironically, as increased numbers have crossed race and ethnic groups to marry, resistance to blurring the racial borders has increased. Affirmation means persons moving in and out of groups freely and without negative repercussions. While the 2000 Census cleverly increased the options for people with multiple backgrounds, it did not support genuine affirmation of multiracial and multiethnic identity, due largely to opposition from minority groups. Apparently, our society is not ready to accept that multiracial and multiethnic persons are real, that people are truly comfortable embracing multiple identities—and, equally important, that others have no business defining someone else's individual identity (Root, 1996).

Today's Multiracial and Multiethnic Children

While we have discussed the tragic legacy of multiracial children born as a result of White slave masters raping Black slaves, we have also discussed the many consensual interracial relationships throughout our history—which increased dramatically after 1967. We cannot let our tragic history prevent us from finally embracing the notions of multiracial and multiracial identities in anyone who chooses to embrace them. We must stop punishing today's multiethnic and multiracial children for the horrible actions of our past. We must place the blame precisely where it belongs—on the power structure of our nation and a history of past atrocities. Preventing multiethnic and multiracial children from fully embracing their total identity not only limits their equal rights and freedoms, but also makes us party to an oppressive, state-sponsored racist social system.

Freedom is about choice, and if two people from different backgrounds choose to have children, those children should be raised with a full appreciation of both backgrounds. We believe that people from different racial/ethnic groups who marry can have equal relationships and raise healthy children. Further, we must correct our negative history by embracing people who celebrate their total heritage and encourage people to explore and embrace their family's rich multiethnic and multiracial past. People from different racial and ethnic groups who freely choose to challenge this county's fixation on exclusive radial categories to marry and have children should be celebrated as having the courage to create a new America.

Where Do We Go from Here?

Multiethnic and multiracial people have not benefited from any racial or ethnic category that acknowledges and describes their origins nonderisively, because, of course, this would jeopardize all single-race categories. Further, mixed-race persons do not have any rights, bearing, and status (Zack, 2002). To benefit from existing civil rights legislation, protected class status, affirmative action, and college scholarships and support groups, the multiracial person must deny his or her White heritage. According to Root (1992), the rigid dichotomy between

White and non-White creates a caste system or vehicle of oppression whereby persons of multiple ethnic and racial heritage experience oppression not only as people of color but also by people of color. Persons of multiple ethnic and racial heritages then hold dual subservient status as both people devalued by the mainstream culture and by members of the respective minority groups in their background. For generations, fear and the "power of silence" have kept multiethnic and multiracial populations private and isolated (Funderburg, 1994) with "little development of a group consciousness" (Nakashima, 1992, p. 177). For too long they have been told that they belong nowhere.

Although progress has been made in the past forty years, we still have a long way to go to fully embrace persons of interethnic and/or interracial heritage. Acknowledgment is related to empowerment (Flores, 1995), and, as Gay (1995) wrote, " 'Voice' is the power of affirmation" (p. 35). Affirmation means valuing and celebrating; it means a positive assertion—which is what the multiracial movement is all about: the books, conferences, and miles of websites. The Internet has become a tremendous boon to the affirmation of multiethnic and multiracial people through the world. Until Whites are ready to openly proclaim their own racial mixing and lack of racial purity, and minorities are willing to adjust their view of group belonging and loyalty, multiethnic and multiracial persons will not find full acceptance and validation. Both groups must come to believe that the perpetuation of the current racial and ethnic categorization system used in this country is deeply destructive to our society.

New Visibility

With increasing numbers and visibility, multiethnic and multiracial persons are breaking the "racial silence" that kept them hidden and are moving to the forefront of educational, social, and political activism to define and assert themselves and challenge the country's definitions of race, ethnicity, culture, and community (Nakashima, 1992; Scales-Trent, 1995). Recognition of multiethnic and multiracial persons will necessarily force radical changes in the way race and ethnicity are defined and perceived in the nation—and the world—and will revolutionize how societies address diversity—especially in our nation's schools—in curricular content, teacher training, research paradigms, and demographic data collection. The challenge of declaring an interethnic and interracial identity remains in a postmodern world still ruled by deeply entrenched traditional definitions and ideologies of race, racial purity, racial labels, and a recent history of White colonization and racism (Zack, 2002). It challenges the arbitrary racial categories and definitions that we have created. Individuals who cross ethnic and racial lines are legitimate and wholesome humans, expanding our understanding of humanity.

Conclusion

Clearly, changing the way we categorize multiethnic and multiracial people is not the final solution, but it is a start. As a multiracial person recently stated, "We may have changed the name of the game but the rules remain the same," referring to the 2000 Census decision to reclassify all mixed-race people as minorities. Multiethnic and multiracial children are particularly vulnerable in a society whose educational approach fails to recognize their full identity and humanity, because it is at school where children primarily develop their identities and their attitudes to their identities. With ever-increasing numbers and combinations of interethnic and interracial children in our schools and society, we must act immediately. At least the 2000 Census has opened the door for research to commence on the home, community, and school lives of these children. We need much more information to support curricular development and intervention strategies than we currently have. The Census change, while not completely satisfactory, is a step in the right direction and the tip of the iceberg. As Cortes (1999) has said, "The time for recognizing, honoring, and responding to racial mixture has arrived" (p. 31).

Questions/Projects

1. Interview family members to develop a personal family tree. Go back as many generations and branch out as much as possible.

2. Study and develop a timeline of the historical evolution of slavery prior to European expansion. Explore the historical evolution of slavery in other parts of the world. How does the evolution of slavery match other developments of the time?

3. Interview several Spanish/Hispanic/ Latinos. Try to interview Latinos of different phenotypes (Black, White, Indian, mestizo, mulatto, zambo,

etc.). Ask them about their own racial and ethnic identification. How do they feel about the U.S. Census labels, and what recommendations do they make?

4. Interview several persons who have been raised and/or lived in highly diverse and pluralistic societies, such as Hawaii, Costa Rica, or Brazil. How do they feel about the U.S. Census labels—and whether we should even have them? Have they changed their identity labels since they came to this country?

Resources

Books

Dramer, K. (1997, September). *Native American and Black Americans: Indians of North America*. Broomall, PA: Chelsea House Publishing.

Graham, L. O. (1999). *Our kind of people: Inside America's Black upper class*. New York: HarperCollins.

Loewen, J. (1995). *Lies my teacher told me*. Carmichael, CA: Touchstone Books.

Russell, K., Wilson, M., & Hall, R. (1992). *The politics of skin color among African Americans*. Harpswell, ME: Anchor Publishing.

Williams, G. H. (1999). *Life on the color line: The true story of a White boy who discovered he was Black*. Boston: Dutton/Plume/Harcourt Brace.

Website

U.S. Census Bureau Home Page
http://www.census.gov/

5

Identity Development of Multiethnic and Multiracial Children

Most of the limited research on multiethnic and multiracial children focuses on their racial and ethnic identity development. In a society fixated on a single-race view and conditioned to believe children with more than one racial or ethnic background will somehow be messed up and dysfunctional, this focus is understandable. However, much of the development of multiethnic and multiracial children is the same as single-race children. All children progress through various physical, social, cognitive, and emotional stages on their way to adulthood. They develop age-specific skills, abilities, and behaviors. Additionally, all children must struggle with developing their unique independence, forming appropriate moral reasoning, and finding and keeping friends. Where multiethnic and multiracial children differ, of course, is in their development toward a healthy multiethnic or multiracial identity.

FOCUS QUESTIONS

1. Why are we in this country so concerned with the identity development of multiracial and multiethnic children?

2. What is the optimum environment for the healthy identity development of multiracial children?

3. What is the role of the school in supporting a multiethnic or multiracial child's healthy identity development?

4. Why is the school's relationship with the interethnic or interracial family critical to the healthy development of children of mixed heritage?

Identity Development: A Definition

"What are they?" "What about the children?" "It's not fair bringing these children into the world." These are all popular sentiments about multiethnic and multiracial children. Much of our society believes our children are confused, messed up, and degenerate. Other beliefs also exist: that in a society fixated on single-race identity, they cannot develop into whole, unified humans—that they will be continually pulled from one side to the other. However, it is important to note the question of healthy multiethnic and multiracial identity development is not an issue in countries where the concept of a mixed identity is common, where children see lots of multiracial role models, and where the government recognizes a mixed-race identity. In Brazil, for example, there is no discussion about the identity development of mixed ethnicity/race children, because the majority of people and children in Brazil are of mixed heritage, and the government recognizes them as such. In Brazil children do not sit together by race or ethnicity in the cafeteria; there is no discussion about whether playing in the band, joining the soccer team, or playing golf is a Black thing, White thing, or Asian thing; or whether someone is "acting White" or "acting Black." It's a little like arguing the value of teaching a second language at an early age to people in European countries where second language acquisition by young children has been conducted effectively for years!

A person's identity is how the person sees himself or herself (Wardle, 1996). A healthy identity is a self-image that is comfortable, positive, empowered, and self-affirming (Curry & Johnson, 1990). For multiethnic and multiracial children the question is "What constitutes a healthy identity?" We believe a multiethnic/ multiracial child with a healthy identity celebrates his or her entire heritage, is comfortable and at ease with his or her total family and cultural background, and is able to flexibly move between single-race groups. Most importantly, we believe the multiethnic and multiracial child does not need to put down, invalidate, or belittle any part of his or her heritage to feel good about his or her identity. While there are certainly healthy multiethnic and multiracial people in this country who embrace only the identity of one of their parents (usually the minority parent, or parent of lowest status), we feel it is far more appropriate to raise multiethnic and multiracial children with a full acceptance, appreciation, and understanding of their entire background. Further, we feel it is easier to create a healthy self-esteem in these children if their full heritage is supported and celebrated (Bowles, 1993; Brandell, 1988; Jacobs, 1977, 1992; Wardle, 1999).

To this end we will discuss a variety of identity development models briefly (see Figure 5.1) then present Wardle's ecological and developmental model (1992) in more detail.

Identity Development Models

A variety of identity development models have been proposed. They are all based on the premise that multiethnic and multiracial children face a unique challenge in developing their sense of racial and ethnic identity—a different and more challenging process than for single-race children (Gibbs, 1987, 1989; Phinney & Rotheram, 1987). Some of these models are developmental stage models that

Name of Model	Poston's Model	Jacobs's Model	Phinney's Model	Kerwin-Ponterotto's Model	Root's Approach	Wardle's Model
Type of Model	Developmental	Developmental	Developmental	Developmental	Ecological	Developmental and ecological
Central Task for the Child	Fully integrate both parents' heritages	Full biracial identity	Achieves secure ethnic or multiethnic/multiracial identity	Comfortable embracing both backgrounds	Positive identity resolution	Healthy multiethnic/multiracial identity
For Which Children?	Black/White	Black/White	Single-race minority and multiethnic/multiracial	Black/White	Multiethnic/multiracial	Multiethnic/multiracial
Ages Covered	Preschool—adult	Preschool—8 to 12 years	Adolescence	Preschool—lifelong	Child—adult	Preschool—end of adolescence
Stages	*Stage 1, Personal Identity* No awareness of race/ethnicity.	*Stage 1, Pre-Color Constancy (0 to 4½)* Knows color of skin but is not aware of its significance.	*Stage 1, Unexamined Identity* Child has not examined his/her identity and is not concerned with it.	*Stage 1, Preschool (up to 5)* Becomes aware of similarities and differences to others.	Four possible healthy identity resolutions: *1. Individual accepts society's definition of his/her race/ethnicity.* Positive if the individual is comfortable and supports it. Label may change.	*Stage 1, Preschool/Early Childhood* Child becomes aware of physical features; aware of similarities and differences between parents and peers. Is often asked, who are you? Needs a label.

Stage 2, Choice of Group Categorization	Stage 2, Post-Color Constancy (4½ to 8)	Stage 2, Ethnic Identity Search/Moratorium	Stage 2, Entry into School	2. Identifies with both races.	Stage 2, Transition Period, Late Elementary
Selects one identity—usually the parent of color.	Learns skin color is permanent. Has ambivalence to own skin color. Realizes identity is different from that of parents.	Child is interested in identity and background, but not ready to select a racial or ethnic identity.	Children are continually asked "what are you" by peers. Needs label to help them.	Moves between groups. Is positive if the person does not have to change values and behaviors from group to group.	Becomes aware of sexuality. Group belonging is important. Interested in competencies and the concept of race.
Stage 3, Enmeshment/ Denial	**Stage 3, Biracial identity (8 to 12)**	**Stage 3, Achieve Ethnic Identity**	**Stage 3, Preadolescence**	**3. Identifies with a single-race ethnic group.**	**Stage 3, Adolescence**
Child experiences confusion from identity with only one parent.	Learns (1) skin color is related to mixed heritage; (2) color of skin does not define race; (3) child is biracial/biethnic because parents are of different races/ethnicities.	Child selects racial/ ethnic identity and is totally at ease with the choice.	More aware of physical features, skin color, hair texture. Becoming aware of racial group membership.	Person makes an active choice to align with one group. Is positive if the person feels fully accepted by the group.	Erikson's identity crisis. Learning to separate out race, ethnicity, abilities, likes, dislikes, career choices. Family and school support non-race-specific groups. Becomes comfortable with mixed identity.

(continued)

FIGURE 5.1 Identity Development Models

Name of Model	Poston's Model	Jacobs's Model	Phinney's Model	Kerwin-Ponterotto's Model	Root's Approach	Wardle's Model
	Stage 4, Appreciation While still holding to one identity, learns to appreciate the background of their other parent.			*Stage 4, Adolescence* Pressured by peers to select a single race/ethnic group.	*4. Individual identifies with mixed-race identity.* Positive if the identity embraces all parts of his or her background. Can move between groups, but maintains mixed identity.	*Ecological Components:* *Majority/Higher Status Context.* White or higher status race/ethnicity. *Minority/Higher Status Context.* Black or lower status race/ethnicity. *Community.* Neighborhood, school, church, Clubs, etc. *Family.* Nuclear, extended, foster, adoptive, etc. *Group Antagonism:* Group racism, prejudice, and dislike.

Stage 5, Integration
Fully identifies with the background of both parents, has integrated both heritages.

Stage 5, College/ Young Adult
Have friends from mainly one side of their background; feel less pressure to choose sides. Comfortable in different race/ ethnicity groups.

Stage 6, Adulthood
Integrate all aspects of their background; feel comfortable in variety of groups/ settings.

FIGURE 5.1 Continued

come directly out of the human development tradition; others are ecological in nature; Wardle's model is both developmental and ecological.

Poston's Model

Poston's developmental model has five levels, or **developmental stages**—the final stage being when the individual "experiences wholeness and integration" (1990, p. 154). This model, like several others, was developed when the terminology for children of mixed heritage was biracial and biethnic; today's terminology is multiethnic and multiracial (which will no doubt change—or be eliminated—in the future). Further, Poston's model is only for children of Black and White parentage. However, we believe it also applies to children with other multiethnic or multiracial backgrounds.

Stage 1. Personal Identity.   The child's sense of self, or identity, does not include the concept of ethnic or racial belonging (see the Chapter Feature "Development of Racial and Ethnic Identity" on page 14).

Stage 2. Choice of Group Categorization.   Biracial children are pressured to choose one background for their identity; a biracial identity probably will not be the choice, due to limited cognitive development; most often the identity choice is the same race/ethnicity as the parent of color. Note that Poston believes mental structures—cognitive development—preclude a child of this age adopting a true biracial identity.

Stage 3. Enmeshment/Denial.   The individual experiences confusion, self-dislike, and guilt from choosing the identity of one parent and denying that of the other parent. This sense of confusion and dislike must be resolved for the child to move to the next stage.

Stage 4. Appreciation.   The individual may still identify with the single group selected in Stage 2, but the child learns about and appreciates more of the background of his or her other parent.

Stage 5. Integration.   At this age the child fully integrates both sides of his or her background and views him- or herself with an identity that includes the ethnic/racial, cultural, and family heritages of both parents and their extended families.

Jacobs's Developmental Model

Jacobs based his model on data he collected from studies conducted using dolls with biracial children of Black and White parentage. While he believes the model may not work for children who come from backgrounds other than Black/White, others believe that it does, in fact, work with multiracial and multiethnic children with a variety of backgrounds (Wehrly, Kenney, & Kenney, 1999). There are two reasons models developed just for children of Black and White parentage might not work for multiethnic and multiracial children. First, there simply is almost no research on multiracial and multiethnic children from different backgrounds to provide any body of knowledge; second, research on the identity development of single-race children suggests a different pattern for children whose physical features—skin color, eye shape, hair texture—are not as salient as other children (Aboud, 1987). Jacobs's model (1977, 1992) has three developmental stages.

Stage 1. Pre-Color Constancy: Play and Experimentation with Color (0–4½ years old).   At around the age 4½ children know the physical color of their skin, but are not concerned with it (it is not a critical feature). Further, they cannot accurately match a doll's color to the color skin of another family member.

Stage 2. Post-Color Constancy: Biracial Label and Racial Awareness (4½ to 8 years old).   Children learn that skin color is permanent—it won't wash off or change. They then show an ambivalence regarding their own skin color, first preferring black, then white. Jacobs believes resolving this ambivalence is required for a child to positively progress into the final stage (much as Erikson does for each of his stages). According to Jacobs, the child needs assistance (parent, teacher) and the use of a biracial label to fully resolve this conflict. The child realizes his or her identity differs from his or her parents; during this stage the child is also becoming aware of racial discrimination.

Stage 3. Biracial Identity (8–12 years old).   If a child reaches this stage successfully, the child has developed three conclusions:

1. The color of his or her skin is related to his or her mixed heritage—based on parents' genotypes.
2. The color of his or her skin does not determine his or her race.
3. The child is biracial because of the different racial heritages of both parents.

Phinney's Model of Ethnic Identity in Adolescents

Phinney's model (1993) applies to single-race minority, multiracial, or multiethnic adolescents and has three distinct stages through which the adolescent progresses.

Stage 1. Unexamined Ethnic Identity.   The child has not examined his or her ethnic identity and either (a) has no interest in ethnic identity at all or (b) automatically accepts the view of the ethnic or racial identity that is assigned by others.

Stage 2. Ethnic Identity Search/Moratorium.   Individual children search for information about their ethnic or racial heritage and try to determine its relevance to them and their personal identity, but they are not yet ready to select an ethnic or racial identity.

Stage 3. Achieved Ethnic Identity.   The individual chooses a racial or ethnic identity and is totally confident and accepting of all aspects of that identity.

Kerwin-Ponterotto's Model

The Kerwin-Ponterotto model (Kerwin & Ponterotto, 1995) is a six-stage life-span model, starting at childhood and progressing to adulthood.

Stage 1. Preschool (up to age 5).   Multiracial/multiethnic children of this age become aware of similarities and differences between their appearance and the appearance of other children.

Stage 2. Entry to School.   At this age multiethnic and multiracial children are asked by their peers, "What are you?" Parents need to give them a term—"mixed," "biracial"—to help them respond proactively to their peers.

Stage 3. Preadolescence.   Multiracial and multiethnic children are increasingly aware of physical differences, including skin color and hair texture, and are beginning to understand cultural determinants of group membership. From research on single-race development we know this is the age when children begin to fully understand the concept of race as a socially constructed concept, not directly and immutably tied to physical characteristics (Aboud, 1987). Multiethnic and multiracial children know their parents belong to different racial groups. A precipitating event, such as racist behavior or entry into an integrated school, seems to force the child to full awareness of his or her multiracial or multiethnic identity.

Stage 4. Adolescence.   Because of the identity crisis of this age and the need for adolescents to associate with similar people (Tatum, 1999)—a group-belonging idea encouraged and reinforced by our schools—multiethnic and multiracial youngsters are often pressured to identify with only one ethnic or racial group. Non-race specific extracurricular activities can help these children deal with this pressure.

Stage 5. College/Young Adolescence.   Young people may have friends mainly from one of their backgrounds, but feel less pressure to choose sides, feel comfortable in groups of different racial-ethnic people, and can generally see things from more than one point of view.

Stage 6. Adulthood.   As they integrate aspects from every part of their heritage, multiethnic and multiracial adults function comfortably in a variety of contexts.

Root's Approach

Maria Root's approach (1990, 1997, 1998) is not a stage model; rather, she is concerned with the impact of ecological factors—family, social ability, school, community, and peers—on the identity a multiethnic or multiracial person selects (1998). We will discuss the ecological aspect of development later in this chapter, detailing the pioneering work of Bronfenbrenner, whose contribution to the field is significant. Root believes that a multiracial or multiethnic person's identity can, and will, change, depending on the ecological context. Further, she believes the central task for the multiethnic or multiracial child is to achieve a positive resolution between a sense of identity and his or her environment (Root, 1990, 1997). Root believes there are four possible healthy identity resolutions for a multiethnic/multiracial person:

1. **The individual accepts society's definition of his or her race or ethnicity.** This is positive if the person is comfortable with this definition, and if the immediate social environment supports it. However, the label chosen may change as the individual moves to a place whose societal context supports a different label—when the ecological context changes.

Several identity development models call for multiethnic/ multiracial children to embrace and integrate all parts of their heritage, including their mainstream White background.

2. **The individual identifies with both ethnic or racial groups.** This is positive as long as the person does not feel pressured to change who he or she is—behavior, language, and personality—as he or she moves from one racial or ethnic group to the other. The person maintains his or her own inner compass.

3. **The individual identifies with a single racial/ethnic group.** In this case the person has made an active choice to align with one of his or her backgrounds—differing from simply accepting society's label. This is a positive choice if the individual feels fully accepted by the group and does not deny, put down, or reject the other side of his or her heritage.

4. **The individual identifies with the mixed-race or multiethnic/ multiracial group that his or her background presents,** which is positive as long as the new identity embraces all parts of the person's heritage. Even though this person can move comfortably from group to group, he or she maintains his or her multiethnic or multiracial identity in every ecological context.

Wardle's Developmental and Ecological Model of Identity Development

We believe all the models discussed have some value. These ideas have been integrated into Wardle's model (1992) and expanded to apply to all multiethnic and multiracial children, not just children with Black/White identity. We believe a model that details the successful development of a healthy multiethnic/ multiracial identity must have two distinct parts: developmental stages (Jacobs, 1977; Kerwin & Ponterotto, 1995; Poston, 1992) and ecological influences (Bronfenbrenner, 1979, 1989; Root, 1990, 1997, 1998; West, 2001). We describe these components in detail and discuss how they interact together to support the healthy development of multiethnic and multiracial children. Appendix A provides an age-related matrix that includes many ideas for parents, teachers, and others to support the multiethnic/multiracial child at each of these stages.

Developmental Stages

Piaget developed a theory of cognitive development that proposes that children progress through a series of invariant, stepwise stages of mental development, culminating with the **Formal Operations Stage** in adolescence (Piaget, 1963). In each of these stages a child thinks and processes information in a unique way, and, while the stages move from simple to more complex thinking, the development is not linear. Children must successfully complete each stage to be able to move to the next stage.

Erikson (1963) developed an eight-stage psychosocial theory that spans a person's life and is thus called a **life-span theory.** Some of the identity theories already discussed in this chapter appear to follow the lead of Piaget and Erikson. Kohlberg used Piaget's theory of mental development to construct his theory of moral reasoning, suggesting that our concepts of right and wrong and good and bad are inexorably connected to the way we think and reason about right and wrong and good and bad (Kohlberg, 1963). The importance of these stages regarding identity development is that (1) children think about the world differently as they mature—including how they think about ethnicity and race—and (2) a child's emotional and psychological development—including the way the child perceives his or her own identity—changes over time.

We believe multiethnic and multiracial children progress through two critical developmental stages in their journey to healthy development: early childhood and adolescence. Like Erikson, Piaget, and Kohlberg, we believe they need to have certain experiences and develop certain beliefs and understandings during each of these stages. However, unlike Piaget, we believe that a child who fails to complete the first stage can return later and make it up, but that it is more effective for a child to fully achieve stage I before going on to stage II.

Thus multiethnic and multiracial children need lots of exposure, discussions, exploration, modeling, and affirmation of their full identity when they are preschoolers. While many parents wait until their children reach the very difficult adolescent years to address their mixed heritage, we believe this is too late. Children need a solid sense of the rightness and normalcy of being multiracial and multiethnic before they have to struggle with what Erikson calls the identity crisis of adolescence (Erikson, 1963).

Stage I: Early Childhood (3 to 7 years)

During this age children explore individual differences, including skin color, hair texture, and eye shape (Goodman, 1964; Katz, 1982). They begin to compare and contrast themselves to their peers: who's tallest, who can jump the highest, who can run the fastest. This is a critical time when children develop feelings about themselves and about others who are different from them. They become increasingly aware of racial, gender, and special needs differences, which is one reason why children this age are so fascinated by the physical features of multiracial children and wonder aloud why they look different from their parents. Multiethnic and multiracial children at this age are discovering their own physical characteristics and also wondering why their hair and skin color do not match those of their parents. They also learn labels and emotional responses associated with various differences (Brandell, 1988; McRoy & Freeman, 1986). Children begin to pick up society's norms and biases and may imitate prejudicial behaviors of others—experiences and attitudes they pick up from peers and adults.

But, according to Alejandro-Wright (1985), a child does not fully understand the concept of race until 10 or 11 years old. A true sense of racial belonging develops from a vague awareness of skin color and other salient physical features, to a primitive understanding of the physical and biological attributes associated with racial categories, and finally to an eventual understanding of conventional racial categories and the notion of individual membership within those categories (see Chapter Feature, page 14).

The young child's sense of self-awareness and self-esteem is not directly tied to his or her sense of racial belonging. The mixed-race/ethnicity child is learning about the differences of skin color, hair texture, eye color and eye shape, and other physical features, but does not fully understand how these refer back to the racial/ethnic groups of his or her biological parents or single-race/ethnicity children he or she knows. It is not unusual for multiethnic or multiracial children at this age to want to look like their mothers. This is also true of adopted multiethnic/multiracial and single-race (transracially adopted) children.

Preoperational Stage. Children at this age are in Piaget's **preoperational stage**; they exhibit preoperational thought, which is very basic, highly influenced by salient and concrete factors, and prone to incorrect assumptions and conclusions. Preoperational children are very egocentric and also have difficulty holding more than one piece of information in their minds at a time—they are centric thinkers. Further, preoperational children have not learned what Piaget calls class inclusion—the ability to place one concept within another. For example, when Francis's children were this age, they could not understand that, while they live in Denver, Denver is in Colorado. They'd say, "No, I don't live in Colorado, I live in Denver!"

The preoperational child has difficulty with the idea that a peer can be Asian and Native American, Black and White, Hispanic and Korean, English and Nigerian, and so on. It is not surprising that a preoperational child's concept of race and ethnicity is unclear and seemingly based on very simplistic, often inaccurate physical cues. It's much like their view of gender identity, which is based on the clothes or hairstyle a person wears and stereotypical gender occupations (Phinney & Rotheram, 1987).

Based on our knowledge of the preoperational child, multiethnic and multiracial children need a single label to describe who they are. They also need lots and lots of opportunities to explore their physical features: mirrors, art activities, dress-up clothes, barrettes, combs, picture books of mixed-race and ethnicity children, stories of interracial families and multiracial heroes, and so on. Further, an understanding of the preoperational child explains why single-race children have such a difficult time recognizing and labeling these children, thus an early childhood program must provide ample opportunities for the single-race child to explore the complexity and variability of multiracial and multiethnic children.

The Initiative versus Guilt Stage. In Erikson's life-span model, 3- to 7-year-old children are experiencing the stage labeled **Initiative versus Guilt**. Initiative corresponds to the child's natural curiosity and experimentation with the larger social world; guilt is based on whether this exploration into the world is viewed by the child as positive and successful or negative and full of guilt. Parents', teachers', and caregivers' responses to the child's initiative will determine whether he or she develops a sense of initiative or guilt. Clearly, Erikson's concept is critical to the healthy development of multiracial and multiethnic children. Adults who openly support their exploration of physical characteristics, diversity, and racial identity development will enhance the progress through this stage; adults who insist that multiracial children identify with only one background, ignore their search for meaning, or exhibit prejudice because of their own biases will produce guilt in these children—especially associated with their unique racial characteristics.

Multiethnic and multiracial children in this stage must be encouraged to ask questions, experiment with a variety of social interactions, be exposed to a variety of live and fictional multiethnic and multiracial families and children, and play with many concepts and labels. Because children this age think in very egocentric and primitive ways, inaccurate and incorrect ideas about race and identity should not be punished, but rather explored though discussion, books, interaction, and exploration (Aboud, 1987). Children 3 to 7 years old must not be expected to understand adult concepts of racial identification, racial and ethnic labels, group belongings, and group loyalties—activities about racial and ethnic diversity should focus on individual differences and the variability of the human condition, not group belonging and reference group orientation.

Transition Period (from age 6–7 to about age 11–12 years)

At this age the multiethnic and multiracial child is progressing through a transition period. This is the time period when single-race children generally develop a secure sense of their socially ascribed racial or ethnic label; they are in Piaget's **Concrete Operations Stage**, which means they can more easily handle abstract concepts, even when they may contradict concrete evidence, and they are in Erikson's **Industry versus Inferiority Stage**, where the child must feel competent in a number of areas, especially in comparison to peers. Thus, children in this transition period are able to think abstractly about racial and ethnic concepts, see themselves and others as members of racial and ethnic groups, and are very interested in how their abilities and appearance compare to their peers (Wardle, 1999). Since children this age are beginning to collect in socially proscribed groups of gender, race, and ethnicity, the multiethnic and multiracial child is beginning to struggle with the question of racial and ethnic group belonging.

Stage II: Adolescence

Erikson (1963) has proposed that the central task of adolescence is to form a stable identity, which he described as a sense of personal sameness and historical continuity. Other important tasks of this stage are to establish autonomy and independence, relate appropriately to members of both sexes, and commit to a career choice (Dworetzky, 1995). Erikson points out that adolescents can be very cruel and fixated on in-group and out-group membership in their attempt to establish their personal identity "in skin color or cultural background, in tastes and gifts, and often in such petty aspects of dress and gestures selected as signs of an in-grouper or out-grouper" (Erikson, 1963, p. 262). This period is often called the period of the identity crisis. Interestingly, Erikson was Danish (Aryan) and

Jewish, and he experienced very keenly the hostility and harassment from single-identity peers during his adolescence. Thus, his observations for this age are particularly cogent for mixed-ethnicity and mixed-race adolescents.

As Tatum (1999) argues, the search for identity at this age is one of the reasons all the Black kids sit together in the cafeteria and why members of other ethnic groups tend to cluster together. Group belonging, group language, and establishing rules for membership in the group are some of the ways adolescents try to come to terms with their unique identity and membership within traditional ethnic and racial groups.

Clearly, adolescence is a critical time for healthy multiethnic and multiracial development (Gibbs, 1987; McRoy & Freeman, 1986). Not only are adolescents of mixed-heritage struggling with their identity crises, but single-race students who are also struggling with their own sense of identity often pressure multiethnic and multiracial children to select the identity of only one of their parents, because this helps single-race children develop their own identity—validating and supporting their search for belonging and affiliation within one reference group. Single-race minority adolescents often accuse multiracial and multiethnic children of being disloyal, wanting to be White—or the identity of the higher status parent—and believing they are better than them. Of course, some White kids will insist that multiethnic and multiracial students cannot claim any White heritage in their identity. Single-ethnicity/race adolescents do not realize that, while they struggle to find their place within a single reference group, this approach is not meaningful or healthy for multiethnic and multiracial students.

Multiethnic and multiracial adolescents need lots of opportunities to discuss race, racism, and racial identity; they need opportunities to explore their own unique identity through art, projects, family genealogy, exploration of multiethnic and multiracial people in the arts and history, and examination of mixed-ethnicity and race people in other cultures. They need positive role models at school, in the community, and in their textbooks.

Avoid Focusing on Racial/Ethnic Groups. Any discussion and presentation of diveristy and multicultural issues at the school during this stage must avoid focusing on groups and group belonging and loyalty, and examine individual identity: everything that goes into defining a person's identity—including, but not limited to race and ethnicity (Wardle, 1996b). Finally, while it's easy and very tempting for single-race/ethnicity adolescents to group by race and ethnicity in schools (Tatum, 1999), schools should explore ways to discourage this temptation and to encourage students to enjoy and explore their racial, ethnic, cultural, linguistic, and other diversity: to share with other students who are different. Adolescence should be a time to expand horizons, challenge ideas and attitudes, investigate the world, and explore what it means to belong to the human race; it is not a time to simply hide in one's own racial and ethnic comfort zone. Schools must not respond to the temptation to group students by ethnicity, race, language, or any other single segregating category—which is not only obviously detrimental to multiethnic and multiracial students, but also limiting to single-race adolescents.

Mixed-race adolescents should be encouraged to explore the positive aspects of their unique identity: as bridge builders, peace makers, people with the ability to move easily within different groups, and individuals who have been exposed to a range of diverse experiences single-race and ethnicity children often don't know (Olumide, 2002; Root, 1996).

Join Non-Race-Specific Groups. Multiethnic and multiracial adolescents have the challenge of developing a secure ethnic and racial identity in a country that truly does not recognize multiracial and multiethnic people as a group. Of course, much of an adolescent's identity is based on characteristics other than race, such as sports, gender, academics, interests, professional status of parents, career goals, and music choices. Mixed-race/ethnicity adolescents should be encouraged to join clubs in and out of school that are not race specific: National Honor Society, sports, art, drama, gifted programs, computer magnets, gymnastics, choir, and so on (Wardle, 1988). Schools should not sponsor race- or ethnic-specific clubs and should challenge racial and ethnic stereotypes associated around certain activities, groups, clubs, and teams. Finally, because much of self-esteem is based on individual competencies and skills, schools and families should focus on developing and supporting multiethnic and multiracial children's unique skills, interests, and abilities.

Chapter Feature
Student Profile: Zack

Zack, 10th grade, White mother/Black father.

I think most teachers know there are multiracial students in their presence, but they don't teach about them and don't teach to them: They teach to the Black kids and to the White kids. You go into the school and you see all the White kids hanging out with White kids, and all the Black kids hanging out with Black kids, and all the Hispanic kids hang out with Hispanic kids. We don't have a diverse school—we have three different schools. When I think about diversity, I think of interchange between different races and cultures. And I think multiracial kids are a prime example of the world of diversity.

I just try to hang out with whomever I want to. I'm in the band; I play basketball. That's like two opposites. All my Black friends ask "Why are you playing music? Why aren't you playing football this season? Why are you being all weak, you're hanging out with all those weak people?" People want you to fit into one group. I don't fit into one group.

I love challenging people's thinking, because if I get one person to acknowledge that people can be multiracial—that they can do totally opposite things—then I am doing something good.

Multiethnic and multiracial children should be encouraged to join race-neutral activities, such as sports.

Because adolescents have the cognitive ability to handle multiple pieces of information simultaneously and to process complex abstract ideas, they can now appreciate the full concept of a multiracial identity (Hall, 1980). They also understand the interplay between physical characteristics, their parents' racial and ethnic backgrounds, and individual and group belonging. Often multiethnic and multiracial adolescents move comfortably from one racial group to another and take on some of the attributes of each group (Olumide, 2002; Root, 1992).

Ecological Components

Uri Bronfenbrenner developed the concept of the importance of the ecological context in the healthy development of children (Bronfenbrenner, 1979, 1989). The **ecological context** is made up of environmental factors that have the most impact on a child's development: family, peers, school, poverty, community, media, and so on. However, children do not simply absorb these ecological components—they use them to *construct* their own view of the world—their reality. Thus, in the process of racial and ethnic identity development, children are continually taking in information from the environment about their racial and ethnic identities and processing it into a unique view of their own racial identity (West, 2001), based on personal experiences and developmental (age) social and mental abilities.

Successful completion of the two developmental stages discussed depends on the child's interaction with the components that make up the ecological model: family, group antagonism, minority/lower status context, majority/higher status context, and community (Wardle, 1992). These ecological components of the model are a liberal adaptation of a model proposed by A. Jones (1985) to work with Black patients in counseling and therapy settings. Figure 5.2 shows the interacting ecological components of this model, each of which has a different impact at the two different stages; for example, the family factor is a much stronger influence during stage I, and community a stronger impact during stage II (Poston, 1990). As Bronfenbrenner points out, each child will interact differently with each factor, using it to help construct his or her own unique racial and ethnic identity.

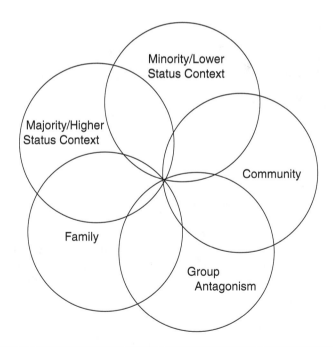

FIGURE 5.2 The Ecological Components of the Multiethnic/Multiracial Identity Model

Family

The family includes biological, adoptive, foster, teen, grandparent, and blended families, plus the extended family—on all sides. The family's impact on the child's multiethnic/multiracial identity depends on the attitude of the family toward a multiracial identity, whether the child's unique identity is openly discussed, discussion by the family about racism and prejudice, and the various ways the family supports the child's identity development (Brandell, 1988; McRoy & Freeman, 1986; Poston, 1990).

Each biological parent's attitude toward his or her own heritage and that of his or her spouse is also critical. It must be open, supportive, and understanding. Interethnic and interracial parents must not only find ways to resolve their own inevitable struggles and arguments, separating out issues of race from other conflicts (Crohn, 1999), but they must also agree about how they will raise their children. Some parents still believe in the view that "society will see them as Black" (Latino, Native American, etc.), so they need to raise them as Black (Latino, Native American, etc.); others seek advice from experts and professionals who generally believe in the orthodoxy that children can only be raised with a single racial/ethnic identity (Wehrly, Kenney, & Kenney, 1999). We believe the best way is to raise the child as proudly multiethnic/multiracial; what is most important, however, is that both parents agree on their approach to this complex issue. Because the family is so critical to the positive resolution of stage I, parents also need to find ways to actively support their children's identity development: discussion, role models, integrated schools and early childhood programs, cultural festivals, multiracial support groups, and so on (Wardle, 1999). Parents need be able to answer children's question about race, racism, prejudice, group labels, genetics, people's fears, diversity, and many other related topics. And, as Poston and Jacobs so accurately point out, children at stage I need a label that can be easily used to answer the incessant questions they will get, both from peers and adults: "mixed," "brown," "biracial," "multiethnic," and so on.

Families also must be comfortable with their interethnic/interracial status and understand that much of society is uneasy about it (Olumide, 2002; Wardle, 1999). They must understand that they are challenging hundreds of years of single-rage orthodoxy in this country and exposing strong emotional feelings in many people. As Olumide (2002) says, "In this way mixed race is the bearer of bad tidings for the race thinker. It carries, like the scapegoat, the sins and ill fortunes as well as the aspirations of the would-be-pure" (p. 2). An interethnic or interracial family—biological, foster, adoptive, or blended—must never retreat into a sense of shame and fear, because this will guarantee that the children will develop the guilt that Erikson talks about at this age, which occurs at exactly the same time the children are discovering their physical characteristics and determining how they differ from peers and parents.

The family is the child's first cultural context (Johnson, 1990) and, as such, provides the multiracial child with a sense of belonging, security, and protection. It functions as a mechanism for synthesizing the different identity contexts of the

The family is the first and most important context in the Multiethnic/Multiracial Identity Model.

child and in helping the child develop a unique sense of being multiethnic or multiracial. The family provides this context by openly discussing all issues around racism and prejudice, by taking up causes around race that affect the child (insensitive teachers, schools that insist on the child's filling out single-race federal forms, etc.) and by responding appropriately to prejudice that affects the family. The family should be the place where all the racial and ethnic backgrounds of the child come together, intermingle, and form a united entity that seems natural and wholesome to the child.

Other family dynamics are also important. Parenting style and competent parenting (Meyerhoff & White, 1986) will have an impact, especially in the area of communication and negotiation. While divorce poses a negative impact on all children (Hetherington, Cox, & Cox, 1978), divorce in an interethnic or interracial family can have an even more severe impact, especially if race becomes an issue, or if divorce results in removal of the child from one of the children's heritages (McRoy & Freeman, 1986). If the extended family of the child's **noncustodial, minority parent** also leaves the scene, taking away the concrete experience the child has with his or her minority heritage, the impact can be devastating (Wardle, 2002d).

Extended family support, attitudes, and involvement are important to the multiethnic and multiracial child. In addition to the normal support all families receive from their extended families, such as approval of a son's and daughter's marriage choice, extended family members of multiethnic and multiracial children need to learn to respect both parents' heritages and to support the multiethnic or multiracial identity of their grandchildren Appendix A provides additional advice for families, along with ideas for addressing issues that may arise within the additional contexts.

Group Antagonism

Multiethnic and multiracial children often must deal with two kinds of group antagonism: the traditional racism that minorities in this country still experience, including in early childhood programs and schools, and the antagonism of all single-racial and ethnic groups toward children and people of mixed heritage. The level of racism multiethnic and multiracial children experience depends to a large degree on their phenotype, but also on where they live, the diversity of educational programs they attend, and the level of training and sensitivity of the programs' staff.

Several researchers have pointed out that it is more difficult for multiracial and multiethnic children to develop a healthy identity than for single-race children (Gibbs, 1987; McRoy & Freeman, 1986). There has been some debate as to why this is—some believe the difficulty is caused by conflict within the child regarding group loyalty (Gibbs, 1987), but a more reasonable explanation is an inability by any of the groups that make up the child's background to fully support the child's multiracial or multiethnic identity (Olumide, 2002). This bias against mixed-heritage students is held by people in every racial and ethnic group—including teachers, administrators, social workers, and psychologists (Wehrly, Kenney, & Kenney, 1999). Furthermore, the general population seems to be ahead of the professionals regarding acceptance and support of multiethnic and multiracial identity. There are a variety of reasons for this attitude; what's important is that group antagonism can have a tremendously negative impact on the multiracial and multiethnic child's healthy development.

Group antagonism has to do with the lack of support from both of the parents' cultural contexts, which may include outright prejudice, exclusion, questioning of loyalty and name calling, and questioning of the child's parents' loyalty and motivations. One parent reported to Francis Wardle that children in her child's kindergarten told her child that she, her mother, was a whore because she was a White woman married to a Black man. When she took up this issue with the school's administration, they refused to address it, telling her it was her problem that she could address, if she chose.

Group antagonism often includes a general dislike or fear of diversity and a lack of recognition by the community at large of the legitimacy of a multiracial/multiethnic identity. Young multiethnic and multiracial children are often required to answer incessant questions from peers and adults about their ambiguous (to the observer) identity; older children must deal with an array of official school forms that have no place for them and that simply ignore a critical part of their family. Multiethnic and multiracial children are also often misidentified with a single-race identity, so they often have to correct the teachers. And teachers often tell these older children "to check the minority box, because that will give you a scholarship and other preferences" (Benjamin-Wardle, 1994). When multiethnic and multiracial students enter college, they can receive all the support and acknowledgment of official minority student organizations if they reject or hide their non-minority backgrounds. Forcing multiracial or multiethnic children to select just one of their backgrounds creates in them guilt and doesn't allow them to develop their full identities (Bowles, 1993; Sebring, 1985; Wardle, 1992).

Cultural Contexts

Cultures operate as context because they fix meaning over time, and each culture has the capacity to fix meaning differently (Johnson, 1990). Individuals and families operate within these cultural contexts and help children find belonging within a specific cultural context. While racial groups are clearly not biological categories, they operate very strongly to define cultural context, often ascribing membership to the cultural group through differences of phenotype (Wilson, 1984). As we have discussed, the assumption is that race and ethnicity provide a cultural context that is essential to a person's identity; the concept of hypodescent places any child of multiple heritages into the cultural group of the parent (or grandparent) of lowest status (Daniel, 1992).

The multiethnic and multiracial child develops within several cultural contexts, including the context of highest status and the one of lowest status. For the child with a Black/mainstream White background, the two contexts are obviously the mainstream White group and the Black group; for a Latino/Black child, it would be the Latino and Black group, respectively; and in a mainstream White/ Latino child, it would be the mainstream White group and the Latino group, respectively. Clearly, there is tremendous cultural diversity within each large population group; further, since contexts are interactive and dynamic, each impacts the child differently, depending on the other ecological factors.

Minority/Lower Status Context.   Multiethnic children with some mainstream White heritage have a distinctive cultural context that includes minority and majority status; children whose parents are from two minority groups also have a lower status and higher status context, based on the position of their parents' race and ethnicity within the strict racial hierarchy. While children with some mainstream White heritage must deal with those who accuse them of wanting to be White, trying to be better, ignoring their roots, and avoiding their real identities, children with two minority heritages will be expected to identify with the race of the lowest status, will be discriminated against by people from the race of their higher status, and will be accused of passing for the race of higher status (Cruz-Janzen, 1997).

Nobles (1976, 1980) defined several factors that positively impact self-concept in minority children. He lists group identification or we-ness, strong extended family ties, a strong emphasis on spirituality, a flexible concept of time, and a general sensitivity to others. Further, all minorities must develop ways to cope with experiences of racial discrimination and determine to what extent they will adopt majority values, goals, and psychological patterns (Jones, 1985). Individual minorities develop a variety of ways to deal with discrimination. Clearly, children with one mainstream White parent and those with two minority parents must also learn to effectively deal with discrimination, which the minority parent or parent with the lowest status can most effectively teach the child. If this parent is not in the picture, members of his or her extended family must step in—especially during stage I, when children are concrete learners and need direct exposure to the minority, or lowest, side of their background (Wardle, 2002a).

Majority/Higher Status Context.   Again, the child with one mainstream White parent will have a strong influence from the majority context, while children with two minority parents will have a strong influence from the race or ethnicity of higher status. The mainstream White context is the dominant value in this society: TV and video images, print advertisements, teachers in schools, most pictures in books and magazines, and so on. Models that are viewed as the ideal or standard are mostly mainstream White (president, lawyers, TV heroes, etc.)—although this is beginning to change. For example, Francis Wardle believes the prototype for woman's beauty is shifting from the blond, blue-eyed goddess to the universal woman that the famous Navaho painter R.C. Gorman has so powerfully developed—Asian/Native Indian features, brown skin, black hair, and a nurturing, but highly independent personality (there are no men in any of Gorman's beautiful artworks)—an ideal that Disney seems to have adopted in some of its latest cartoons, along with the redo of the movie, *Charlie's Angels*. Minority fashion models—especially women—have increased dramatically over the last few years. White images are also the dominant images in magazines, books, TV, movies, and advertisements in Mexico and Latin American countries, including Brazil.

As we have discussed already, much of the curricular content and materials in schools disproportionately reflect the dominant society. Thus, mainstream White children receive daily feedback that they count, that they belong to the most powerful group, and that non-Whites don't count as much (McIntosh, 1988). The White context develops in White people a pattern of assumptions: a sense of control, a feeling of being able to succeed according to White standards, and the ability to make the system work for the individual (McIntosh, 1988). Whites also believe that success is based on individual merit, and that individuals, not systems or institutions, perpetuate racism.

Mainstream Whites can choose what to escape and what risks they choose not to take. (Francis Wardle, who is White, was once told to shave his beard to more closely match the image of the company for which he worked. He could choose to do so, although he did not; a person of color cannot chose to change his or her color.) The dominant context is often sought after by non-mainstream Whites, including the more negative values, such as greed, violence, and sexism.

In families with a mainstream White parent, multiracial children can learn to come to terms with majority interests and values—to become multicultural and work effectively within the dominant society (Banks & Banks, 1997; Jones, 1985). The mainstream White parent may also assist the family in understanding that, to a large extent, interethnic/interracial families do not have a strong reference group in which to find orientation and meaning—unlike traditional single-race minority groups—and therefore must take on the more majority view of identity and meaning—an "I can do my thing" approach (Nobles, 1980). This lack of a strong reference group in which to belong is one of the reasons why multiethnic and multiracial families start support groups in their communities (Brown & Douglass, 1996) and why the Internet has become a virtual reference group.

The child with two or more minority heritages will have to find other ways to develop a multicultural style regarding the dominant context. Children whose parents are both minorities are exposed to one background that is considered more powerful, more popular, and more desirable. They must, however, guard against the belief that aligning only with the higher status side of their heritage somehow places them more in favor with that group and the dominant culture.

Community

The community represents the most important ecological impact on a child after the family (Bronfenbrenner, 1989) and includes school, church groups, immediate peers, and neighborhood groups—scouts, gymnastics team, track team, church choir, soccer, baseball, and so on. For older children, especially middle school and high school students, formal groups within the school are important sociocultural factors: athletic teams, gifted clusters, National Honor Society, science organizations, and service organizations. Informal groups are also important: cliques, peers, political action groups, gangs, and neighborhood friendships.

The neighborhood in which the interracial or interethnic family live will have a different influence, depending on its character and how dependent the family is on the neighborhood. Some neighborhoods are tight, self-sufficient communities of homogeneous populations; in other neighborhoods people share little beyond the streets and trash collectors. Often children do not attend neighborhood schools and families may attend a house of worship across town.

Three factors play heavily on the impact of the community on healthy multiethnic and multiracial identity:

1. Does the family feel it belongs?
2. Is the community accepting of a range of diversity?
3. Is there minority representation and multiracial/multiethnic children in at least some of the community groups the child attends: childcare, school, church, dance clubs, neighborhood soccer teams, and so on?

Furthermore, the age of the child is a factor: During stage I, children need to have positive exposure to ethnic and racial diversity, know others they can identify with, and be around similar families (Derman-Sparks, 1989; Wardle, 1987). During stage II, children use friends and groups to define their similarities in relationships to others. Most teenagers are also fairly mobile and can move out of their neighborhood to find peers they want. Erikson (1963) points to many criteria for group selection—race only being one—and Cross (1987) makes the distinction between personal identity (the child's sense of who he or she is) and reference group orientation (the groups the child identifies with). Because of the comparatively small number of multiethnic and multiracial children in most communities, non-race criteria are generally used for adolescent group selection. These children switch comfortably between different single-race/ethnicity groups, without denying either side of their heritage, becoming anti- one side or the other, or becoming confused (Root, 1996).

Integrating the Ecological Components

Bronfenbrenner (1979) suggests that each child integrates all of his or her experiences within his or her own unique context. The related strengths of each of the child's experiences will differ from child to child, as will the way these experiences interact and influence each other, resulting in the child's constructing his or her own unique, integrated contexts (West, 2001). Thus, each multiracial and multiethnic child will integrate all the factors of the model, both during stage I (early childhood) and during stage II (adolescence): The impact of each factor will differ at each stage. While each child will integrate these factors differently, the totality of the child's multiracial or multiethnic identity will depend on positive experiences, interactions, opportunities, reinforcements, and processes with each of these factors (West, 2001) and the extent to which each contexts either supports or contradicts each other.

Conclusion

Considerable attention and concern has been focused on healthy identity development of multiethnic and multiracial children—although most of the research has been conducted on Black/White children. In fact, it seems that almost all research on multiethnic and multiracial children is narrowly directed to this one topic. Reasons for this focus include a historical view that children of multiethnic and multiracial backgrounds must be raised with a single identity—usually of the lowest status parent—or they will become confused and disoriented; current beliefs by many professionals that single-race identity development is still the most appropriate—the prototype; and the fact that our contemporary society is fixated on a single-race perception of people. Countries that have a history of multiethnic/multiracial acceptance and a contemporary view of the normalcy of mixed identity, such as Brazil, do not place the same focus on a healthy identity development of multiethnic and multiethnic children. Regarding the healthy identity developed in this country, we know that (1) the developmental process for multiethnic and multiracial children is different from that of single-race children, and (2) the various contexts a child experiences—family, group antagonism, majority/highest status context, minority/lowest status contest, and community—determine the success or failure of the healthy multiethnic or multiracial identity process. A part of the community context, the early childhood program and school are extremely powerful factors in the development of healthy multiracial and multiethnic children. These programs can also determine whether group antagonism will negatively affect these children—through the attitudes of teachers, staff, and peers—and whether the school is a context that supports the child's healthy integration of his or her majority/higher status background with his or her minority/lower status heritage.

Questions/Projects

1. Do you know a family with multiethnic or multiracial children? If so, interview the parents to determine how they are raising their children.

2. Are the issues around identity development of multiethnic and multiracial children the same in all countries and societies? What are factors that might change how parents raise their multiethnic/multiracial children in different countries?

3. Are the identity issues of a child of Black/White background the same as those of a child of Navajo and Black background or Korean, Japanese, and White background? What are factors that parents, teachers, and professionals should consider in working with these children?

Resources

Book

Tomorrow's children: Meeting the needs of multiracial and multiethnic children at home, in early childhood programs, and at school
Center for the Study of Biracial Children
2300 South Krameria Street
Denver, CO 80222

Article

Wardle, F. (1999, September). The color of love: Finding the face of multicultural love through the eyes of family. *Mothering, 96,* 68–73.

Websites

Biracial Kids
A place for multiethnic/multiracial kids, with articles and links

http://www.biracialkids.org

Interracial Families
Center for the Study of Biracial Children

http://www.csbc.cncfamily.com

Beautiful Biracial

http://beta.communities.msn.com/
BeautifulBiRacial

6

Families and Communities

In examining interethnic and interracial families, each unique combination of couples brings to the family different strengths and challenges. A family whose father is Jewish and mother Puerto Rican has different issues from a family whose mother is Navaho Indian (Dine) and father Black. The combinations are endless, the issues complex. And all of these nuclear families bring with them diverse and varied extended family contexts. Add to these family structures foster and adoptive families, teens and grandparents raising children, and blended families, and the diversity of issues is immediately apparent. Additionally, the communities in which these families live have a profound impact on interethnic and interracial families. Francis Wardle just visited the Crow Indian Reservation in southern Montana and learned of a family living on the reservation that has one parent who is Crow and the other parent who is Korean. The experience of the children in this family will be very different from their experiences if they lived in a Korean community, a mainstream White community, or an integrated community.

Early childhood programs and schools are vital community institutions. They have a responsibility to support all the families they serve and to provide a safe and secure haven for struggling families. For interethnic and interracial families, the role of the early childhood program and school has added significance, because these families often feel lost and lacking the support and acceptance they need and deserve. This chapter examines a variety of factors that impact interracial and interethnic families and explores ways communities, early childhood programs, and schools can support these families as they challenge one of society's most intractable biases and prejudices.

FOCUS QUESTIONS

1. How do religious differences impact a family's life?

2. Why does the early childhood program and school have a unique role to play in nurturing and supporting interethnic and interracial families?

3. How can schools support the interracial and interethnic family in its sincere effort to provide a psychologically safe and nurturing place for multiethnic and multiracial children?

4. What are the issues a blended family faces when one of the children from a previous relationship is multiethnic and/or multiracial?

The Multiethnic and Multiracial Family

Multiethnic and multiracial families face a variety of challenges as they strive to raise their children. Clearly, most of these challenges are the same issues that singe-race families struggle with. However, here we will touch on some of the more critical issues that are unique to these families as they raise their children, work with their children's early childhood programs and schools, and sometimes struggle with relatives and members of the extended family. Appendix A provides a way to view many of these issues thoughout the interethnic/interracial family's life.

The Child's Ethnic or Racial Identity

The question of how the family will raise its children—as members of the minority or lowest status race, as proudly mixed-ethnicity or mixed-race, or as human above anything else—is one of the most difficult issues all interethnic and interracial families face. This decision is, of course affected by extended family opinions and pressures, experts parents seek out for advice, books the parents consult, and the community in which they live, work, and worship. Parents—biological, adoptive, foster, and extended family parents—seem to take one of several approaches to the issue of their multiethnic or multiracial child's identity:

- Raise the child with the identity of the minority parent, or parent of the lowest status (Daniel, 1992).
- Raise their child as a member of "the human race" above all racial labels.
- Let the child decide—usually during the difficult and confusing adolescent years.
- Don't really know—confused by all the pressure and contradictory advice—from family, friends and experts.
- Raise the child with a proud multiracial and multiethnic identity.
- Support the child's changing of his or her identity as age and context dictates (Root, 1992).
- Label and identify their child based on his or her phenotype—if he or she looks "Black," "Hispanic," "Native American," "Asian," etc.

Further, parents will have different understanding about the nature of ethnic and racial identity development, the developmental nature of all identity development, including race and ethnicity, and the importance of the environment—discussed at length in the previous chapter.

Chapter Feature
Excerpt from *Tomorrow's Children*

Myth: Interracial marriages fail. As a result of the myths about the incompatibility between people from different racial and ethnic backgrounds and the belief that partners in successful marriages must have similar backgrounds, it is widely assumed interracial and interethnic marriages fail far more often than marriages of people from the same racial or ethnic group. This myth is further supported by the myth that people from different racial and ethnic backgrounds marry for "unnatural reasons." For Black/White marriages, these "unnatural reason" include:

- Black men marry White women because they represent ideal female beauty.
- Black men marry White women for status.
- Black men marry White women to get back at White society.
- White women marry Black men because they are sexually superior to White men.
- White men marry Black women because they are exotic.
- White men marry Black women because they are good in bed.
- Whites marry Blacks because they feel guilty about White racism and want to get back at a racist society.
- Black women marry White men to improve their economic and social standing.
- Black men marry White women because Black women emasculate Black men.
- Black women marry White men because Black men are sexist and chauvinist.

Clearly, marriages based on these and other ulterior motives cannot succeed.

Reality: Interracial marriages are as successful and unsuccessful as other marriages. We don't have much information about the success or failure of interracial marriages. A study conducted in midwestern states showed interracial marriage to be more successful than Black-Black marriages, but less successful than White-White marriages. Another study of interracial and interethnic marriage, conducted in Hawaii, suggested interracial and interethnic marriage to be more successful than same-race marriage. This study also found that people who marry interracially were more independent than those who did not, because people willing to cross racial and ethnic barriers to marry are more secure of themselves and able to make personal choices despite societal pressure. A third series of studies suggest that interracial partners tend to be urban, of the same religious background, and well educated.

Many contemporary interracial couples enter into a relationship fully aware that society predicts it will fail and that their children will have problems. They know they are challenging deep-seated taboos and therefore work very hard to make sure their children have a secure home to shelter them from the negative pressures of society. Many of these interracial couples are actively involved in local support groups and are also actively involved in their children's schools and childcare programs. (Wardle, 1999, pp. 90–91)

Many first-time parents of multiethnic or multiracial children are at the "don't know" stage, struggling for advice and support. It is our experience that almost all "experts"—psychologists, social workers, adoption specialists, multicultural educators, school counselors—advise interracial and interethnic families to raise their children with the single identity of the parent of color or the parent with the lowest status. These professionals need to become knowledgeable about the latest research and theories about multiethnic and multiracial identity development. They need to explore their own biases and the biases of the education they received about multiethnic and multiracial families and provide parents with enough information so that they can make their own reasoned decisions. Alternatively, they should refer these parents to books, Internet sites, and people in the community knowledgeable in this area. Schools can be invaluable places for providing accurate and objective information to help parents come to terms with this difficult issue and to help them make up their own minds. Further, early childhood programs and schools should provide these families with access to community resources.

Often the minority parent in the relationship insists the child be raised with the minority label. This is also true for relationships between two minority parents—say Latino and Black—where the parent of lowest status insists on the child's being raised with his or her identity. There are a variety of complex reasons for this insistence, including:

- A belief that identifying with the minority will enable the child to learn techniques needed to resist White racism in this society.
- A deep-seated antagonism toward people who have "passed as [mainstream] White." Obviously, many multiethnic and multiracial children could pass as mainstream White. Thus, the minority parent may not want to be accused by others of his or her ethnicity/race of trying to have his or her child pass.
- Complex issues around color. All races and ethnic groups have distinct hierarchies around color—usually with light being better (and straight hair, European features, etc.), dark being worse. However, overlaid on this issue of colorism is a sense of ethnic and racial pride—of being Chicano, Native American, African American, Asian, whatever—especially since the civil rights movement of the 1960s. These two apparently opposing values can cause complex reactions to the notion of a multiracial/multiethnic identity. One response by minority parents is that since their child could be lighter than them, they must actively affirm the child's minority identity to maintain their own racial and cultural pride and a sense of group belonging. Francis Wardle, who advises interracial families, has often responded to Black fathers upset with the lightness of their children. (Ironically, many multiracial babies are very white and some tend to get darker with age.)
- Loyalty and reference group orientation. All minorities who date and marry "outside their group," be it to a mainstream White person or another higher

status minority, are accused at one time or another of being disloyal to their group and wanting to escape the oppression and racism experienced by members of their group. One way minority participants in interracial and interethnic marriages respond to this accusation is to strongly assert the single minority identity of their children, thus proving loyalty to their own group.

- Probably the most often heard rationale for raising multiethnic and multiracial children with only the identity of the minority—or lowest status—parents, is the statement, "but society will see your child as Black (Latino, Asian, Native America, etc.)," so you must raise him or her to meet society's expectations. We have both heard this argument repeatedly, from experts, ethnic studies professors, researchers, psychologists, parents, and the average person on the street—of all races and ethnicities.

- Politics of numbers. Most civil rights activists in this country believe the only way to produce positive change is through the political process, which can only occur through numbers. Thus, keeping up the numbers of various minority groups is critical for the struggle of equality, and identifying as multiethnic or multiracial is "siding with the enemy."

- Mainstream White parents don't want to be seen as racist. Some of these parents (and other minority parents of higher status) are not sure themselves whether a multiethnic or multiracial identity is a good idea and don't want to be accused by minorities of wanting their child to be multiracial or multiethnic—or, more damaging, of not wanting their child to be perceived as Black (Native American, Japanese, Latino, etc.). Clearly, many White parents don't want to be accused of this attitude.

Interracial and interethnic couples must struggle with the issue of the ethnic and racial identity of their children and must come to a position they can both support. And, as we have already suggested, we believe parents must make this decision before the children become preschoolers. Parents should carefully discuss the various options. It's not OK for the minority parent to simply say, "You don't know because you have not experienced racism (it's a Black thing, you won't understand!)"; it's also not OK for the White parent to say, "we're all human beings who are equal, so race doesn't matter," because the minority parent knows that, in this society, race *does* matter (Crohn, 1995).

Religion

Probably the most difficult aspect of family diversity, even beyond race, is religion. This is because religion is the basis of each individual's set of value and attitudes, which then determines his or her response to all sorts of activities, issues, and conflicts. Religion very much defines how we see the world and our view of knowledge. Adults bring their religious beliefs, values, and viewpoints to their marriages and other adult relationships. In many marriages religious differences cause the major conflicts (Crohn, 1995), so much so that some experts discourage interfaith marriage altogether (Gordon, 1964). While religion does not directly correspond to race and ethnicity, there are tendencies—many Latinos are Roman Catholic, some Blacks are Moslem, most Jews in this country are White, many mainstream Whites are Quaker, Unitarian, Protestant, or Catholic. Thus many interracial and interethnic marriages are also interfaith marriages. Clearly, couples must very carefully understand and separate out these two potential areas of conflict (Crohn, 1995).

The first real stuggle for Francis and his wife was a religious disagreement. As a lifelong Catholic who had attended Catholic schools and who was herself baptized, Ruth assumed their children would all be baptized, and so expected a baptism shortly after the birth of their first child. Furthermore, since this was the first grandchild, she wanted to please her mother by baptizing her first grand-daughter. Francis, however, was raised in a radical Anabaptist faith, whose historical ties come out of an opposition to both Catholicism and the Lutheran reformation. His faith believed very strongly in adult baptism. Although he is no longer a practicing Anabaptist, professing atheist beliefs, his upbringing still prevented him from supporting infant baptism. Additionally, he did not want to lose the support of his extended family, who were all still active Anabaptists.

Couples who come from different religious backgrounds must carefully and diligently address the issue, hopefully exploring their differences before they commit to marriage. If one or both parents are no longer active believers, this may help, although our deep-seated values are based on our religious upbringing. Further, because extended family support is so critical for the interracial and interethnic family (Wardle, 2002a), the possibility of losing extended family

Ruth Benjamin-Wardle's mother is Catholic, so Ruth intended to baptize her first child. Her husband disagreed. Religious disagreements can make interracial and interethnic marriage more complex.

support because of religious conflicts with in-laws should not be underestimated (Crohn, 1995).

Both parents must be open to compromise and must discuss the issue in good faith (Crohn, 1995). It is not OK for the Latino parent who is Roman Catholic to simply say, "My family has always been Roman Catholic and expects my children to be Catholic," or a Black parent who is a Moslem to say, " Blacks in this country must be Moslem to fight White oppression," or the Quaker partner to suggest, "My family heritage is based on pacifism and nonviolent resistance, so we must continue that tradition." When people from different backgrounds marry, everything must be open to discussion and negotiation. (It should be noted that many marriage partners of the same race and ethnicity must grapple with similar conflicts around religion, values, and educational expectations for their children.) One real problem with interfaith marriages is that some religious leaders and advocates for certain religious groups belittle parents for not raising their children in the faith of one particular religion. The more traditional Jewish groups require children of interfaith marriages to be raised Jewish, and there is considerable debate within the overall Jewish community regarding raising children with more than one faith.

Clearly, interethnic and interracial marriage can increase interfaith tensions, although it doesn't automatically have to do so. However, couples must find ways to keep these issues of race and religion separate and find supportive people (such as religious leaders and interracial support groups) who can help them explore both their interfaith relationship and their interracial/interethnic experience.

Selecting Schools and Early Childhood Programs

Selecting early childhood programs and schools is one of the first critical decisions all couples must make. This decision is fraught with a variety of issues, including religious values, the kind of schools the parents attended when they were young, neighborhood options, transportation, and academic expectations. If the children have special needs or are gifted, this adds an additional wrinkle. What makes the decision different and more complex for interethnic and interracial families than for single-race families is that ethnicity and race must be a consideration. Multiethnic and multiethnic children need to be around other children like them; they need appropriate adult role models, and they should be in programs where considerable racial, ethnic, national, linguistic, and other diversity is present (Wardle, 1999).

Young children are concrete learners, so children up to about 8 years old need to be in programs where they can see and relate to other children like them. Older children are less concrete learners, but need schools where they are not the token minority and where there is open discussion about racial and ethnic diversity. Obviously, these schools must exhibit tolerance to all racial and ethnic differences.

However, homogeneous minority early childhood programs and schools are problematic also, because they lack diversity and because attitudes of minority children—and sometimes staff—toward children of mixed heritage are often as intolerant, if not more so, than those of mainstream White children and staff. While anti-racist statements and behaviors on the part of mainstream White people and children are not tolerated in our schools, insensitive and downright racist remarks by minorities toward multiethnic and multiracial students and their families are often accepted within all-minority schools. Cruz-Janzen recalls many very cruel incidents of students' degrading mixed children, with little or no staff concern or intervention (Cruz-Janzen, 1997).

The racial and ethnic makeup of the early childhood program and school is particularly critical if the children are living with only one side of their heritage—particularly the White side. White parents must make a special effort to find educational programs for their children that include a healthy and diverse mix of ethnic and racial backgrounds. Schools near universities with strong international programs are often wonderful places with a rich variety of international families that bring different traditions, languages, nationalities, and races and ethnicities to the school community.

How Schools Can Support Multiracial and Multiethnic Families

Schools are often the most immediate and direct contact multiethnic and multiracial families have with official, mainstream society. Thus, they carry a huge responsibility regarding meeting the unique needs of these families. In Chapter 9 we discuss the kinds of training educational personnel need to be able to meet this responsibility. Some of the other things schools must do to support these new, and often struggling, families, include:

1. *Be supportive.* Often interethnic and interracial families are struggling with many issues, above and beyond the typical struggles single-race families must face.
2. *Be nonjudgmental.* Unfortunately, in this country many people of all races and ethnicities have very strong opinions regarding interracial marriage and mixed-race/ethnicity children. School personnel, especially social workers, counselors and psychologists—who often meet with families in crisis, or children with school-related behavioral or social problems—must come to terms with their own biases, and often inaccurate and blatantly racist training, and make sure their own opinions do not affect the way they work with multiethnic and multiracial children (Wehrly, Kenney, & Kenney, 1999).
3. *Provide resources and referrals.* Most multiracial and multiethnic families lack information about how to raise their children and find knowledgeable, sympathetic professionals in the community. Schools need to provide this information for these families.
4. *Support the family's choice of identity for their child(ren).* As we have discussed throughout the book, many multiracial and multiethnic families struggle with the OMB racial categories and the ways schools implement them. At

best, schools should provide multiethnic/multiracial choices for the child; at a minimum, the school must be highly sensitive to this issue and understand why these forms cause so much concern to many of these families. Further, schools should immediately implement the new Census approach, which allows parents—and older children—to select as many ethnic/racial categories as they feel represent their child's full identity. Denying the child a multiethnic or multiracial label is denying the child his or her full identity and heritage, which can have lasting negative affects (Bowles, 1993).

5. *Respond to each parent and family as unique individuals.* School personnel can never assume the dynamics of an interracial family are a cause for the child's problems, or presume that academic or behavioral problems of a child are automatically caused by mixed-family status. At the same time, however, schools must recognize the unique issues and the stress many of these families must deal with (Wehrly, Kenney, & Kenney, 1999).

6. *Find out from the family the identity they have chosen for their child, how they support that identity, and how they would like the school to support it.* The best time to get this information is when the family initially enrolls their child.

7. *Provide multicultural and diversity activities in classes that include multiethnic and multiracial children.* At the same time do not provide-single race activities and celebrations that communicate to these children that they are somehow abnormal, messed up, freaks, or that they are only acceptable when they reject part of their background.

The Benjamin-Wardle family explores both sides of their heritage. This is a maternal great grandfather.

Chapter Feature
Excerpt from *Raising Healthy, Happy Interracial Children:*
Supporting Your Biracial Child

On the U.S. Census, 6.8 million Americans checked more than one box when asked to identify race. The number of interracial and interethnic families and children is steadily increasing and multiracial/multiethnic people are becoming more and more visible in entertainment, athletics, and political arenas.

In the past, individuals of two or more races were often pressured to identify with their minority race and were rarely given the opportunity to embrace their multicultural heritage.

Today experts are telling us that it is not only acceptable for interracial/interethnic children to identify with all parts of their heritage, but imperative for their emotional and social well-being (Nishimura, 1995).

Since schools, institutions, and communities are often not prepared to support interracial/interethnic children, it is up to you, the parent, to provide the accepting, loving environment your child needs to reach his or her full potential. There will be times when you will be your child's most important advocate.

Raising the Multiracial/Multiethnic Child
Most of the time raising a mixed-heritage child is the same as raising any child. There are, however, some things that parents or caretakers of these children should keep in mind:

DO—Put race in its proper perspective. Though it is important to deal with, it is not everything (Wright, 1998).

DON'T—Link self-worth with appearance or race. Rather, focus on people's personal characteristics.

DO—Talk about race and ethnicity at home. Make it part of regular conversation.

DON'T—Assume that your children will have the same experiences as you did growing up. Your children have the unique quality of having different experiences than both of their parents.

DO—Create a label for the family and your children that they can use with peers.

DON'T—Worry when your children go through stages of wanting to be different.

DO—Expose your children to all races and acquaint them with all kinds of people, especially multiethnic/multiracial role models.

DO—Teach them their family history.

DO—Provide a variety of dolls, books, and toys that represent all shades of people.

DO—Learn how to style your child's hair. Get advice from hairstylists if necessary.

DO—Get involved in non-race/ethnic specific activities.

DO—If possible, live in a diverse neighborhood. If you cannot, join or create a support group.

From Beane (2001).

Different Family Structures

Interracial and interethnic families come in all sorts of diverse structures, just like single-race families. Each of these diverse structures adds a unique twist and different challenges to raising multiethnic and multiracial children. Further, as we have said, these various structures come with their own unique extended family configurations, which add to the family's diversity. Next we touch on a few of these different multiethnic and multiracial families.

Transracial Adoption

Because of the dearth of eligible mainstream White babies to adopt, and lots of minority children who need homes, many mainstream White couples adopt minority children. And, of course, many of these children are multiethnic and multiracial—for a variety of reasons, including the taboo against mixed-race children in this country and many other countries. A recent study conducted in Britain showed that a child of mixed race is two and one half times as likely to end up being cared for by the state's social service system than a single-race child. One implication of this statistic is that the system intrinsically believes mixed-ethnicity and mixed-race families are more pathological than single-race families and therefore will produce more "at-risk" children who will need the help of the state (Olumide, 2002). Additionally, in countries such as Brazil, children of mixed heritage make up a significant part of the number of adoptable children because the mixed race population is so large.

Domestic Adoption.   Ironically, while dating interracially and interethnically has gained some acceptance in this country—especially in high schools, colleges, and between minority men and White women—mixed-race/ethnicity children are not as readily accepted (Wardle, 2002d). The result is that many of these children are given up for adoption—what we call **domestic adoption**. Further, as with other White and minority children, some mixed-race/ethnicity children end up being taken from their parents by social services and then become available for adoption.

Mainstream White families who adopt mixed-race/ethnicity children face many hurdles. This may be the first time they may have come to close contact with minority issues and experiences, and they may not have been prepared to help their children deal with a racist society. Further, when a mainstream White family adopts a multiethnic or multiracial child, it becomes a minority family and must learn to deal with this new—and often uncomfortable—status (Wardle, 1999).

Many mainstream White adoptive families are so conscious of the minority status of their child, and so concerned with trying to expose their child to what they perceive as his or her minority culture, that they don't even recognize the child is multiracial or multiethnic—and therefore may have some physical and cultural attributes similar to their own. What confounds this issue is that the vast majority of adoptive workers—especially those working for state, county, and city programs—tend to believe in the one-drop rule, insisting adoptive parents raise their child with the single identity of the parent of color or the parent with lowest status (Melina, 1989; Powell, 1988). Even when parents seek out advice and training on how to raise multiethnic and multiracial children, they will usually be told to raise them with a single-minority heritage (Melina, 1989; Wardle, 1999).

Added to all these issues is the position taken in 1976 by the National Association of Black Social Workers opposing the adoption of Black children by mainstream White families. Native American tribes have a similar position, except in the case of the tribes, the rule is codified in federal law, giving the tribe first rights in adopting a child with any heritage from that tribe. The British Association for Adoption and Fostering (BAAF) also supports a complete ban on transracial adoption—believing that transracial adoption creates the process of "pathological bonding" (Olumide, 2002, p. 54). The BAAF also believes "Children of mixed parentage who have a White parent and Black parent are no different from other Black children. . . . The child is a Black child and should be treated as such" (BAAF, 1995). Further, The National Association of Black Social Workers strictly follows the one-drop rule—thus labeling multiracial and multiethnic children as children who should not be adopted by White families (Wehrly, Kenney, & Kenney, 1999), and tribes use the federal quantum percentage to determine tribal membership (Wilson, 1992).

Mainstream White adoption organizations, such as the Child Welfare League, Adopted Child, and American Family Association (AFA), have generally accepted the ban on transracial adoption and have fully adopted the view that multiracial and multiethnic children are single-race/ethnic children with the identity of the parent of color or lowest status parent (Melina, 1989; Powell, 1988)—a position also supported by the BAAF (Olumide, 2002).

Many social workers who work directly with families who have adopted transracially are members of the National Association of Black Social Workers (NABSW), or are social workers who believe in their same-race adoption position. White adoptive parents also often experience other professionals—school counselors, school psychologists, Head Start officials—who either believe strongly in the position of the NABSW, Indian Tribes, and adoption agencies, or who simply do not know any better. Most colleges that teach social workers also adhere to this same position; the home of the NABSW is the University of North Carolina School of Social Work.

All new adoptive parents must learn a great deal of information about being adoptive parents. Parents who transracially adopt—single-race or multiethnic/multiracial children—also need to learn about the unique needs of their children. Books and other resources designed to help biological interracial and interethnic families are also helpful to adoptive families. Mainstream White families who adopt multiethnic and multiracial children must explore a variety of concrete ways to expose their children to positive aspects of all of their backgrounds. This takes tremendous effort, especially for families who have never had much contact with minority peoples, cultures, and communities.

Foreign Adoption.   Families who adopt multiethnic or multiracial children from other countries—**foreign adoption**—have to confront all the issues addressed already, plus a few more. They must find ways to expose their child to his or her native culture—language, food, customs, national treasures, history, and the arts. They need to find ways to make contact with people from the country of their child's origin. Establishing contact with people from the child's home country can be extremely difficult and tricky if the child's country of origin has a history of prejudice against mixed-race people, such as Japan and Vietnam. Further, many countries are extremely class conscious and do not look kindly on children from lower-class peoples joining their native groups, even in this country. Native Indian children from Peru, Bolivia, Guatemala, and Columbia are often not welcome in national social groups from those countries in this country; children with part-Black heritage from Mexico and Latin American countries will not be welcome in many national groups either.

The other challenge for these families is to understand the cultural difference between the same racial and ethnic groups in this country and those in the child's country of origin. For example, there is considerable distrust and hostility between African Americans and Africans, and some third- and fourth-generation Latinos aren't very welcoming to new immigrants from Mexico, Central and South America, etc. Adoptive parents cannot assume their mixed-race or mixed-ethnicity children will be accepted by the child's minority group in this country—even if the adoptive parents raise the child only with the identity and heritage of his or her minority side (Wardle, 1990).

How Schools Can Support Adoptive Families and Their Children.   Adopted children often struggle with belonging to their families. This struggle can be far more difficult for children who look physically different from their parents. Early childhood programs and schools need to find ways to support the child's sense of belonging to the adoptive family and not focus on the child's physical difference. As with biological interethnic/interracial families, schools should ask parents how they want the child's multiracial heritage supported at school (Wardle, 1993)—along with his or her foreign culture, if the child is a foreign adoptee. Schools should not be tempted to automatically assume that adoptive students who have problems in school are suffering because of their adoptive status (Wehrly, Kenney, & Kenney, 1999).

Just as parents should not assume that foreign adopted multiethnic and multiracial children will be accepted by single-race minority children in this country, schools should not make the same mistake. They need to understand the child also has a national identity—which is probably more important to the child than his or her racial/ethnic identity, because many other countries do not place the emphasis on race and ethnicity that we do. However, since most foreign children are adopted when young, the school should not assume the child knows the language, customs, religion, politics, and traditions of his or her nation of birth. An example of this problem occurred when a child adopted as an infant from China was embarrassed by her elementary school teacher when the teacher asked her to demonstrate how to write in Chinese on the board. She did not know Chinese or how to write in Chinese!

Of course, the school must determine from parents how—and when—to address with the child the issue of the child's adoptive status and how they want the school to support this unique part of the child's identity (Wardle, 1990). The school must always be fully sensitive to the fact these children are adopted, from another country, and multiethnic or multiracial—and that the child's integrated view of this complicated identity depends on his or her age and a variety of ecological contexts (Wardle, 1992; West, 2001).

Foster Families

Unlike transracially adoptive families, who are mostly mainstream White individuals or couples, foster families come in every racial and ethnic group—including interracial and interethnic families. However, regardless of their ethnic background, all these families work very closely with the state or city social workers or contracted private substitutes. Many social workers believe in the one-drop rule and the rule of hypodescent. The result is that foster parents are often instructed to treat mixed-ethnic and race children as single-race children with the identity of the lowest status. Another result is that placement workers try very carefully to match multiracial/multiethnic children with minority families—thus ignoring the White side or the highest status side of these children. This position is even more extreme in Britain (Olumide, 2002).

Like biological and adoptive parents, foster parents themselves tend to take several different views regarding the ethnicity and race of the children they care for. Some believe ethnicity and race are very important; others believe the most important thing is that their children receive a warm, secure, loving environment. Some, of course, believe both are important. However, very few foster parents know much about the needs of multiracial and multiethnic children (Wardle, 1990, 1993).

Children in foster care are struggling with a whole range of issues. These include separation and sometimes abandonment from their biological family, along with behaviors and severe psychological conditions resulting from being foster children. Many of the children yearn to be reunited with their parents, even parents who may have abused them. Further, most of these children experience considerable dislocation, not only by being placed in a new family, but also by entering a new childcare program and/or school and being given new adults—social workers, therapists, and advocates—that they must relate to. They have lost their parents, their friends, and sometimes their siblings. Unfortunately, foster children are often frequently moved from foster family to foster family, which aggravates all these negative experiences, such as abandonment and rejection.

How Schools Can Support Foster Families and Children. More than anything, foster children seek stability in their school experiences. So many things have changed in their lives that they need one place that is relatively stable. Further, because foster placement is temporary, there is a need for frequent and quality communication between the school and the foster home. To maintain this sense of stability, the school and home must stay on the same page regarding homework, behavioral expectations, discipline, academic expectations, and medications, for example. And the role of the teacher—especially at the early childhood and elementary level—is even more one of nurturer and provider of security and assurance.

The school has two primary functions when it comes to the needs of multiethnic and multiracial foster children: (1) to work closely with the foster family in supporting the child's unique identity and (2) to educate foster parents about the unique needs of the child—to have his or her unique identity supported (the world is not color blind) and to give foster parents information, advice, referrals, and resources to help them support the child's full racial and ethnic identity (Wehrly, Kenney, & Kenney 1999). Fulfilling this function may sometimes place the school in direct conflict with the child's social worker and/or therapist, who may not recognize the need for the child to embrace his or her full multiracial and multiethnic heritage.

Specific ways schools can help foster parents support their students' multiethnic and multiracial identity development are discussed elsewhere in the book and include knowledge of the various developmental models (Chapter 5) and providing appropriate curricular materials and other resources (Chapter 7). Often the foster parents of multiracial and multiethnic children are of different racial and ethnic backgrounds than their foster children. This places a burden on the school to help these children understand social, political, and self-care (haircare, for example) issues around race and ethnicity. The kind of information children need depends, of course, on their developmental age. However, regardless of age, teachers, counselors, and psychologists need to be knowledgeable and well prepared to work with the parents and children (Wehrly, Kenney, & Kenney, 1999).

Foster parents—along with adoptive parents—can benefit from interracial/interethnic support group activities (Brown & Douglass, 1996). Schools should discover whether support groups exist within their communities; if not, they might support these parents in starting their own groups. These groups have been very successful in meeting the unique needs of multiethnic and multiracial foster and adoptive families (Brown & Douglass, 1996).

Blended Families

There are a growing number of blended families with one or more multiracial or multiethnic children. While the most obvious of these families are mainstream White parents who have a mixed-race child from one of the parent's former marriages or relationships, these families can also be a minority family (two of the same race/ethnicity parents) with a multiracial child from a previous relationship or an interracial or interethnic couple with a multiracial child from another relationship.

Obviously, these families must struggle with the challenges all blended families face: agreeing on child raising and discipline approaches, addressing the typical child's response of, "I don't have to listen to you because you are not my father," helping children from both marriages learn to get along with each other, and sometimes dealing with the ex-partner and ex-extended families. But, beyond these issues, the blended family with a multiethnic or multiracial child family must deal with race, ethnicity, and multiracial/multiethnic issues.

This is particularly an issue for two mainstream White parents of a multiethnic or multiethnic child. These parents must find ways to make sure the multiethnic/multiracial child feels that he or she belongs, does not feel inferior to White siblings, and also has some positive contact with minority students and other multiethnic and multiracial children. It is our experience that this latter issue is particularly difficult. Often single White parents with multiethnic or multiracial children return to their mainstream White world of relatives, friends, neighborhoods, and social groups for support and comfort (Wardle, 2002d). When they remarry another mainstream White person, their return to the White world is complete—except for the fact that they have a multiethnic/multiracial child whose healthy development requires exposure, contact, and involvement with the minority part of his or her heritage.

These White families must make a continual and conscious effort to find ways to expose their multiracial or multiethnic children both to other multiethnic and multiracial children and to people and groups who represent their minority heritage—through school choice, neighborhoods, recreation, and afterschool groups, playgrounds, sports clubs, for example. Mainstream White blended families cannot simply ignore the children's minority heritages and multiethnic or multiracial identities and try to treat them as White. The rest of the world—including their school peers—sees them as minority and multiracial or multiethnic.

Clearly, minority blended families of one racial or ethnic background who have multiethnic or multiracial children have similar issues they must face. They must work equally diligently to make sure the racial/ethnic part of the child that is not represented in the home is positively and frequently represented in other ways. Even if the new family is a minority family, the multiracial/multiethnic child must have his or her unique identity supported, celebrated, and acknowledged. A multiethnic or multiracial child's identity will always be partly based on the combination of her racial and ethnic backgrounds.

Multiethnic and multiracial children in any blended family—White or minority—should never feel they represent the past mistake of one of their parents; they should never feel like a bad reminder of past indiscretions.

How Schools Can Support Blended Families.   The school must do its part in helping multiethnic and multiracial children in blended families feel they are an important part of the family and that they have equal status with the single-race children in their family and in the school. The school should carefully discuss with parents how to support their children and how to help the child develop a minority

Multiethnic and multiracial children in all family structures must have positive inter-actions with grandparents on both sides.

and multiethnic/multiracial identity without developing a dislike or hatred of their single-race family and siblings—especially if their family is mainstream White.

Clearly, children in blended families—especially young children—need to see examples of their kind of blended family throughout the early childhood program and school in books, curricular materials, posters, films and video programs, student- and teacher-created materials, and so on. And they need teachers who are both sensitive to their unique family structure and knowledgeable in the ways of supporting children in blended homes. Finally, as we have discussed regarding children from other family configurations, support staff—social workers, counselors and psychologists—must never assume problems these children have are automatically caused by their unique family structure, but must also be fully aware of the challenges and difficulties these children face at home, in the community, and at school (Wehrly, Kenney and Kenney, 1999).

Single-Parent Families

Francis Wardle, who runs a web page that supports parents and families nationwide, receives by far the most requests for information and advice regarding raising multiethnic and multiracial children from single, mainstream White mothers (Wardle, 2002d). As we have pointed out, our acceptance as a society of interracial dating and relationships has not yet advanced to societal acceptance and support of interethnic and interracial families, for a variety of reasons. Of course, this state of affairs also reflects our society's acceptance of birth out of wedlock and of divorce. Regardless of the specific causes, today there are many mainstream White female-headed households with multiethnic and multiracial children. And these families have their own unique needs and struggles.

The major task of these single women is to garner the social and financial support needed to raise a family, while maintaining positive contact with the child's minority heritage. This is, of course, difficult to do, because single parents often retreat to their mainstream White neighborhoods and extended families to raise their children, and because minority families often sever their relationships with the White families. A single White parent of a multiethnic or multiracial child must find ways for the child to interact with minority children through choice of neighborhood, schools, school clubs, and sports and recreational activities, for example. And every attempt must be made to maintain regular contact with the children's minority parents and extended families.

Of utmost importance is that the parent not blame the breakup of the marriage or relationship on the race or ethnicity of the other parent. Further, the child(ren) should never believe that the minority part of their background is somehow to blame for the breakup, therefore representing some kind of failure— that the other parent's race is the reason why the marriage or relationship failed. The single White parent cannot afford to become a racist; a single minority parent cannot do so either, because the result of this would be that the multiracial child will come to dislike—or even hate—the race or ethnicity of his or her background represented by the absent parent.

How Schools Can Support Single-Parent Families. Unfortunately, often multiethnic and multiracial children with a single, mainstream White parent end up in all White—or nearly all White—schools and early childhood programs. Often these educational programs know little about minority children, let alone multiethnic and multiracial children. A program that serves single parents with multiethnic and multiracial children must become knowledgeable of their needs, train staff, purchase appropriate materials, and develop concrete ways for children to be exposed to minority and mixed-race children and adults—field trips, classroom visitors, community projects, pairings with more diverse educational programs, for example.

These all-mainstream White schools must not fall into the temptation to view these children as single-race minority children or as tokens for diversity efforts. Teachers must be very careful not to treat these children as somehow representative of their minority communities. Many of these children are, culturally and ecologically, more White than minority. The school should also support and embrace the White side of multiethnic or multiracial children who have some White heritage.

Grandparents Raising Children

For a variety of reasons, including drug abuse, death, incarceration, poor parenting, teen parentage, and parents who simply refuse to take responsibility for their children, more and more grandparents are raising their grandchildren. Clearly, this poses a variety of unique challenges. Adding children of mixed heritage to the mix simply increases the complexity of the issue.

Some of these grandparents belong to mainstream White families, some to minority families. For the mainstream White families, raising children with some minority heritage often challenges deeply seated racist assumptions and behaviors; almost always it places the White parents in situations they have never faced before—dealing with minority teachers, school administrators, and social workers. They suddenly become a minority family. Not only must they deal with things like hair and skin care, but also racism toward their grandchildren and the possible loss of long-time friends and social contacts as well.

The minority grandparent must learn that views regarding multiethnic and multiracial children have changed considerably since they were young and that these children do not represent illicit or immoral relationships. Further, minority grandparents need information about the choice to raise these children as proudly multiethnic or multiracial—an option that was not available when they were raising their children.

As we have mentioned under the section discussing single parenting multi-ethnic or multiracial children, the part of the child not represented in the grandparent's home (minority in the White home, White in the minority home) should never be ignored, belittled, or put down.

How Schools Can Support Grandparents Raising Children.   More than any-thing else, grandparents raising multiethnic or multiracial children need support and advice. They need to know about haircare and skin care, parenting advice, local support groups, and culturally competent therapists. They need to know websites, magazines, advice books, and places to turn to when they need help. And they need support in their valiant efforts to raise another family. Use of the last of Erikson's (1963) stages—Ego Identity versus Despair—might be helpful in this endeavor.

Schools need to be clear about the legal guardians for these children and make sure they have frequent, open, and supportive communication with the grandparents.

Teen Parents

Teen parents raising multiethnic or multiethnic children must cope with the varied challenges of teen parenthood—for example, staying in school, learning parenting skills, finding childcare, transportation, financial support, and work-ing things out with the child's other parent. The adolescent years are a very precarious time period. While these teens have their own children, they are devel-opmentally still adolescents, struggling with all the issues Erikson (1963) so accurately addressed in his identity versus role confusion stage. Many teens have not achieved Piaget's stage of formal operations, where they can make rational, informed decisions about their future and the future of their children. Part of this struggle of role confusion includes ethnic and racial identity. Just because an ado-lescent has a child with a person from another ethnicity or race does not mean that he or she doesn't have racist or prejudicial feelings, especially if the person, like most teens, functions almost exclusively within single-race/ethnicity social groups (Tatum, 1999). Thus—as with other single parents we have discussed— teen parents must be careful not to put down, disparage, or otherwise devalue the racial or ethnic part of the child they don't represent.

Even if teen parents eventually decide that interracial or interethnic relationships are no longer for them, they cannot ever ignore or dislike their children's multiethnic or multiracial identity. They must also be taught how to celebrate and support the children's full identity (Wardle, 1999).

How Schools Can Help Support Teen Parents. Schools need to make a conscious effort to include the children's multiethnic and multiracial identities with the myriad of other things they do for teen parents. Guest speakers, support groups, other interracial families, for example, should be invited to talk to these parents about their child's unique needs. Further, the school should encourage the extended family on both sides to provide support and interact with the child: Fathers should always be encouraged to be involved with their children—and to take responsibility for them. We believe this responsibility is even greater for minority fathers of multiethnic and multiracial children, because these children need direct, concrete exposure to their minority heritage (Wardle, 2002a). And the teen parent should be encouraged to join an interracial/interethnic support group.

School should also work with the teens around issues of ethnicity and race. For White teens, this should include exploring the rich history and diversity of their own background; for minority teens, it should include the negative impact of strict group membership during the adolescent years, the fact that race and ethnicity are social rather than biological constructs, and knowledge about how to raise their children with a full racial and ethnicity identity. Both minority and White teen parents of multiethnic and multiracial children should be exposed to all sorts of examples of interethnic and interracial families, such as live role models, books, films and videos, and speakers.

Many teen parents are very fascinated with the physical appearance of their children and which characteristics the child receives from each parent. This fascination is even more exaggerated with teens who have multiethnic or multiracial babies. These parents need a lesson about genotypes and phenotypes, and they also need to understand that the child's physical features may not be an obvious reflection of either parent because phenotypes do not match genotypes.

As children in teen homes get older, they should be exposed to all the experiences, activities, and groups that we have talked about in this chapter under many of the other family structures.

Conclusion

Interethnic and interracial families challenge every part of our society. For children of these families to develop into healthy, contributing citizens, the rest of society must change. Because schools are the institutions of society that have most direct impact on children and families, the societal responsibility falls first and most strongly on early childhood programs and schools. This is a tremendous challenge, because interethnic and interracial families come in all forms, including two-parent, single-parent, blended, adoptive, foster, teen, and grandparent—necessitating that the program become knowledgeable in a vast variety of areas. But early childhood programs and schools need to find ways to support these families, provide them nurturance and understanding, give them resources and community contacts, and help them develop support groups to help meet their needs and the needs of their children.

Questions/Projects

1. See whether there is an interracial support group in your community. If there is, find out what services they offer and when they meet.

2. Does your college have a multiracial/multiethnic student club? If so, invite one of the members to give a class presentation.

3. Collect a list of websites that provide information and services to multiethnic and multiracial children and their families.

4. Talk to several ministers about how they advise potential marriage partners who have different religious backgrounds; also what they advise them regarding raising children. Include a Jewish rabbi, a Catholic priest, and a Protestant minister.

Resources

Books

Beane, H. (2001). *Raising healthy, happy interracial children: Supporting your biracial child.* (Brochure). Washington, DC: Author.

Gaskins, P. (1999). *What are you? Voices of mixed-race young children.* New York: Henry Holt & Co.

Wehrly, B., Kenney, K. R., & Kenney, M. E. (1999). *Counseling multiracial families.* Thousand Oaks, CA: Sage.

Websites

Bahai world

http://www.bahai.org/

Pact Adoption Alliance
Adopted children of color

http://www.pactadopt.org/

Curriculum

Serving Biracial and Multiethnic Children and Their Families: A Diversity Curriculum for the Training of Childcare Providers
Childcare Health Program
2625 Alcatraz Avenue, Suite 369
Berkeley, CA 94705
Includes a video, teacher's guide, and family portraits.

Video

Counseling the Multiracial Population: Couples, Individuals, and Families by Kelley Kenney.
Micotraining Associates, Inc.
25 Burdette Avenue
Framingham, MA 01702

7

Curricular Approaches

A school's curriculum provides the most formal and tangible evidence of what and how schools teach our children. It includes goals and objectives, the learning environment, curricular content, curricular materials and activities, and the teacher's role—setting up the environment, structuring the activities, instructing the students, facilitating learning, and assessing the entire learning process. To this end the curriculum allows us to directly address the issue of positively including multiethnic and multiracial children. It also includes the hidden curriculum. In Chapter 8 we will discuss the teacher's specific approaches to instruction; the rest of the curriculum will be covered in this chapter. We break down our discussion of curriculum by age groups: early childhood (up to age 8 years old), late elementary age (8 to 11 years old), middle school, and high school. We will discuss the characteristics of each age as they relate to identity development and learning, present appropriate goals for the age group, and discuss the environment, curricular content, and curricular materials.

FOCUS QUESTIONS

1. Why do multiethnic and multiracial children rarely see themselves in their educational programs' curricula? Why is it important that they do see themselves?

2. How does the educational programs' hidden curriculum negatively impact multiethnic and multiracial children?

3. What are ways by which schools can make interracial families feel they belong?

4. How do the curricular needs of multiethnic and multiracial children differ from single-race children? How are they the same?

Early Childhood (up to 8 Years Old)

Beginning at the elementary level, school curricula should provide opportunities for students to investigate their individual heritages and to develop an understanding

149

of the relationship of their unique pasts to U.S. and global history. The pedagogical process may include creating family trees, conducting oral history interviews with relatives, collecting family artifacts, perusing family records, writing family histories, and studying local communities. It should also include learning about the experiences of various racial, ethnic and religious groups to which members of their families belong. . . . The curriculum should also involve the history of interracial contact and exclusion, the development and use of U.S. categories . . . and the ramifications of all these developments on American life. (Cortes, 1999, p. 31)

Children at this age are becoming aware of their own physical characteristics and how they are the same and different from their peers, siblings, and parents. The child is primarily in Piaget's preoperational stage and two of Erikson's stages, initiative versus guilt and industry versus inferiority. Thus, preschool and early elementary children are very primitive thinkers who have difficulty holding more than one piece of information at a time in their minds, are highly egocentric, are very inquisitive and creative, and are committed to master all sorts of skills and tasks. Early childhood and elementary children do not have a true concept of race and racial belonging (Aboud, 1987).

Goals for Early Childhood Curricula

Multiracial and multiethnic children should achieve the goals and objectives set for other children of this age, such as gaining important self-help skills, social skills, and academic achievements. Additionally, specific goals for multiethnic and multiracial preschool and early elementary children include:

- Exploring their own physical characteristics.
- Exploring how they are alike and different from other children.
- Beginning to explore their own unique racial/ethnic identities.
- Learning to talk about their identities.
- Using terms when talking about their identities.
- Reading/viewing/listening to books that honor and celebrate diversity.
- Reading/viewing/listening to books that honor and celebrate interracial families and multiethnic/multiracial children and people.
- Engaging in creative activities to explore and express their unique identities.
- Being exposed to multiracial and multiethnic role models and biographies.
- Having a positive attitude toward their unique identities.
- Having a positive attitude about their families.
- Participating with other children from a variety of racial/ethnic backgrounds.
- Being able to defend themselves from harassment from adults and children.
- Having a primitive understanding that their physical characteristics come from both biological parents.

Learning Environment

Multiethnic and multiracial preschool and elementary students need the same **learning environment** as single-race children, with some important additions and modifications. These additions include visual images of interracial families and multiethnic and multiracial children and adults—all the various combinations we covered in the previous chapters. These images can be photographs, drawings, original art, posters, books, book covers, illustrations in instructional materials and on game boxes, and bulletin boards created by teachers and children. Images that children create themselves of their families and extended families should also be prominently displayed. Critically, these images should exist throughout the building: classroom, hallways, kitchen, office, lunchroom, counselors' offices, cafeteria, and so on (Wardle, 2003). Multiethnic and multiracial children need to see enough images of themselves and their families to learn that they and their families are normal.

Further, the environment must provide lots and lots of opportunities for multiethnic and multiracial children to explore their unique physical features and backgrounds. Children at this age need to experience mixing colors, looking at themselves in mirrors, and braiding their hair. They must have lots of opportunities to paint and engage in other expressive art activities; the dramatic play area should include mirrors, hairbrushes and combs, lots of colorful barrettes, and a variety of dressup clothes and hats—also for the boys (Wardle, 2003). This area must be large enough and have a variety and diversity of materials so that children can naturally engage in dramatic play representing their own unique experiences at home and in the community.

Curricular Content

Curricular content specifically targeted to the needs of the young multiracial and multiethnic child includes exploring all kinds of diversity, engaging in multicultural activities that go beyond a single-race approach to diversity, reading a variety of books that celebrate diversity (including multiethnic and multiracial

Chapter Feature
Student Profile: James S.

James S., 10th grade, White mother, Black father.

The first experience I had with this (dealing with misunderstanding from single-race children) I was in elementary school—second grade. This kid was like—when he saw my mom—

"So, are you adopted or something?" My mom's White, and my dad's Black, and he was, "Oh, that's strange, I never heard of that before!" It was like weird—I (realized) I guess I'm kind of different.

diversity), and engaging in accurate discussions of the genetic basis for physical characteristics—at the child's developmental level (Bredekamp & Copple, 1997). Curricular themes around families—all kinds of family structures—communities, culture, and the arts must include a variety of multiracial and multiethnic families and people.

Social science content should not simply present people in this country within single racial and ethnic groups or teach that Europe is all White, Africa all Black, and Central and South America all Latino (Wardle, 2003). "Schools that examine racial and ethnic diversity, yet avoid the theme of racial mixture, distort the American experience. Moreover, such schools do serious, if unintentional, injustice to students of all backgrounds who need to be weaned from their rigid reliance on old categories when grappling with changing realities" (Cortes, 1999, p. 31). Schools must:

1. Cover the racial and ethnic diversity that makes up this country—including mixed people.
2. Discuss the ethnic and racial diversity that comprise many other countries today, such as England, the Netherlands, Brazil, South Africa, Germany, Costa Rica, Mexico, and so on.
3. Cover the concept that multiethnic and multiracial people have existed throughout our history and the history of the world.

If an early childhood program or school celebrates ethnic/cultural specific holidays—Cinco de Mayo, Martin Luther King Day, Black History Month, Chinese New Year—it must focus on the contributions of a diversity of people to this country, the struggles for equality of all peoples, and the racial and ethnic diversity that exists within traditional social/political groups. These celebrations must never be presented as racially, culturally, or ethnically exclusive.

The curricular content for children at this age should include multiethnic and multiracial families and people—stories, biographies/autobiographies (Cortes, 1999) of famous multiracial people, classroom visitors from multiracial families and community people proud of their multiracial and multiethnic heritage, child-developed journals and publications about each child's family, histories of groups working together for liberty and justice (e.g., Seminole Indians and Blacks during the Civil War, Blacks and Jews during the Civil Rights Movement), and use of diverse cultural images, symbols, and styles. For younger children much of this content will be in pictorial and simple-story form; for older children, more complexity and detail is effective.

Curricular Materials

Unfortunately, there are very few curricular materials that positively reflect multiethnic and multiracial children, families, and people for preschool- and elementary-age children. School publishers and educational materials companies see little need to create materials that reflect the rich diversity of multiethnic and multiracial populations. They believe there simply is no market (Wardle, 1996). This deplorable situation will only improve when parents, activists, and, most importantly, teachers who are members of curricular materials selection committees insist on these changes (see Chapter Feature "How to Evaluate a Textbook/Reading Book for P–12 Programs" on pages 156–160). In a university diversity class Francis teaches, the students were assigned the task of assessing instructional materials for racial, gender, and disability bias and/or omission (Grant & Sleeter, 1998). On completion of this task, several students reported they had recently been on book selection committees and had approved books that they now believed to be very sexist, racist, and discriminatory. Unfortunately, the checklist used in the class did not address multiethnic and multiracial people

Like the learning environment, curricular materials must exhibit lots of examples of multiethnic and multiracial families and people—for example, dolls; little-people sets; puzzles; books; song books; book illustrations; illustrations in workbooks and instructional materials; computer programs; games; basic math, science, and literacy instructional materials; and test items.

Whenever people are used in curricular materials, there must be examples of interracial and interethnic people and families; whenever there is content about people—for example, community helpers, immigrants, artists, famous people, discoverers, minority groups—multiethnic and multiracial people must be represented. Teachers need the knowledge to be able to correct inaccurate information and to enhance and elaborate content with additional materials about multiracial and multiethnic peoples.

Multiethnic and multiracial children must see themselves, their families, and their extended families throughout the school day equally as much as single-race children see themselves and their families.

Late Elementary (8 to 11 Years Old)

Curricular approaches for this age child build on ideas discussed for the early childhood age. The late-elementary-age child is functioning in Piaget's concrete operations stage and is still in Erikson's industry versus inferiority stage. Thus this age child understands sophisticated concepts, can handle more than one piece of information at a time, and is less egocentric; the child loves to continue to master new skills, concepts, tasks, and abilities (arts, sports, academics, social skills), but also must be successful in his or her attempts at mastery, otherwise the child will develop a sense of failure and inferiority. Late-elementary-age children tend to compare themselves with other children based more on abilities, accomplishments, and skills than on physical characteristics.

Chapter Feature
Student Profile: James S.

James S., 10th grade, White mother, Black father.

In late elementary school, I kind of accepted I couldn't pick one side. You try to pick one side, and it just flat out didn't work. I don't pick either side—I do what I want to do, because I figured pretty early on it was going to have to work for me, or it wasn't going to work at all. That's how I decided.

I have my dad's half, which is Black, and I have my mom's half, which is White. So, I can't just deny my mom's half by saying I am Black, and I can't deny my dad's side by saying I don't have any Black in me. I kind of feel I have to identify with both sides, because that's who I am. If (people) don't like it, they'll just have to deal with it.

When I brought one of those (school) forms home my mom was outraged because there was nothing, not even, "other." There was Black, White, Hispanic, and a couple of other choices, but nothing for a mixture of cultures. So she sat there and checked every single box, because, "people are more than just one thing."

That's how I kind of look at school forms. If I have a choice I check both Black and White.

Goals for the Late Elementary Curriculum

Curricular goals for this age multiethnic/multiracial children—in addition to those already discussed in the previous section—include:

- Exploring membership in different racial and ethnic groups.
- Exploring the movement of people across the globe and the interaction (marriage) of people through trade, migration, war, and domination.
- Beginning to understand the sociopolitical nature of race and ethnic belonging.
- Being able to accurately discuss their unique heritage with peers and adults.
- Becoming more sophisticated in defending themselves from harassment from single-race peers and adults.
- Being able to explore school-related and extracurricular activities based on their own interests, friends, and abilities, and not based on perceived racial/ or ethnic ascriptions.
- Being positive about their physical features and racial/ethnic identity.
- Being able to move comfortably between different racial and ethnic groups of children.
- Being competent academically, physically, and socially.
- Feeling positive about their family and extended family.
- Advocating for the rights of other multiracial/multiethnic children in the school.

Children 8 to 12 years old need to learn to feel positive about their family and extended family.

Learning Environments

Most of the suggestions for the learning environment are the same as for the early childhood years—just more complex, more integrated, and more "academic" (Wardle, 2003). Basic instructional materials—for example, social sciences, math, literacy, science—must include illustrations and examples of multiethnic and multiracial people and interracial families; books, magazines, videos, computer programs, games, reference and resource materials must all reflect this population.

The visual environment in the school must also include multiethnic and multiracial heroes, interracial families and multiethnic and multiracial children: posters, artwork, teacher- and student-created bulletin boards, and "inspirational messages," etc. Further, materials the school creates to communicate with parents and the community—web pages, newsletters, official reports, end of the year progress reports, and so on—must include illustrations and graphics that include these children and families. The school should also highlight any live models who are proudly multiracial/multiethnic or involved in multiracial relationships—staff, school, and classroom visitors—and give positive exposure to interracial parents. Live models are very powerful teaching approaches for showing multiethnic and multiracial children they are normal (Bandura, 1965).

As with the early grades, the learning environment must also provide lots and lots of opportunities for these children to explore their unique identities and backgrounds.

Curricular Content

Specific curricular content for this age will be mostly in the social science and literacy areas. In social science, content must include the nature of racial, ethnic, and other groups in this country and around the world, the tremendous diversity of people in most countries, and the concepts of migration, cultural exchange, trade, and religious movements. Critically, the content must convey the diversity and variability within geographic areas, such as mixed-race people, Blacks, Indigenous people, Asians, Jews, Italians and other northern Europeans in all South American countries; also the diversity within ethnic and racial groups, which is larger than the diversity between them (Zack, 2002). Finally, the content should examine the history of racial mixing (Cortes, 1999).

Literacy content should include famous multiracial/multiethnic people—Frederick Douglass, Ralph Ellison, Bob Marley (Stephens, 1999), Maria and Marjorie Tallchief, Rosella Hightower, and Yvonne Chouteau (Livingston, 1997); Alexander Dumas, James Audubon, the founder of Georgetown University, etc. Fictional and nonfiction accounts of interracial families must be included and work by multiracial authors provided.

Curricular Materials

As with the early childhood age, there are very few curricular materials for the late elementary age that include positive portrayals of multiethnic and multiracial people and issues. Teachers must scrounge the Internet and their community for local resources, consult with interracial parents and local support groups, and make their own materials. Further, teachers need to encourage multiethnic and multiracial children to create their own curricular materials as they explore their

Chapter Feature
How to Evaluate a Textbook/Reading Book for P–12 Programs

Information about the Book
Title
Author(s)
Date of publication
Grade level and/or the
grades/ages/learning styles for which
the book can be differentiated.

There are five different evaluations that can be conducted, depending on the book being evaluated. Use all the approaches that apply (obviously a picture critique would not be conducted on a book with no illustrations). These five evaluations are Picture Critique, People/Heroes Critique, Anthology Critique, Language Critique, and Story Critique. The student/teacher will then combine all the data to determine the book's appropriateness.

Current P–12 teachers, teachers on materials' selection committees, teachers in training, and teachers taking graduate classes can all use this tool.

Chapter Feature   Continued

Picture Critique
Using the chart below, tally the pictures by race, ethnicity, mixed ethnicity/race, gender, disability, and age. The pictures may show individuals or groups. Make a judgment—a few separate individuals doing their own thing is not a group; a group will generally be doing the same thing together (building a house, debating a topic, etc.)

Note any racial or ethnic stereotypes.

Note any multiethnic/multiracial stereotypes.

Note any gender role stereotypes.

Note any disability stereotypes.

Are there any age/old age stereotypes?

	Female	*Male*	*Child*	*Adult*	*Over 60*	*Disability*
Asian individual						
Asian group						
Black individual						
Black group						
Latino individual						
Latino group						
Native American individual						
Native American group						
Mainstream White individual						
Mainstream White group						
Multiethnic/ Multiracial individual						
Multiethnic/ Multiracial group*						
Mixed race or ethnicity group**						
Race/ethnicity of people unclear						

*Members of the group appear to be multiethnic/multiracial.

**Members of the group appear to have different single racial or ethnic identities from each other.

(continued)

Chapter Feature   **Continued**

People/Heroes Critique
This approach is to be used for critiquing the text of science, social studies, and history textbooks.

	Main part of text			*Supplemental text*		
	Male	*Female*	*Disabled*	*Male*	*Female*	*Disabled*
Asian						
Black						
Latino						
Native American						
Multiethnic/ Multiracial						
Mainstream White						
Not clear						

Distinguish between important famous people—in the main part of the text—and those simply added in boxes or as supplements that appear to be an afterthought—a token, if you will.

Anthology Critique
This approach is to be used for literature texts, arts books, Pre-K and elementary stories.

Title of book.

Race/ethnicity/gender of author.

Race/ethnicity/gender/disability of characters.

Are all the characters of the same race/ethnicity? (Yes/No)

Does the story/theme relate to one racial ethnic group or to a multiethnic/ multiracial experience? (ME/R). Which?

Does the story/theme communicate a need for group belonging/loyalty/ solidarity? (Yes/No)

If the story/theme is about one group, does it imply it is better/more successful? If so, which one?

What is the context? urban (U), rural (R), another country (AC), not clear (NC)

Are there race/ethnic/multiethnic/multiracial stereotypes? What are they?

Are there gender stereotypes? What are they?

Are there stereotypes based on wealth/poverty? What are they?

Are there disability stereotypes? Explain.

Chapter Feature **Continued**

Code for the Anthology Critique

AAM Asian American male

AAF Asian American female

BF Black female

BM Black male

NAM Native American male

NAF Native American female

LM Latino male

LF Latina female

MWM Mainstream White male

MSF Mainstream White female

ME/RM multiethnic/racial male

ME/RF multiethnic/racial female

Add D (disability), G (gay), L (lesbian) to any that apply.

Language Critique

This should be conducted for all books that include words.

Record answers on a separate sheet of paper.

1. Does the book use nonsexist language or just male words to refer to both genders? If just male words are used, list them.
2. List any stereotypical words and the person's race/ethnicity/mixed ethnicity/ race they are linked to. What adjectives are used to describe non-mainstream White and multiethnic/racial people? Are these words positive or negative?
3. Observe adjectives used to describe women and men. List those that are stereotypical.
4. Look carefully for words like *progress, successful, cultured, improved, civilized, brought religion,* etc., and the race/ethnicity/ mixed ethnicity/race of individuals that they relate to—is it always mainstream White men?
5. Look carefully for words like *deprived, bad, revolt, hostile, unrest, unreasonable, reduce, dishonest, threaten,* and the people/individuals they are usually associated with. Is it usually the poor and minorities?
6. Look carefully at words like *confused, marginalized, need to belong, sense of not belonging, coping, disloyalty, racially ambiguous, ashamed, need to classify racially, conflict, making choices,* and the people/individuals they are associated with— is it always multiethnic/multiracial?
7. What image is portrayed by the use of dialects, accents, non-English phases, etc.?

Story Critique

For history books, long stories, and novels.

1. People of what race/ethnicity/multiethnic/multiracial/gender/disability receive most attention throughout the book?
2. List the major problems that are resolved and tasks accomplished in the text, and the race/ethnicity/mixed ethnicity/gender/disability of people who accomplish these.
3. What other people appear in the book—race/mixed race/ethnicity, gender, and disability? How much attention do they get and what do they accomplish?
4. To what extent do they cause the problems; to what extent to they resolve them?

(continued)

Chapter Feature   **Continued**

5. To what extent do the people in items 1 and 2 present problems for others? With how much accuracy is this detailed?
6. Which people does the author intend the reader to sympathize/relate to and respect? Give race/mixed ethnicity/gender and ability/disability.
7. What people—race, gender, disability—does the reader learn most about?
8. Is the author(s), as far as you can tell, the same race/mixed-race/ethnicity/ mixed ethnicity, gender, or disability as the people featured most in the text? Why is the author qualified to write from that particular perspective?

Analysis of the Results

Consider people with these backgrounds in analyzing the results of this critique, but remember that each of these single categories can interact with the other; for example, a person could be a mainstream White female who is a lesbian and has a disability.

> Multiethnic/multiracial
> One of the many Native American nations
> One of the various U.S. Asian groups
> Latinos
> Mainstream White
> Black
> Women or men
> English as a second language speakers
> Lower class, middle class, or upper class
> Gay/lesbian/bisexual
> Disability

1. Determine how much space and attention—both text and pictures—is devoted to each category.
2. Determine how the text depicts the experiences and challenges of each category and how these challenges were overcome.
3. Does the book (text and pictures) provide an opportunity for a student who identifies with the characters of the book to have positive and empowering impressions?
4. Does the book (text and pictures) provide roles and characters with whom students can identify and who give the impression that students can aspire to anything and achieve their goals?
5. Does the book provide complex characters who give richness and diversity around racial/ethnic/gender/disability/income, or do they simply focus on one category, and one narrow view of that category?
6. To what extent does the text positively portray people with different backgrounds as equals experiencing life and solving problems together?
7. Does the text (book/pictures) openly or subtly imply that people must join similar groups to live their lives and solve their problems (gender, race, religion, disability, economic status, etc.)?

unique backgrounds, heritages, and identities (Wardle, 1996a). Teachers should never assume that materials claiming to be multicultural—in catalogues, books, museums, textbooks, etc.—include multiethnic and multiracial children and their families. Most do not (Wardle, 1996b, 1999, 2001).

Middle School

According to Erikson, children this age are in the **Identity versus Role Confusion Stage**; in Piaget's theory, most of these children are in the Late Concrete Operations Stage. Thus, while this age child is able to cognitively handle the concept of a multifaceted identity with a variety of attributes and characteristics, he or she is entering the identity stage that includes what is referred to as the identity crisis. The big question for the child at this age is "what am I?"—sexually, socially, academically, ethically, religiously, likes and dislikes, abilities, and ethnically and racially. Middle-school students begin to congregate with "like students," based on a whole variety of criteria—for example, dress, music preference, sports teams (sports jackets), race, ethnicity, language, athletics, and clothing. The pressure to belong to one of these groups is extreme; the pressure for multiethnic and multiracial children is even stronger. One way students at this age define their sense of belonging is by defining who they are not—a common intellectual activity that is part of a process called **concept formation** (Ormrod, 1999)—not a jock, not a nerd, not a punk. Unfortunately, this negative approach can be very destructive, often leading to lack of tolerance, and it is one of the principal reasons why some minority adolescents do everything they can to prove they are not mainstream White—avoiding certain clubs and sports, avoiding some friendships, and often avoiding academic classes and pursuits (to be Black or Latino or Asian or Native American, one must *not* be White).

Goals

Goals for multiethnic and multiracial children of this age include:

- Increasing understanding and acceptance of their full identity.
- Increasing understanding of the construction of race and ethnicity within a sociopolitical context.
- Choosing friendship groups based on nonracial/ethnic factors.
- Defending themselves from putdowns, harassment, challenges to their loyalty and integrity, and intimidation from peers and staff.
- Exploring multiethnic/multiracial heroes.
- Exploring their family's rich history.
- Using creative exploration to express their identity and feelings about who they are.
- Understanding that the world is not broken into neat racial and ethnic groups.

- Understanding the fluid, dynamic, and multidimensional nature of culture.
- Being positively involved in the school's culture.
- Communicating to the school community the positive value of being of mixed heritage.
- If the student is part of a special population (special needs, behavior problems, gifted student), understanding that this is not a function of his or her racial/ethnic background.
- Proudly acknowledging and celebrating their entire biological, cultural, and social heritage; being proactive.
- Engaging in a variety of nonracially specific extracurricular activities

Learning Environment

Much of the learning environment at the middle school level that impacts multiethnic and multiracial students is the human environment—teachers, administrators, support professionals and other students. Because of the temptation for race/ethnic specific groups, activities, and celebrations at this age (Tatum, 1997), the school must make every effort to create and support interest/skill/ability groups, provide activities that stress service, cooperation, and universal values, and group students in ways that don't reinforce racial/ethnic stereotypes. Schools should never appear to support or condone single-ethnicity/race groupings or activities.

Curricular Content

Curricular content for this age student should include contributions to the country's history and the world's progress by people of color, as well as multiethnic and multiracial people. Further, the content must stress the many examples of people from different groups and backgrounds helping each other in times of need—overcoming group differences and hatreds for the greater cause—for example, the collaboration of free Blacks and mainstream Whites in the Under-

Chapter Feature
Student Profile: Sarah

Sarah, 8th grade, Black father, German/White mother.

Instead of classifying kids as that little Black girl or that little White girl . . . they (teachers/administrators) can try not to look at the child's outward appearance. Try to let everybody get to know each other for who they are on the inside of the person. Also, try to get more diversity in the clubs.

They should take the categories away—it doesn't matter what color we are, so long as we learn.

ground Railroad; the collaboration between different Native American tribes and Black runaway slaves during the Civil War; and the assistance provided by Native Americans during the Potato Famine (1840s) in Ireland.

Content must explore all the ways people have used cultural, linguistic, historical, religious, and other differences to create great music, art, dance, architecture, and drama. There are millions of examples of this fusion—the use of jazz and folk music in classical music; inclusion of folk and "primitive" art in the turn of the twentieth-century modern art movement, the use of various literacy traditions and folk traditions in great literary works, and the influence of African dance and religions in Brazilian art, music, and dance. Finally, students this age should explore their own family's cultural and traditional family genealogy, customs, countries of origin, and important people.

Curricular Materials

Curricular materials for this age student must:

1. Challenge the narrow group and individual identity thinking of this age.
2. Show students positive ways to define their full identity.
3. Encourage students to consolidate around projects, issues, and activities, not racial or ethnic group identifiers.

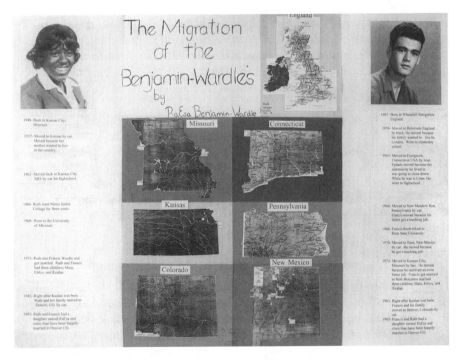

The migration of Ruth Benjamin-Wardle and Francis Wardle—RaEsa's middle-school project.

Chapter Feature
Student Profile: Sarah

Sarah, 8th grade, Black father, German/White mother.

The schools consider diversity to be just because they have a variety of African Americans, Caucasian, Hispanics, and we all happen to be in the same class. But they're not teaching us, "We have some people who are mixed." One of my teachers said we had to write an essay about a race, but it couldn't be our race. We had to choose between Black, White, and Hispanic. And, I was, like, "I'm all three of those." It sort of left him speechless. He didn't know what to say, so he just said, "You should do (write about) White." "Why should I do White—I am White?" If they (teachers) just learn diversity is not just a bunch of people of different colors in the classroom; that people are actually mixed with other things, too."

There is a need for lots of images—books, posters, artwork, student/teacher made bulletin boards, live visitors, and role models—that

- Challenge gender, racial, ethnic, and disability stereotypes.
- Show positive examples of interracial families—biological, adoptive, blended—and multiethnic and multiracial people.
- Include many different ideas, attitudes, and values—that are difficult to categorize by race, ethnicity, gender, culture, and so on— such as Black kids succeeding academically, Asian kids involved in sports, multiethnic and multiracial children engaged in a variety of activities, girls farming and fixing cars, and people with numerous disabilities succeeding at a variety of occupations.
- Stress the universal aspects of people—the ways we are all the same.
- Stress the content of character, not the way people look.
- Show a variety of people from around the world enjoying the same things—family, music, dance, arts, the outdoors.
- Show a variety of the same cultural artifacts that are produced by very diverse groups of people—beadwork, basketry, quilts, dolls, pottery, weavings, etc. (Wardle, 1999).

High School

High school students are more sophisticated than their middle-school counterparts. Most are in Piaget's concrete operations and formal operations stages and Erikson's identity versus role confusion stage. This means intellectually most high school students can predict the consequences of actions and decisions—such as selecting certain classes and engaging in certain at-risk behaviors; emotionally, high schoolers are still concerned with who they are and what they will do in the

Chapter Feature
Multicultural School Activities

We must carefully select events we take our children to and those our schools and communities officially sponsor. One such positive cultural presentation is the International Folk Art Museum in Santa Fe, New Mexico. The perspective of this museum is to show that people throughout the world are joined by common human experiences and emotions. Dolls, toys, religious icons, decorative cloth, and important cultural celebrations illustrate this universality.

The museum also has exhibits that show how contemporary cultures are based on many different cultural influences. One exhibit shows the impact of Jewish, Christian, English, African, and Moslem beliefs on Ethiopian cultures (they even have St. George and the Dragon motifs in some of their art!); another exhibit displays beautiful beadwork from Native American Nations, Zimbabwe, Nigeria, Russia, and Czechoslovakia. (pp. 97–98)

From *Tomorrow's Children*, © 1999. Reprinted with permission from Francis Wardle.

future. While group belonging is still very important, high school students are now more able to select groups based on their own needs and cognitively determine the value of various group memberships. As high school students progress through their studies, they become concerned with post–high school choices and potential careers. They can see the consequences of working hard and achieving academic success.

Goals

Goals for multiracial and multiethnic high school students not already mentioned include:

- Selecting extracurricular activities based on personal interests, abilities, friends, and career interests.
- Moving freely between different groups in school.
- Consolidating a secure and positive sense of their full identity.
- Exploring the politics of race in this country and the world.
- Having friends from different racial and ethnic groups and of different genders.
- Exploring the historical development of the concept of race and racial categories—in this country and other countries—and fully exploring the reality that race is not, and never has been, biologically defined (Fish, 2002; Zack, 2002).
- Advocating for multiethnic and multiracial issues in the school, such as a multiethnic/multiracial category on all school forms.

- Protesting any single-race clubs, groups, sports, activities, and so on—either formal or "hidden"—in their school.
- Engaging in discussions and activities that enhance diversity, choice, and student empowerment in the school.
- Engaging in a variety of community service activities.
- Engaging in creative activities and research projects—art, dance, drama, history, psychology, theory of knowledge—that enlighten the child about his or her own heritage and identity, as well as the heritage and identity of other students.

Learning Environment

High school must be a place where students are supported in developing a secure racial and ethnic identity and where students learn to appreciate, enjoy, and work collaboratively with people who are different from them. Further, any environment that directly or indirectly supports single-race and ethnicity grouping forces multiethnic and multiracial students to make difficult choices and to feel that they must hide part of their background to belong (Cortes, 1999). In most high schools there are not enough students of multiracial/multiethnic backgrounds to "sit together in the cafeteria"; further, as we have suggested, these children come from such diverse backgrounds that to assume they all belong to the same group simply makes no sense.

As with the middle school environment, high school environments must stress admission and involvement into groups, classes, sports, and programs and be based on ability and interest, not race or ethnicity. Administrators and teachers must actively find ways to integrate official school-sponsored events, destroy racial and ethnic stereotypes within the school, and expose hidden curricula that communicate to students that Advanced Placement programs are only for White students, track and basketball for Black students, swimming and lacrosse for White kids, and golf and tennis for Asian students, and so on.

The multiracial daughters of Francis Wardle and Ruth Benjamin-Wardle attended the International Baccalaureate program in an integrated city high school. This program is an international precollege curriculum with headquarters in Cardiff, Wales. The local school in which the program is housed has a large and diverse minority population; however, the IB program is almost exclusively White and only has one minority teacher, who is from India. Francis Wardle has been informed that prospective minority teachers are warned by minority teachers in the school not to apply to teach in the program, because "it's a White program." This is an example of what should not take place in the high school environment.

Role models who visit the school and classrooms should continually destroy stereotypes—of women, minorities, and people with disabilities—and should celebrate people who have a multiethnic or multiracial heritage.

The learning environment at the high school level also includes the way staff respond to multiethnic and multiracial children, how the school addresses single race/ethnicity celebrations, and how the school collects official OMB data. Further, support staff—social workers, counselors, and psychologists—must be fully supportive of multiethnic and multiracial families and students and must be very careful to avoid labeling these children as being abnormal or dysfunctional because of their ethnic and racial status (Olumide, 2002; Wardle, 1999; Wehrly, Kenney, & Kenney, 1999).

Learning environment ideas regarding visual images are the same as those discussed in the middle-school section.

Curricular Content

Curricular content at the high school level must include all sorts of diversity—religion, language, national origin, abilities, gender, and race and ethnicity; but this must be done in a way that highlights movement between groups, various splinter groups, individual diversity within broadly defined groups, and the tremendous diversity within groups—for example, all the different Protestant faiths, the variety of disabilities, and the different languages spoken in countries like Guatemala and Peru, not to mention the variety of Native American languages. Additionally, content must explore the rich history of multiracial and multiethnic people around the world, as well as writings about being multiracial—historical (Douglass, 1994/1845/1855/1893; Stephens, 1999) and contemporary.

One example of curricular content would be to develop a unit around the great Brazilian artist Antonio Francisco Lisboa (1738–1814), also called Aleijadinho "little cripple," because of the deliberating disease he contracted in midlife. Antonio Francisco Lisboa was born a slave, the son of a Portuguese architect and one of his slaves. He was apprenticed to his father and to a local painter and draftsman. He became the most celebrated artist of the Brazilian colonial era, and his works can be seen throughout the state of Minas Gerais, Brazil. Among other buildings, he designed the church of Sao Francisco.

Chapter Feature
Student Profile: James S.

James S., 10th grade, White mother, Black father.

I've yet to see one textbook do something about a multiracial person. I'm like, "Are there no multiracial people in the world? Did they crawl into a hole and not do anything all history?" Schools try to promote diversity—everybody getting along. But, when you only learn about this side, it defeats the whole purpose. Like—Black History Month all the Black kids say, "Yeah, we're finally going to learn something about Black history." And all the mixed kids are like, "Sure, its another kind of history... there's nothing for us to relate to, so let's go with them." I don't hear anything about mixed people.

Church of Sao Francisco in Ouro Preto, Brazil. Designed by Antonio Francisco Lisboa, a Portuguese/Black sculptor and architect.

> Of all Western monuments, the church of Sao Francisco in the town of Ouro Preto is perhaps one of the most perfect. It was entirely conceived by a single man, the architect and sculptor Aleijadinho, who created this monument in its plastic totality, designed the floor plan, sculpted the entrance façade and the soapstone pulpits, and together with his pupils produced all the wood carving in the chancel. (Bazin, 1975, p. 223)

Students could research Aleijadinhos' life, the rich Baroque art period in Brazil, the impact of the European Baroque on Brazilian architecture and art, the differences between English and Portuguese approaches to New World conquest, and the Black brotherhoods in Ouro Preto at that time. They could also compare and contrast the condition of Brazilian slaves to those in this country. The possibilities are endless.

Curricular Materials

At the high school level the challenge is the same as the other levels—almost no curricular materials celebrating and addressing multiethnic and multiracial issues exist. However, at the high school level teachers are free to augment and

Chapter Feature
Comments about Interracial Marriage and Multiracial Identity by Frederick Douglass and Bob Marley

Douglass: I would not be understood as advocating intermarriage between two races. I am not a propagandist, but a prophet. I do not say that what I say should come to pass, but what I think is likely to come to pass, and what is inevitable (*The Life and Times of Frederick Douglass*, originally published 1893, pp. 438–439). Hence I have often been bluntly and sometimes very rudely asked, of what color my mother was, and of what color was my father? In what proportions does the blood of the various races mingle in my veins, especially how much White blood and how much Black blood entered my composition? ... Whether I considered myself more African than Caucasian, or the reverse? ... Whether persons of mixed blood are as strong and healthy as persons of either of the races whose blood they inherit? ... Whether they inherit only evil from both parents and good from neither? ... Why did I marry a person of my father's complexion instead of marrying one of my mother's? (Douglass, 1893, pp. 438–439).

Bob Marley: I don't have prejudice against myself. My father was a White and my mother Black. ... Me don't dip on the Black man's side nor the White man's side. Me dip on God's side, the one who create me and cause me to come from Black and White. (R.A. Allen, *Caribbean Times*, 1975, as quoted in the movie, *Time Will Tell*, 1991. From Stephens, 1999.)

enhance their materials with their own resources. Thus, teachers must become aware of resources that are available to explore the topic: Internet sites, books, magazine articles, local support groups, local community resources, and people and role models within their school. They also need to insist that curricular materials the school adopts truly reflect the contributions, struggles, and courage of interracial/interethnic relationships and families throughout history and the world.

Hidden Curriculum

While much of a school's curriculum is a direct outgrowth of the school's mission statement, policies/procedures, goals, and individual content plans, there are many things that occur in schools that are not written down or that directly contradict the written plans and policies. This is called the **hidden curriculum**—and is an integral part of the school's overall curriculum (Doll, 1970).

We are interested in the hidden curriculum that affects multiethnic and multiracial children and their families. The most obvious example is forcing interethnic and interracial parents and their students to select only one single-race identity—usually the parent of color or of lowest status—communicating to families and children that their school and government do not recognize their right to choose their own identity and do not support the healthy development of children with a mixed heritage. Other hidden curricula include single-race groups, single-race celebrations, programs that staff and students believe are exclusively for one race or ethnicity, the disproportionate number of minorities in lower ability classes and mainstream Whites and Asians in AP and gifted programs, and the disproportionate number of boys and children of color in special education. As a special education teacher recently e-mailed to Francis Wardle, "There are a lot of confused biracial children in special education." The hidden messages here are that (1) biracial children are confused, and (2) more biracial children than single-race children are in special education because they have more problems than single-race children (Wardle, 2002c).

Clearly, a school curriculum that totally ignores multiethnic and multiracial students—content, illustrations, discussions—is providing a hidden curriculum message that multiethnic and multiracial children and people are invisible. This conveys the message that there is something wrong with being multiethnic or multiracial, and therefore we must not discuss them. Schools must very deliberately examine and address any hidden curricula that undermine the healthy development of multiethnic and multiracial children and jeopardize a positive relationship between the school and interracial/interethnic families.

Multicultural Model

To help teachers, schools, and early childhood programs respond to the increasing diversity of their students, including those with mixed heritage, Wardle developed the **Anti-Bias and Ecological Model of Multicultural Education** (1996) (see Figure 7.1). This anti-bias and ecological model proposes that each child's background should be viewed using seven distinctly different factors: race/ethnicity, culture, gender, ability/disability, community, family, and socioeconomic status. These seven factors differ in weight and influence for each child and interact uniquely to define each child (West, 2001). For example, for some children family is the most important influence on their identity, for others it is ethnicity/race or gender, for still others their disability is most relevant. A description of the seven factors follows.

Race/Ethnicity

Traditionally, in this country the government and "the folk" divided our population into five general categories: American Indian or Alaskan Native, Asian or Pacific Islander, Black, Latino (any race), and White (non-Latino). While throughout this book we have discussed the limitation of these groupings, they are still very powerful concepts for Americans in the twenty-first century. The racial and ethnic group a family belongs to has a profound impact on a child's

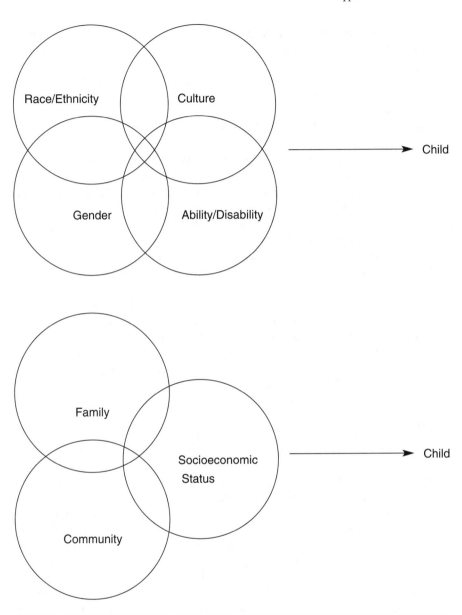

FIGURE 7.1 Anti-Bias and Ecological Model of Multicultural Education. From Francis Wardle, *Introduction to Early Childhood Education: A Multidimensional Approach to Child-Centered Care and Learning.* Published by Allyn and Bacon, Boston, MA. Copyright © 2003 by Pearson Education. Reprinted by permission of the publisher.

experiences. These factors include a common history, including a history of persecution, oppression, stereotypes, and personal degradation, a lower position in relationship to the country's mainstream, and a specific government status, such as a protected class, affirmative action, scholarships, and membership in an Indian Nation. For adoptive or foster children, racial/ethnic identity has specific implications, as we have discussed. Belonging to a racial or ethnic group also includes certain expectations, both from within the group and from without.

Families within these groups may exhibit certain characteristics that differ from other groups. For example, many Latino families speak Spanish, are large and religious and extended, and teach respect for elders; Asian families tend to be extended and teach respect for elders; Native American families also teach respect for elders and treasure cultural values and traditions; Black families often have extensive extended family support and some are very religious; and many mainstream White families place a great deal of emphasis on education. But we must be very careful about these generalizations, because there are always group and individual examples that don't fit the norm and because values, attitudes, expectations, and behaviors continually change. Further, there is considerable variability within these broad categories—of religion, values, life experiences, and so on. Finally, each member of these groups is also a member of the larger "American" culture. Francis has some Pueblo Indian friends from Taos who regularly visit Europe to expose Europeans to our Native cultures. When he meets with his Pueblo friends, their discussions invariably focus on how European and "American" culture differs.

Culture

Over the last years there has been a growing tendency in this country to define culture with race and ethnicity: that racial and ethnic belonging determine unique and exclusive cultural differences. Some school districts are even using the term "culture" in place of race and ethnicity (Black culture, Latino culture, etc.). Francis has a good friend from Sierra Leone, Africa. She was a member of her country's 1996 Olympic track team. The other day she told Francis that she cannot return to her country because she belongs to its lowest class, and even though she has lived in Europe and the United States and has a computer science degree, she will never be accepted by her country's upper class. The separation between the upper and lower class in her country is so great that marriage across class is taboo. The ruling class of Sierra Leone are descendants of former Black slaves from the United States who hold the political jobs and own most of the land; the lower class are Native Africans who never left their country. While these two groups are viewed as belonging to the Black racial group, they comprise two distinct social and cultural groups in Sierra Leone.

We have talked at length about the different cultural groups that exist within the broad Latino label.

Having a separate cultural category allows for the distinction between American Blacks and first-generation Blacks from Africa and the Caribbean; Spanish Americans living in the mountains of northern New Mexico who are direct descendants of original Spanish settlers, Puerto Rican immigrants in New York, first-generation immigrants from Brazil, and mestizos from Mexico; third-generation Chinese Americans and first-generation Hmongs, Cambodians, and Vietnamese; and White Southern aristocratic families and poor Appalachian Whites. It also allows us to appreciate the rich differences of customs, religions, art, dance, houses, and languages of various Native American Nations in this country and throughout Central and South America (Sample, 1993).

A central component of a child's cultural experience is religion. Does the family regularly attend a synagogue, mosque, or church? Are they active members in their religious community, and do they send their children to religious early childhood and school programs?

Culture describes those parts of a child's experience that frame the way the child views the world. This includes child-rearing practices of the family, ideas, expectations—including gender, education, beliefs, different groups the family associates with, involvement in local and national politics, and many others. Of the seven categories in this model, culture probably is one of the most important. Talking to an Amish child about the importance of college education will not be effective, because Amish children finish school after eighth grade. Trying to use rap and hip-hop music with a young gifted Black student studying cello at a local college may not work either.

Gender

The gender category is obvious. What is not so obvious, but very powerful, is how schools, early childhood programs, parents, toy and materials marketers, and teachers respond to children based on their gender (Wardle, 2003). This category is also very important in relationship to other categories, such as ability/disability (more boys are in special education than girls), culture (some cultural groups raise boys and girls with distinctively different roles and expectations), and family.

Ability/Disability

A child's unique strengths, competencies, and physical, mental, and emotional challenges are covered here. Strengths include artistic and musical abilities, excellence in dance and physical activities, specific academic strengths, and other unique abilities covered by some of Gardner's (1983) eight intelligences. A child might be learning ballet and gymnastics, be on a soccer team, or may be identified through a gifted and talented search. Challenges include diagnosed special needs, potential special needs, and behavioral and social problems that pose difficulties for the child at school.

Community

The category of community includes small college towns, suburbs, inner cities, Native American reservations, small rural communities, segregated and integrated neighborhoods, ethnic sections of town, and religious communities such as the Amish. The influence of community also addresses movement between communities. For example, many low-income families move from one community to another within a school year. Some families, such as the new Mayan immigrants in Houston and some recent Mexican immigrants, have two communities—in their native country and in this country. And some third-culture children have two distinctive communities (West, 2001).

Communities include a variety of components that directly impact families. These include opportunities for children, including schools, early childhood programs, and club activities and recreational centers. They also include services and supports for the whole family, such as health clinics, bookstores, and playgrounds. Finally, communities include a variety of different media outlets and services. And, of course, religious institutions are a vital part of each community.

Family

The family is the most critical influence on young children (Bronfenbrenner, 1979, 1989). Family diversity includes all the different family structures we discussed in Chapter 6, along with the amount and quality of extended family support. Parenting styles—**authoritative**, **authoritarian**, and **permissive**—and various forms of family dysfunction (alcoholism, domestic violence, drugs) also influence a child's family experience. Of course, all these factors interact with and overlap each other. For example, a child could come from a mainstream White teen family with lots of extended family support, a permissive parenting style, and a hardworking, motivated single parent.

The family component also includes media and computer use at home. Homes where TV is used as a babysitter are very different from homes where TV is carefully monitored or where there is no TV at all. Homes that have computers and Internet access not only enable their school-age children to do sophisticated homework projects, but parents of these children often pressure their children's educational programs to provide computers and computer access.

While religion is part of the culture category, the family is the prime place where children experience religion: traditions and celebrations, practices, values, attitudes toward gender roles and people who are different, and views of history, science, and society.

Socioeconomic Status

Socioeconomic status has a powerful impact on the healthy development of all children. Lack of health insurance, poor food, homelessness, welfare, crime, poor quality early childhood programs and schools, and lack or recreational choices are all results of poverty. Even the kind of childcare programs a child attends is largely a function of the income of the family. Poor families use subsidized non-profit programs, Head Start programs, relative care, or home-based care. Middle- and upper-class children will stay at home with a parent; attend university lab programs, commercial childcare programs, home-based programs, or public and

Chapter Feature
Case Study of the Anti-Bias and Ecological Model of Mulicultural Education

---

Case Study Example. Joao Meira, father of first-grader Isabella, complained to the principal that his daughter was very unhappy in her public-school classroom. She had few friends, disliked the teacher, and was struggling with reading and math. Isabella complained that the teacher used her as an example when teaching some Spanish words and expected her to be friends with the Hispanic girls from the neighborhood. The teacher gave Isabella basic instruction in computer use and seemed confused when Isabella asked the teacher if she could do a computer Internet search for the project. Isabella could not find the books of interest to her in the classroom. She was looking for books about female doctors, dentists, and lawyers, but could only find ones about famous athletes and African American and Hispanic American heroes. And she was very upset that the teacher limited her time painting and drawing, her favorite activity. A student could use the art area only when she finished her academic subjects, which Isabella had a difficult time doing.

Because Isabella is dark-skinned in a school that served primarily children from a low-income Hispanic area of town, the teacher made some inaccurate assumptions about her. Here is a brief use of the model to help the teacher more effectively meet Isabella's educational needs.

- *Race or ethnicity.* The teacher assumed Isabella was Hispanic; the reality is that she is Brazilian, speaks Portuguese, and has a Portuguese colonial heritage.
- *Culture.* Again the teacher assumed that the child came from a low-income, Hispanic background and spoke Spanish. The reality is that she is from a middle-class professional family and speaks Portuguese.
- *Gender.* The teacher assumed Isabella's role models for women were mothers, aunts, and elder sisters who primarily care for children—an inaccurate assumption even for other children in the class. The reality is that Isabella comes from a home that expects girls to become professionals.
- *Ability or disability.* The teacher believed Isabella was not good at anything in particular. In reality she is quite competent in computer skills and gifted artistically. Unknown to the teacher, she has a learning disability that hinders her learning reading the way it is taught in the classroom.
- *Community.* Unlike her classmates, Isabella comes from a middle-class, integrated community.
- *Family.* Isabella comes from a professional family in which education is stressed and children are expected to go to college. Homework is more important than any other expectation or activity.
- *Socioeconomic status.* Isabella's father is a doctor who recently immigrated to this country. He teaches at the local university hospital.

Clearly, Isabella is going to continue to struggle in school, and may even drop out, if teachers do not change instructions, expectations, and approaches, based on the components of the Anti-Bias and Ecological Model.

private school tuition-based programs; or use nannies (Wardle, 2003). A family's early childhood choices are not just a function of tuition cost, but are also a function of availability, location, transportation, hours of service, and parents' comfort with the programs' approach and philosophy. Kealan, the son of Francis Wardle, attended first grade on a scholarship at an expensive, private program for gifted students. It was a very negative experience for the family, who felt they were not allowed to voice concerns and were looked down on by the paying parents—partly because they could not fully contribute to the frequent school fundraisers.

In this society we tend to segregate children by income, starting in early childhood and continuing through high school (and, to some extent, college). Public schools tend to come in two economic levels: poor city schools and many rural schools, in contrast to wealthy suburban schools and schools in university and college towns. Clearly, more minority students attend poorly supported programs, and more White children attend well-supported schools.

Application of the Model

A good teacher can use the framework of the model to effectively support each child in the classroom and challenge his or her own cultural and individual framework. Instead of trying to learn everything about every community, culture, home, family, and so on, the teacher will learn to "read" the child. If a child doesn't seem to respond to certain stories, ask why. If a child is uneasy in engaging in certain activities or participating in certain field trips, find out the reasons. If the child seems to be reticent in relationships with other children in the classroom, investigate the possible reasons. Teachers will also learn to read the family and community of their students. What encourages the family to come to the program? What things keep them away? What do they expect the program to do for their child? What materials do they want their child to use? What TV shows will they let them watch at school? And many other questions. An initial needs assessment when the children first enroll in the school is a great way to begin this process.

The use of the model requires the school to know about the children, community, and families they serve before purchasing curricular materials. Further, because curricular materials still tend to support socially preferred points of view, programs must be very selective when purchasing materials and may have to make some of their own. They certainly will need to be knowledgeable of local resources and be able to collect materials that are not commercially available. Curricular materials, classroom activities, and community outings must address all seven factors of the model in a way that teaches the variability and diversity of each factor, not the idea of one standard or norm: Professional occupations are the best kind, suburban homes the preferred place for an American family to live, mainstream White people the ideal, and boys the preferred gender.

Also, we cannot teach that the prevailing characteristics in any program are somehow automatically the best, whatever they are. For example, if the program is primarily Latino, it cannot teach the idea that Latinos are somehow better than

Native Americans, Blacks, or people of mixed heritage. This exploration of the variability of each factor should occur in all schools, whether they are diverse or homogeneous.

Conclusion

Early childhood programs and schools play a vital role in the healthy development of multiethnic and multiracial children. While multicultural education has helped schools respond to diversity beyond mainstream White middle-class students, it has done little to help schools meet the needs of families and children of mixed backgrounds (Cortes, 1999). Because a program's formal curriculum is the place where its official mission is carried out, P–12 schools must make a concerted effort to adopt and implement curricular approaches that actively include multiethnic and multiracial children, families, people, and experiences. And, because the school environment is a vehicle for implementing the curriculum, it must also reflect the needs of multiethnic and multiracial students and their families. Finally, schools must very carefully examine their hidden curriculum to make sure it supports all students, including multiethnic and multiracial students.

Questions/Projects

1. Use the instrument *How to Evaluate a Textbook/Reading Book for P–12 Programs* to evaluate a book used in the classroom.

2. Procure a curricular materials catalogue. Discuss to what extent these materials meet the needs of multiracial and multiethnic children and their families.

3. Use the Anti-Bias and Ecological Model to create a profile of yourself. Then compare your profile with a colleague's.

4. How would you help a class develop an anti-bias activity to increase the number of curricular materials that reflect multiethnic and multiracial children and their families?

5. How should a high school resolve the apparent conflict between minority children needing a sense of group identity and multiethnic and multiracial children having their full identity supported?

Resources

Books

Steichen, E. (1983). *The family of man*. New York: The Museum of Modern Art.

Szumski, B.F. (Ed).(1996). *Interracial America: Opposing viewpoints*. San Diego, CA: Greenhaven Press.

Website

Composers of African descent from around the world, many of whom are multiracial

http://chevalierdesaintgeorges.homestead.com/others.html

8

Instructional Strategies

The early childhood and school curriculum is adapted and modified into a written instructional plan: thematic units, unit plans, and lesson plans. Teachers use these documents as blueprints to implement the curriculum in the classroom. They use their knowledge from teacher education, past experience as teachers, and unique teaching styles to implement these lessons. As they teach, they learn from their students, observing their diverse background experiences, cultural patterns, and learning styles. Teachers must constantly differentiate their teaching in order to meet the developmental and educational interests and needs of each student in their classes. Similarly, students learn through building on experiences and mental schemas they have developed, challenging their knowledge base, and broadening their view of the world.

While teachers are limited by the state and district curricula, which in recent years have been influenced by the standards movement, teachers make many choices as they implement the curriculum in the classroom, including setting up the environment, selecting appropriate materials, providing opportunities for all children to succeed, working effectively with each child's family, and tailoring their individual approaches to match each student's interests and learning styles. The teacher's role in implementing the curriculum is the focus of this chapter.

FOCUS QUESTIONS

1. To what extent do national educational standards negatively impact teachers' ability to most effectively teach all their students?

2. How can teachers work effectively with multiethnic and multiracial children in their classrooms?

3. How can teachers make classroom instruction meaningful to each student?

4. Why do all teachers need to carefully examine their own racial identity, background, and values to be effective teachers of students who are different from them?

5. How can a teacher respond to the unique needs of multiethnic and multiracial children without making negative assumptions about these children, based on their unique backgrounds?

The Impact of Standards on Instruction

Before we look at how teachers can use various instructional approaches to teach a diverse student population, we will address the impact of the **educational standards** movement. The use and adoption of content standards throughout our public schools has produced administrators and teachers whose survival is dependent on children's test scores on standardized tests. The natural—and logical—result of the standards movement is that teachers are expected to teach to the test. Instead of assessments being used to evaluate the quality and effectiveness of the curriculum and its implementation—the traditional role of assessment (Wiles & Bondi, 1998)—they are now used to judge administrators and teachers. The net result is that anything not specifically addressed by the standards is eliminated from the curriculum: art, music, emotional intelligence, social development, and physical education. Further, teachers who stray from the "curriculum by the test" approach, at best, are reprimanded and, at worst, may lose their jobs. And school administrators are pressured to "stick to the test" in order to raise their school's scores and avoid low ratings that are highly publicized.

The very purpose of standards is to control what is taught in our schools, with the obvious result that areas not included, such as multicultural education, suffer (Berlak, 1999; Bigelow, 1999). Content standards become guidelines that detail the "body of information to be taught," including specific content and skills to be taught in every school subject area at every grade level. These guidelines aim to standardize not only curricula but also pedagogy—how the content is taught—prescribing both the legitimate knowledge and areas of study, and at what depth these areas should be examined—very similar to the E.D. Hirsch Core Knowledge approach to curriculum and teaching (Hirsch, 1987). It is no accident that E.D. Hirsch calls his curriculum content **cultural literacy**.

Thus, standards codify a culture's knowledge, totally eliminating the "vibrant cacophony of views about what constitutes truth, knowledge and learning, and about what children ought and ought not to learn in school" (Berlak, 1999, p. 2). This debate, of course, about what should and should not be covered in our schools has raged since the inception of public schools, with the inclusion of religion—and, ultimately, whose religion—being one of the areas of most heated discussion. The very standards movement has produced its own series of debates, especially around the proposed history and social studies standards.

The current standards movement evolved out of the **Goals 2000** legislation, one of the many attempts to create national goals (Wardle, 2003). The logical next step after national goals is national standards, and after standards, tests to evaluate student proficiency on those standards. (Standards are meaningless unless we know how well students are doing on them.) Many believe the final step will be a national curriculum, an educational approach used by almost all other countries in the world. Our challenge, however, is to find ways to marry this movement toward a national curriculum with the ever-increasing diversity of our students. The fear is that a national curriculum would codify the Eurocentric approach to curricular content, delivery, and outcomes, thus further disenfranchising students of color, mixed-ethnicity and mixed-race students, disabled students, and students whose preferred learning style is not logical-mathematical (Gardner, 1983).

The Influence of the Teacher

Clearly, the movement toward national standards contradicts many things we know about effective education, based on the reality that teachers, students, and students' families are all unique entities. Further, more and more research is confirming that knowledge is constructed differently by each student, based on his or her cultural experience, family backgrounds, and learning styles (Gardner, 1983; Wardle, 2003). Just as each person possesses unique likes and dislikes and learns in a unique fashion, each teacher implements the curriculum in a uniquely different way, based on acquired social patterns, ideas and values, including attitudes toward gender, race, ethnicity, language, religion, and social class. Teachers bring all this psychological "baggage" with them to the classroom.

Many teachers unknowingly have preconceived notions of people different from them. While most people become teachers because they care about children and want to provide them with a good start in life, these same teachers sometimes express contempt, low expectations, and unconscious biases toward some of their students and their families. Marta Cruz-Janzen was an elementary school principal in a very poor, predominantly Latino and African American community in a large Western city. Most of the school children lived in a public housing project. When Marta tried to organize a walk of the school's teachers through the neighborhood to meet the children's parents, introduce themselves, and personally invite them to visit the school, she experienced considerable resistance, with teachers claiming the neighborhood was unsafe. Finally, several teachers agreed to walk in small groups along the streets, but insisted some of the children's homes were not "very sanitary" and would expose them to the probability of "catching something."

It was disappointing that some teachers were unwilling to leave the safety of the school building—their perceived domain—to meet parents in their communities and homes. Although research indicates positive impact of increased parent–teacher interaction and communication on student success (Powell, 1998), and that many Latino parents respond well when schools make direct, face-to-face contacts with them, many of the teachers felt that it was the parents' responsibility to come to the school and not the other way around.

On other occasions teachers made derogatory comments about their students and their families, including that "They [the children] all belong in juvenile hall." When new and used coats were donated to the school, a teacher distributed the used and unwashed coats to the poor Black and Latino children from the housing project and the new coats to the mainstream White children and Latino children from more affluent areas. When asked the reason, the teacher explained "They [the children from the housing development] will destroy the new coats in no time."

These kinds of attitudes by White, middle-class teachers have as much—if not more—to do with middle-class lifestyles and poverty as they have to do with people of color. Francis Wardle experienced the very same attitude from his Head Start staff (comprised of diverse ethnic and racial backgrounds) toward Head Start's required home visit policy. Further, many of his staff, who had recently been in poverty themselves, freely expressed very personal and negative views of poor families and the parenting style of many Head Start parents.

Teachers' personal views and attitudes have a direct impact on their ability to work with students who are different from them, and who come from homes, communities, and cultures that differ from theirs. Since most teachers are middle-class, White, and female, this poses a barrier to working effectively with minority students. Further, since very few teachers are multiethnic or multiracial, mixed-race/ethnicity students experience further alienation.

Chapter Feature
Student Profile: Eric Chavez

Eric Chavez is a fourth grader in a predominantly Latino urban school. He is very disruptive in class and frequently erupts in unexpected fits of anger, screaming obscenities and throwing things around while striking at anyone near. Each year his temper seems to get worse and he has been recommended for evaluation to determine whether he should be in special education or on medication. His parents claim that Eric is a very obedient and loving child at home, where he plays well with friends and relatives. They recall how excited he was to start kindergarten; yet now have difficulty getting him up in the mornings. The teachers feel that Eric's parents are in denial about his disabilities and emotional problems. Eric's father is Latino Mestizo (Mexico) and his mother is mainstream White American.

After years of turmoil, Eric sits in the principal's office sobbing. "I hate my parents for having me. Nobody likes me. Why can't I be like everybody else?" Eric has been the subject of constant abuse and exclusion by his peers since he started school, including Latino students. They often call him "White boy." His parents, especially his White mother, are the subjects of offensive jokes. Many teachers are aware of the abuse but simply tell him that he has to learn to ignore it and control his temper, claiming that, he will have to deal with that [being mixed] all his life.

When the Teacher and Parent Disagree

Throughout this book we have used the phase, "multiethnic and multiracial children *and their families*." This emphasis on the families of students is no accident. Perceptions parents hold toward schools shape students' perceptions of teachers and schooling as a whole and impact the way students view their education (Cruz-Janzen, 1997; Epstein, 1984, 1985; Powell, 1998). A student of African American and Native American heritage commented: "My mother always told me not to ditch classes or leave the campus but not to take mainstream White teachers seriously." His mother told him stories about how Native American students were mistreated by teachers in the **Mission/Indian boarding schools**. His parents taught him that they [mainstream White teachers] were smarter than anyone else "in the book sense" along with the belief that they were not as smart when it came to "interacting with families." His parents taught him that these White teachers lacked the significant knowledge of the elders who honored the "oral history" tradition without relying on formal documents and references. This student felt that mainstream White teachers and schools were cruel in forcing them to learn what they learned in school. "I would take bits and pieces from them. In my mind I was always off doing other things. I dedicated myself to just sitting there throughout the class. I went to class but I wasn't doing the work."

In an interracial family with a mainstream White member and a parent of color, parent attitudes may well conflict, leading to a perceived inconsistency by the teacher. Multiethnic and multiracial children with two minority parents may have parents who both distrust the school, but for differing reasons. Also, interracial parents who have had negative experiences with their children's schools—which many have had, including both authors of this book—may appear to the teacher or administrator to be overly sensitive and hostile. The principal of a school where Francis Wardle's children attended told his teachers that the author was "uptight about his children's racial identity."

It is, therefore, imperative that teachers actively find ways to communicate with parents, work out problems and disagreements, and express an interest in their families' unique educational needs. As Epstein has clearly shown, teachers who expected parent involvement from all parents found their parents became more involved (1984, 1985).

Teachers and the Hidden Curriculum

Teachers are very powerful in implementing the hidden curriculum that we discussed in Chapter 7. Examples of this include lining children in boy-girl lines, having boys move books (perceived as heavy) and expecting the girls to clean areas of the classroom, and referring more boys and minority students to special education than girls and mainstream White students (Wardle, 1991). Teachers uncomfortable with math and science will transmit this dislike and inadequacy to their students. They will avoid the subjects and/or appear nervous teaching them.

Francis conducted an action research study on his Head Start program and determined that the teachers (female) preferred to sit at tables and do table activities with students rather than play on the floor with blocks in the block area. He also discovered that all the woodwork tables were being used as desks or stands for fish aquariums. Thus, teachers in the program preferred working with quiet, compliant girls and not active, loud boys: an obvious strong bias against boys (Wardle, 1991).

The personality of teachers becomes apparent the minute a person walks into a classroom: Is it colorful and full of teacher- and student-made projects and artwork or a very rigid classroom covered with commercial posters? A classroom full of science, including live animals and plants, will convey a different message than one without them, and a classroom arranged to encourage small group work versus a classroom with desks lined in rows radiating out from a central teacher desk communicate different images of the role of the teacher to students and parents. The materials and resources teachers select and how they use them in their classrooms also convey to minority and multiethnic and multiracial children whether they belong and are important.

Role of Teachers' Ethnicity and Race

Many studies document the different perceptions and interactions of teachers toward students, according to students' race, ethnicity, native language, gender, socioeconomic status, and other forms of diversity (Sadker & Sadker, 2002). Similarly, teachers who are uncomfortable with children who are not from their own backgrounds are not going to be effective—or supportive—of them. Since overall diversity in schools is a very positive factor for all learning, we must find ways to increase the number of minority teachers in our schools, at every level. Further, as Bandura (1965) has consistently shown in his research, positive adult role models are people who have credibility in the eyes of the students—especially credibility in what they teach or expect of students. Many White middle-class teachers lack credibility in the eyes of minority students. But we cannot make the mistake of trying to match staff ethnicity and race with student ethnicity and race. This would not only further the resegregation of our schools, and segregation or ethnic and racial groups within our schools, it would also deny mainstream White students the value of minority teachers—particularly as the number of minority students increase and minority teachers proportionally decrease.

Many teachers, both mainstream White and minority teachers, have strong beliefs about interracial relationships and multiracial and multiethnic children (Wehrly, Kenney, & Kenney, 1999). The special education teacher discussed earlier who professed the belief that multiracial children disproportionately belong in special education is just one example. Once a mainstream White teacher in Marta Cruz-Janzen's schools stated that she would not date an African American because "I would look ridiculous!" When asked how she defined ridiculous, it was clear that she disapproved of interethnic and interracial marriage. When further queried whether the children of interracial marriages also looked "ridiculous," she remained silent, realizing the impact of her prejudices on her classroom. Many interracial parents have reported problems their children have experienced in schools. Often the school's response has been "That's not our problem"—resulting in the agonizing experience of people like Eric Chavez (Student Profile on page 181).

Teachers must be prepared to work in affirming ways with all students, even when they come from family structures and lifestyles not openly embraced by mainstream society. In fact, a central role of a teacher preparation program must be to provide tools, techniques, and approaches to assist teachers in working with all children and their families and to prepare them for culturally diverse class-rooms (Stachowski, 1998). When training future teachers, Marta Cruz-Janzen reminds her students, "We must leave our biases and prejudices at the school door. Once inside, we must be responsible for the equitable—fair, reasonable, and just—education and protection of all children entrusted to us. Public school educators cannot choose who to teach and cannot penalize children based on our prejudgments of their home lives."

Teachers as Products of Culture

The challenge, of course, is that teachers are products of this society and the individual cultures in which they were raised, thus holding all the values, biases, and limitations that come with growing up in this country. This is true of minority teachers also. From an early grade, children discover whether their education includes them and their families. If it does not, it devalues them. A third-grade African American student once asked very poignantly, "Is Martin Luther King the only Black who ever did anything good?" Another African American fourth grader asked a guest speaker to the school who was telling them, "If you try hard enough, you can be anything you want to be," to "name one woman or Black president." Russell, a Black/Navajo Indian male who is now in college, expanded on this problem:

> Russell began to question what he was being taught in elementary school. He recalls losing interest in history because he knew that most of the stories were untrue and all the characters had "blond hair and blue eyes." "They say these things happened in Africa. Look at these people in Africa. They are dark. Black with dark skin." He states without hesitation that he hated school and was a poor student. Yet, his family's support for and affirmation of his dual heritage helped immensely in combating the negative images and ideas he was being taught at school. "You have to have an understanding of both. I know it's not really told in classrooms. I know the contributions of the In-dians and the Blacks to the development of this supposedly great nation; that we have, that I have ownership from both sides that apply to me." Foremost, because he was part of both, Russell felt like a "bigger person." "Wow! I am a combination of both! They (other people) are one person and I am two per-sons inside." He explains that his public school experiences left him very "lacking" and "hungry for knowledge."

Because most teachers know little about non-Eurocentric history, art, literature, and science, they need to be very motivated to discover and learn on their own. Teachers need to also find ways to continually differentiate their instruction, based on what they know about each student's learning needs and interests.

Addressing Bias and Prejudice

Many teachers often don't know where to begin or how to go about addressing bias and prejudice in their classroom. Of those who are not themselves resistant to change—in themselves and/or their practices—many fear anger and resistance from parents, colleagues, and supervisors. Most of the elementary and high school student participants in a study conducted in 1997 (Cruz-Janzen) agreed that teachers "were aware of racial things going on" in the schools but "acted like they didn't notice." The children teased—indeed abused—each other and used derogatory names. "Teachers in elementary school don't deal with differences. Instead teachers pretend that the kids are not any different from each other." They agreed that teachers are not prepared to address racial diversity, even though it is increasing. Data also suggests that administrators ignore the issue—often believing it is outside of their responsibilities, or simply waiting until it erupts.

Children need opportunities to explore all aspects of their multiethnic/ multiracial heritage.

From our experience we believe many teachers are fully aware of their woeful inadequacies, but lack adequate undergraduate preparation and do not receive training and added support in their schools (Stachowski, 1998). Further, these students often express that classes and workshops dedicated to teaching about diversity often fixate on White guilt and the victimization of minorities but provide little or no direct assistance for helping teachers respond to diversity in their classrooms. Almost no college multicultural courses discuss the unique needs of multiracial and multiethnic children (Cortes, 1999).

Understanding Racism

Teachers need to stop saying that they "don't see race"—for indeed they do—everyone does. As an African American mother pointed out to her child's White teacher, "What rot," said Mrs. Hawkins. "My children are Black. They don't look like your children. They know they are Black, and we want it recognized. It's a positive difference, an interesting difference, and a comfortable natural difference. At least it could be so, if you teachers learned to value differences more. What you value, you talk about" (Paley, 1979, p. 12). People, including teachers and children, look at each other and make judgments based on physical appearances. These racial judgments are often incorrect—and stereotypical—especially regarding multiethnic and multiracial children. But they are continually made, nonetheless.

Teachers cannot effectively affirm diversity in others until they can affirm it in themselves: what we call true diversity. Mainstream White teachers cannot see or understand the subtle and underlying layers of racism permeating U.S. society until they understand how they themselves became racial beings. As a mainstream White teacher, Howard (1999) emphasizes, mainstream White teachers cannot improve schools until they look within themselves and examine their "deepest assumptions and perceptions" about their Whiteness in their minds, hearts, and habits—and the invisible privileges it confers on them: "We can't teach what we don't know."

By the same token, minority teachers need to examine their own racial socialization. Many minority teachers believe that, since they are a minority, they cannot be racist. This simply is not true—especially toward people *and children*—from other minority groups. When Marta Cruz-Janzen was an elementary teacher in New York City, she was shocked when told by a friend who visited her class for several days and observed her that she discriminated against Dominican children in her class. "You don't interact with them. You avoid them and keep your distance." Marta had to get past her initial denial and do some soul-searching to admit that in her home country, Puerto Rico, she grew up with many internalized negative biases toward persons from the Dominican Republic, which were limiting her effectiveness with some of her students! She was saddened that she may have hurt some children, but glad that she could correct her biases.

Further, many people from single-race groups—including minority groups—distrust and look down on interracial relationships and children from these relationships. Issues of colorism in the Black community, acceptance of African and African American influence in the Latino community, interracial marriage, and other racial issues should also be explored by teachers of color.

We must acknowledge that a person's race and ethnicity do make a difference and that many people—including many teachers—are uncomfortable with these differences. Further, children of color and multiethnic and multiracial children internalize the message that their physical differences are very real to some and make some people feel uncomfortable. Students internalize these fears, uncertainties, and discomforts and begin to see themselves with uncertainly, displeasure, and inadequacy. Thus some multiethnic and multiracial children are marginalized by all single-race teachers and staff and begin to see themselves as confused, marginal, and "not normal."

As teachers of all backgrounds gain self-understanding as racial beings, they also learn the importance that race plays in other people's lives and how to respond appropriately to children whose racial and ethnic experiences are different from their own.

Changing Teachers' Attitudes

To help teachers genuinely and realistically know themselves, they should engage in honest soul-searching and introspection, by analyzing:

- **How did I become who I am?** How did I learn what is expected and appropriate for me as the person I am—my language, behaviors, expectations, friends, interests, etc. (based on my gender, race, ethnicity, language, socioeconomic status, religion, physical appearance, abilities/disabilities)? What did I learn? What messages did I receive about people who are not like me? Are my beliefs (about self and others) biased and, if so, how?
- **How do I define/identify people I feel are like me?** People who are not like me? Which diverse (human and/or physical) attributes about those persons do I find distinguishing from myself? In other words, how are people who are different from me, different?
- **What values and ideals do I hold that are like those of the main or dominant culture, and which are different?** In what areas do I subscribe to mainstream values (say religion) and in what areas do I not subscribe to mainstream values (say value of money, home life, etc.)? How do those values and ideas match and/or differ from persons who are not like me? People who are not full members of the mainstream? How do I really feel when in the company of people I consider like me? When in the company of people I consider different from me?
- **How do I feel about single races?** How do I feel about my race? Ethnicity? If I had a choice, which race or ethnicity would I choose for myself? Why? Knowing that there are no pure races, how do I feel about my own mixed racial history? Am I willing to openly proclaim my own racial mixing? How do I feel about affirming my own interracial heritage?

Francis Wardle's parents. "My father was a pacifist during World War II; one of his relatives was a Labor MP. My mother's father was a foreman in the cotton mills. What did I get from my parents?"

- **How do I feel about interracial and interethnic marriages and families?** Would I be involved in an interracial or interethnic relationship? Why or why not? Do I have a friend or relative involved in an interracial or interethnic relationship? How do I feel about it? As a minority teacher, how do I feel about multiracial and multiethnic people affirming their full identity, not just the identity of their parent of color or of lowest status?
- **Why did I choose to become an educator?** How do I feel about working with children, families, and communities that differ from me?

By engaging in this process, teachers will begin to recognize how societies, institutions, and single-race groups transmit the messages of superiority and inequity in multiple ways. Some of these ways are very apparent and easy to challenge, but most racist behaviors are ingrained within cultures and are not as easily discernible.

Biased Instructional Materials

In Chapter 7 we discussed the examination of biased materials as part of appropriate curricular approaches. Here we add a useful tool to help teachers select appropriate classroom materials. Naturally, many of the areas addressed overlap.

Forms of Bias in Curricular Materials and Programs

Sadker and Sadker (2002) have identified seven forms of bias in curricular materials and programs.

Invisibility.   A fundamental form of bias in instructional materials is the complete omission of representatives of a particular group or groups of people from the text narratives and illustrations in all content areas. Today, multiracial and multiethnic persons remain invisible in all textbooks and other curricular materials.

Stereotyping.   Assigning rigid and even traditional roles and characteristics to a group in complete disregard for individual attributes and differences denies students knowledge of the diversity, complexity, and variability between individuals within groups. Typical stereotypes include:

- African Americans as criminals, servants, and professional athletes.
- Asian Americans as laundry workers and cooks or as the "Model Minority"—gifted, mathematicians, and scientists.
- Latinos as non-English speakers, drug dealers, migrant workers, or welfare recipients.
- Middle-class mainstream Whites as always successful in their professional and personal lives.
- Men in traditional occupational roles and as strong and assertive, but rarely as loving husbands and nurturing fathers—especially to daughters.
- Women as passive and dependent mothers and wives.
- Multiethnic and multiracial persons as confused, unhappy, and pathological, as well as tragic, exotic, immoral, oversexed, and promiscuous. Additionally, showing the Black/White person as the only form of mixing that exists in our society and the world.

Imbalance and Selectivity.   Only one interpretation of an issue, a situation, or a group of people is presented. As we have mentioned throughout the book, curricula is grounded on a White male Eurocentric perspective, presented from the dominant White Anglo Saxon, Protestant male perspective. For example, the origins of European settlers are emphasized, with little mention of people of other racial and ethnic groups, and all racial and ethnic groups are presented as a single race with no racial mixing. We don't present the various interactions including intermarriage of White settlers, men and women alike, with Native Indians, Africans, and people from others racial groups (Spickard, 1989). This approach distorts complex issues by omitting different perspectives and robbing students of the richness of our diverse society.

Unreality.   Instructional materials tend to only present the positive side of history and persons we are comfortable with, while ignoring or glossing over facts that are unpleasant, sensitive, or discomforting and that document negative actions by individual leaders or the nation as a whole. For example, we rarely discuss the internment of Japanese U.S. citizens during World War II or that Hitler masterminded the Holocaust based on the manner in which the United States dealt with Native Americans (Loewen, 1995). When we discuss Andrew Carnegie, we don't explain that his father died destitute in this country and that he built his fortune on the backs of Eastern European coal miners and steelworkers. We also do not discuss that the word *slave* comes from *slav*, a White European; that White Europeans were also sold as slaves in the United States; and that slavery exists today in too many countries. We do not discuss racial mixing, particularly among mainstream Whites, and the fact that most mainstream Whites are not White at all. We rarely discuss that one of the reasons most African Americans have White bloodlines is because of the vast racial mixing, mostly through rapes, that occurred during slavery. And we don't discuss the non-White heritage of many Blacks—especially that of Native Americans (Forbes, 1993; Katz, 1996).

Unreality is evident when we ignore the existence of prejudice, racism, discrimination, exploitation, oppression, and sexism in today's society. Examples are found when all people of color and women are portrayed as having economic and political equality with mainstream White males, the assumption all mainstream White men, "have it made," and when we ignore conflict and bias within and between groups—including within and between groups of color—thus denying students the ability to recognize, understand, and solve the problems of society.

Fragmentation and Isolation.   Fragmentation occurs when issues related to people of color and women are separated from the main body of the text, physically or visually presenting material separately, at the end of the chapter or text, or on the sides of the page(s)—thus implying they are less important and not part of the regular curriculum. Individuals from racial and ethnic groups are often depicted as isolated from other groups and interacting only with persons like themselves, ignoring dynamic group relationships and conveying that non-mainstream Whites are peripheral members of society. If multiracial and multiethnic people are discussed at all, they are covered separately from, and usually after, discussion of the individuals from single-race groups.

Linguistic Bias.   The popular expression: "If thought can shape language, language can equally shape thought," conveys the significance of language in every culture. Choice of language conveys bias in both blatant and subtle forms: Use of only English in society creates bias and discrimination against non-English speakers; providing bilingual instruction in only two languages, when students in the classroom speak a variety of non-English languages, is also a bias. Other examples of linguistic bias include:

- Use of the word "he" as "generic" and inclusive of males and females.
- Imbalance in the "male and female" word order and the use of unparallel terms such as "girls and young men."
- Terms such as *forefathers, mankind, fireman, policeman,* and *businessman* that deny the contributions and existence of females.
- Native Americans are frequently referred to as "roaming," "wandering," or "roving" across the land. These terms are more appropriately applied to animals that have a strictly physical connection to the land rather than a

Chapter Feature
Materials and Activities Checklist

For the first section, a "yes" answer is required.

- Do the materials and activities enhance children's self-acceptance, knowledge, and understanding of their heritage and identity by showing their culture in a positive way?
- Do the materials and activities enhance children's understanding and acceptance of people and cultures different from them by showing those cultures in a positive manner?
- Do the materials and activities expand the children's view of the world by exposing them to new ideas, people, and viewpoints?
- Are the materials carefully designed with sensitivity and respect toward children and diversity through the use of acceptance and understanding?
- Do the materials and activities address several areas of diversity in a positive manner?
- Are the materials and activities part of the overall curriculum and classroom materials, and do they integrate naturally into classroom activities and experiences?
- Does the activity require children to face prejudices, stereotypes, labels, assumptions, and misconceptions that they are developing by challenging their thinking and behaviors?
- Does the activity show diversity in realistic, contemporary settings (for example, Native Americans doing real jobs in contemporary clothes, rather than dancing in headdresses)?

The following questions should be answered with a "no."

- Is the material or activity a token? (for example, one minority doll, one book representing each traditional racial group, one day a year to celebrate Asian cultures)?
- Do the materials and activities emphasize differences among groups and cultures without addressing common bonds, histories, and aspirations (e.g., collaborations between Blacks and Native Americans, Black-Jewish cooperation)?
- Do the materials and activities convey that people who belong to the same ethnic or racial group are all the same (no diversity of diversity)?
- Does the activity stress membership in a particular culture group at the expense of each child's total and unique background, including language, culture, family, nation of origin, community, religion? Does it imply that racial and ethnic diversity are the most important, or the only, areas of diversity?
- Does the activity force multiracial and multiethnic children either to be invisible or to choose an incomplete identity? Must they select only one of their backgrounds?
- Do the activities and materials indicate in some way that one group, culture, religion, language, or art form is the best or better than another (for example, the preferred jobs are held by White men, the less preferred by women and minorities)?

From F. Wardle, *Introduction to Early Childhood Education*, 2003. Used by permission.

social or purposeful one. This language justified the taking of native lands by "more goal-directed" mainstream Whites, who "traveled" or "settled" their way west.

- Referring to multiracial and multiethnic persons as ambivalent, unhappy, dysfunctional, maladjusted, mixed up or messed up, tormented, and pathological "tragic mulattoes."
- Using the word *bilingual* to mean English and Spanish, as opposed to *any* two languages.

Cosmetic Bias.   This bias offers the appearance of inclusiveness and creates the "illusion of equity," luring consumers into purchasing books that appear current, diverse, and balanced. However, beyond the superficial appearance biases prevail—for example, in a science textbook that features an attractive pullout of female scientists but includes little about the scientific contributions of women, or a music book with a bright, multiethnic cover that belies the White male composers dominating its pages. Further, textbooks and popular media present images of lighter-skinned persons of color, who tend to be more "palatable" to mainstream Whites, and often their own group, yet they rarely discuss these people's multiracial heritage.

Culturally Authentic Bias

Unfortunately, just because a book is "multicultural" doesn't mean it is free of bias. In fact, the very labeling of curricular materials as multicultural is **tokenism** of its own kind. Many curricular materials from other countries are full of gender, racial, and socioeconomic biases. For example, most folktales and children's literature from Latin America and Latino communities in the this country present White Europeans, usually Spaniards or Portuguese, in position of authority and wealth, while portraying people of color as powerless and poor. White characters are presented as the models of beauty, intelligence, courage, righteousness, and enterprise: the preferred race. Characters of color are ugly, dumb, cowardly, superstitious, and lazy. Materials for government schools in these countries reflect these biases.

Authentic literature, the common stories and folktales of various cultures and countries, often presents women in subservient roles and focuses on the importance of women's beauty and servitude to men. The book's illustrations reinforce these gender inequalities.

As teachers become more sensitive to the diverse needs of these students, they must learn how to select bias-free materials (see Chapter Feature on page 191). This is particularly important when it comes to multiethnic and multiracial materials, because very few cultures have developed a healthy acceptance of these children and people—and thus they are not reflected in a positive light in songs, artwork, stories, and classical literature. It is dishonest and lazy to simply assume that because a piece of material is not mainstream White and is "culturally authentic" that it is unbiased.

Chapter Feature
Culturally Authentic Bias

Growing up biracial in Puerto Rico made me aware at a very young age of the racism in Latino culture. Although my family and friends called me "trigueña" (wheat-colored), I recall classmates' and even teachers' calling me "negativo" (photo negative) because, while I resemble my mother, she is White and I am dark-skinned. Because I attended a predominantly White school they told me, "Eres una mosca en un vaso de leche" (You are a fly in a glass of milk), which also meant that I was Black/White biracial. Children laughed and called me "Cucarachita Martina" (Martina Cockroach), a very popular folktale character most Puerto Rican children grow up with. Historically, Spanish women (as do other women around the world) powdered their faces to appear lighter. Even today in Puerto Rico, Black women are mockingly called "Cucarachas empolvás" (powdered cockroaches), which means that Black women have to and want to lighten themselves. I was reminded "No eres arroz con leche" (You are not rice with milk). Rice with milk is a hot cereal for children in Puerto Rico. It is also a popular expression for light-skinned and often preferred children—as white as rice and milk and just as desirable or sweet. This is not uncommon to other cultures. In the United States light-skinned children with rosy cheeks are often called "peaches and cream," blond children are "milk and honey."

When I dressed in my best, I was taunted, "La Puerca de Juan Bobo" (Juan Bobo's Pig), which is another popular folktale. Juan Bobo is a mentally disabled and poor child living in the mountains of Puerto Rico. He does nothing right. In several stories, Juan Bobo dresses the family pig with his mother's clothing. Juan Bobo represents a mockery of the poor mountain folk and of people with disabilities. The jíbaro is also the true Puerto Rican and a racially mixed person; the product of three cultures: Taíno Indian, African, and Spaniard.

Arroz Con Leche, Cucarachita Martina, and Juan Bobo are part of the rich Puerto Rican oral tradition. I grew up disliking those stories and characters and shied away from using them in my own classroom when I became a teacher, because they always brought back painful memories of how I was abused in school—memories of how people of color, and even racially mixed people, are outcasts in their own countries. Each time I looked into the faces of my students—faces that mirrored the Black, Indigenous, and racially mixed heritage of Latin America—I was reminded how deeply racism hurts.

From *Rethinking Schools* (Fall 1998), reprinted with permission of Marta Cruz-Janzen.

Making Learning Meaningful

One of the most effective instructional techniques for all students is meaningful learning—making the activity of interest to every child. Meaningful learning is effective because it involves intrinsic motivation and continually challenges the child, and because information that is meaningful to the learner is more easily remembered (Ormrod, 1999). This technique is particularly effective with multi-ethnic and multiracial children, because so little of what they learn directly relates to their own unique experiences. Teachers can use meaningful learning by finding out each child's interests, discovering as much as possible about the child's home and family life and spending individual time discussing the child's hobbies, dreams, loves, and fears. Teachers can also conference with parents about student's individual interests and aspirations.

Another way to encourage meaningful learning is to provide learning opportunities with lots of real choices—how a project is to be conducted, materials to be used, and the content to cover. When choices are provided, students select the content and approach that is most meaningful to them. Finally, meaningfulness is achieved by a teacher and student working together to create the goals and objectives of a project, collaboratively deciding on the end product, and then deciding on the rubric to be used to evaluate the task (Clark, 1997). Students gain ownership of their learning, which always makes it more meaningful.

Specific Suggestions for Instructional Techniques

Once teachers have selected their materials, they then develop activities to implement the curriculum. Clearly, there are many more ideas than we can present here, and we encourage teachers to creatively develop their own. Further, there is also some natural overlap between ideas presented in Chapter 7 and those discussed here. Finally, teachers will have to creatively adapt and differentiate these ideas depending on the age of their students, but most can be used with children from preschool to twelfth grade.

Support Different Learning Styles

Make sure you use all eight of Gardner's intelligences—logical-mathematical, linguistic, spatial, musical, bodily kinesthetic, interpersonal, intrapersonal, and naturalist—as well as various learning styles when teaching students (Gardner, 1983). In this way each child has the opportunity to succeed, regardless of the student's individual form(s) of intelligences and learning styles. Further, this approach helps develop the whole child, and not just specific, narrow aspects of his or her abilities. Allow students to show knowledge and mastery using the intelligence they are most effective with, while also encouraging them to expand their repertoire of skills. Students can demonstrate what they have learned through art, drama, writing, constructing, mathematics, logic, music, group presentations, or individual projects.

Support Healthy Racial Identity Development

Create opportunities to openly discuss racial identities in realistic and affirming ways. But remember many of the students will have multiethnic and multiracial

Chapter Feature
Analysis of a Teaching Unit

1. **Do the lesson content and strategies promote or impede educational equity?**
The approach should allow all students to learn using the approach they are most effective and most comfortable with: learning styles (Gardner, 1983), enactive, iconic, or symbolic representation (Bruner, 1972); language; small group cooperative, or individual activity. Parents of every child should be able to contribute as a resource for the activity, and students should be given the opportunity to show what they have learned in a way that maximizes their performance (Clark, 1997). One way of achieving all of these approaches is for the teacher to meet individually with each student to plan the activity, develop the mode of assessment, and discuss the rubric used to access the student's accomplishment. This way the teacher can ensure he or she is meeting content and other standards, while the child will feel some direct involvement in the content and activity (Clark, 1997).

2. **Do the lesson content and strategies make use of or help to develop collaborative, empowering relationships among parents, students, and teachers?**
All students should expect to work in a variety of groups that are racially, ethnically, gender, and ability heterogeneous. The lesson should involve research that uses parents and extended family members as resources—material and human—to collect historical and cultural information. Forms should be sent to parents about the unit and ways they can contribute to its fruition. These communications must be in the parents' familiar language and be written in a user-friendly way that is both easy to understand and empowers the parents. A culminating community activity where students can present products they created should be part of the unit.

3. **Do the lesson content and strategies promote cultural pluralism in society or intergroup harmony in the classroom?**
Efforts must be made to provide a variety of viewpoints for every curricular unit. A unit on Westward expansion must include the view of Western Native tribes; Latinos living in what became New Mexico, California, Texas, Arizona, and New Mexico; and various immigrant groups who were enticed to this country to help build the railroads, build cities and grow crops, and mine gold. These viewpoints must include the issues of race, ethnicity, culture and language, and various religions (Native American, Latino Catholicism, various religions from China, Japan, and the Philippines, and, of course, mainstream Protestantism). In any study of cowboys, Black cowboys must be significantly represented (Katz, 2002). A discussion of the contribution to the development of the West by newly freed slaves after

(continued)

Chapter Feature Continued

the Civil War must also be included. Students should also study the various ways these groups worked together and intermarriage between people from different ethnic, racial, national, and religious groups. Finally, the forced movement and resettlement of Native Americans along the Trail of Tears must be included. The goal is to provide multiple perspectives—those that represent the students' backgrounds, and those that represent other backgrounds.

4. **Does the lesson content help to increase student's knowledge of various cultural, ethnic, religious, national, and linguistic perspectives?**

One major goal of an educational unit is to advance students' understanding of fundamental concepts beyond their current knowledge: religion, history, creation of the world, art, race/ethnicity, political and economic structures, national approaches to education, history and equality, immigration, democracy, family structures, etc. However, the teacher must avoid the temptation to teach about racial, cultural, and ethnic groups; rather, the teacher should help students deconstruct conventional notions of racial, ethnic, and cultural boundaries (Root, 1996). All students in U.S. schools need knowledge about the movement of cultures, religions, languages, and people across the world; the interactions of cultures, religions, and languages, and the rich history of people overcoming artificial "group" boundaries.

All students in our schools need accurate information about the world's peoples, such as the Mayan Indians in Guatemala.

Chapter Feature **Continued**

Students can study the impact of jazz and folk music on western classical music, and the influence of folk, tribal, and religious art in twentieth century visual arts; the number of native words in Brazilian languages (*para*= water; *catu*= beautiful: *Paracatu*= beautiful water) and non-English words in contemporary American; the adoption and success of European games such as cricket, baseball (from a game called rounders), soccer by countries colonized by European countries (the success of Brazilians in the game of soccer, originally brought to Brazil by a British soccer enthusiast, is a well-known example), and the adoption of non-European games, such as polo, by Europeans. The possibilities are endless!

From Davidman & Davidman (1997).

identities. Never present race or ethnicity as a single-group idea. Honestly deal with students' queries about racial issues in developmentally appropriate ways, using books, other people, and developmentally appropriate responses.

Use art activities that encourage children to represent people of diverse racial backgrounds and to explore their own unique physical characteristics. Encourage children to experiment with human physical characteristics, especially skin color, hair texture, and others. For younger children, mirrors are a must! Find ways to affirm every child's unique identity—mainstream White students, students of color, and multiethnic and multiracial students. Make sure all students understand that their unique background is rich with diversity, culture, and uniqueness that should be proudly displayed for the whole world to see. Provide activities that involve the child's home language, nation, profession, race and ethnicity, history, and immigration status in these projects. Create family trees using resources such as *Do People Grow on Family Trees? Genealogy for Kids and Other Beginners* (1991) and *Are Those Kids Yours? American Families with Children Adopted from Other Countries* (1990).

Never, ever, put down White people when trying to elevate the self-esteem of children of color. Remember, many multiethnic and multiracial children have some White heritage; further, building up the self-esteem of one group by putting another group down is a very dangerous practice, especially around children who are in the process of developing their biases toward people who are different from them. *Never, ever*, expect multiethnic and multiracial students to ignore part of their background to engage in a classroom activity. And, never let other students expect them to do the same.

Provide Adult Role Models and Use the Community

Present real-life role models of multiethnic and multiracial persons in the classroom. Also present symbolic role models in books, movies, plays, and videos. Seek advice and support from interethnic and interracial families in your class, school, and community. Constantly find ways to confer with parents of multiracial and multiethnic children about their needs, concerns, and strengths they can contribute to the program. Talk to the parents of interethnic and/or interracial children in your class about how to best address issues of racial identity with their own children as well as their children's classmates.

In the article "Student Teachers Efforts to Promote Self-Esteem in Navajo Pupils," Laura Stachowski (1998) writes, "Other activities included interviewing elders; bringing in local Navajo artists, historians, and others to talk about their work; researching contemporary issues affecting Navajo people; presenting historical information from a Navajo-American perspective; and researching the Anasazi's complex knowledge and use of constellations." Overall, student teachers heeded Gilliland's (1995) recommendations that, "the Indian culture should become an integral part of the basic instruction"—including cultural concepts, values, and historical and contemporary contributions (p. 11). "In so doing, the student teachers also became learners in the process, with their pupils often leading the way" (Stachowski, 1998, p. 343). In the same way, teachers must allow multiethnic and multiracial students to lead them in learning about their history, values, and the culture of multiethnic and multiracial peoples: history, heroes, contemporary contributions, and issues.

Treat All Children as Unique Individuals

Interact with every child as a unique individual with personal needs that can be met by a kind and sensitive teacher. Always relate to your students as individuals who have unique ethnic, racial, and cultural characteristics and experiences, never as "members of such and such a group." Be supportive of interethnic and interracial parents; give them resources to help provide a healthy home to raise their children; help them find resources in the community to support their families and help raise their children.

Don't Allow Biased Behavior or Language

Confront any student who questions the loyalty or ethnic pride of a multiethnic/ multiracial student (or his or her parents); confront any student who uses biased, racist, or sexist language; and confront any school employee—teacher, administrator, or support staff—who says derogatory things about interracial relationships, expresses the belief that interracial relationships are a sign of minority disloyalty, undermines minority cultures, and weakens the marriage market (Kennedy, 2003). If derogatory language persists, and multiethnic, multiracial children continue to experience harassment and put-downs, you have a professional responsibility to address the problem with administration—who have a responsibility to do something about it!

Do not allow single-race students to continually question multiethnic and multiracial students with "Well, what are you anyway?" Use Maria Root's Bill of Rights for Racially Mixed People (see page 11) to help single-race children understand multiethnic and multiracial children. Respond immediately if you hear students say things like "You can't play basketball, that's for the Black kids" or "Why are you playing soccer? That's a White game."

Provide Small Groups and Cooperative Learning

Create plenty of opportunities for children of diverse backgrounds to interact cooperatively with each other, and make sure you don't perpetuate the hidden curriculum that students of the same race should always be together. This is particularly critical in middle and high school. Provide opportunities for children to learn in small groups and in pairs.

Protest strenuously any time the school sponsors any event—guest speaker, conference, lecture, etc.—that supports single-race/ethnicity as the preferred way of grouping students. For example, several years ago the Denver Public Schools sponsored an event only for Black male students. No one else was allowed to attend. This is obviously unacceptable in any true approach to diversity and multicultural education.

Provide Lots of Opportunities to Explore Race and Racism in This Country

Point out to students any curricular content that is biased and prejudicial—also when it is from so-called respected and famous people.

Help students understand that all people have biases and prejudices, that power and control come in every color, and that no group is exempt from racism.

Help and support multiethnic and multiracial children in filling out official school forms. Advocate for them with the school administration; let the students know that providing "racial and ethnic identification information" is voluntary; support them if they choose not to fill in the forms or choose to write in "multiethnic" or "multiracial." If the school administration insists they fill out the traditional OMB forms (allowing for only one race, or the "other" choice), organize multiethnic and multiracial students in an anti-bias attempt to resist this unacceptable requirement.

Don't Stereotype Any of Your Students

Challenge all your students to do their very best at all times. Never allow students to make excuses, such as "my teacher doesn't like me because she's White," for not doing their best.

Read stories featuring characters—and families—that are interethnic and/or interracial. This is particularly important for multiethnic and multiracial children who have little direct contact with children like them. Gay's *Rainbow Effect* (1987), *Of Many Colors* (Kaeser & Gillespie, 1997), *You Be Me, I'll Be You* (Mandelbaum, 1990) are a few examples.

If a multiethnic/multiracial student is having problems at school, do not automatically assume these problems are caused by the child's background. At the same time, understand that the child's background poses unique challenges for the child—especially in defining his or her identity in relationship to single-race peers and teachers (Wehrly, Kenney, & Kenney, 1999).

Be very careful when referring multiethnic/multiracial children and children of color for special education services. Remember, once labeled, these children often remain labeled for the rest of their school experience; further, the label often solidifies for the school community the belief that these children cannot succeed. Make sure you fully challenge special education students in your classroom. If any of these children are twice exceptional (special education and gifted), find ways to meet their unique challenges. These children have a tremendous need for positive self-esteem, healthy racial identity development, and meaningful and challenging activities, projects, and integrated learning opportunities.

Determine with the parents and special education teacher whether the placement is truly accurate, and/or whether it is time for the children to re-enter the general school population. Suggest to the parents that they investigate a 504 placement, which allows the child's unique needs to be met without a special education label. Kealan, the son of Francis Wardle and Ruth Benjamin-Wardle, was labeled with a disability. After many arguments with his son's school—and actually becoming so disillusioned that he would no longer even meet with teachers at conference time, Francis finally succumbed to his son's request to be taken out of the special education category and had the school assign a 504 designation instead. (Special education requirements are part of the IDEA law; 504 is a component of the Civil Rights requirement that all students must be treated equally, and it is enforced by the U.S. Department of Justice.)

Create Appropriate Instructional Materials

Help students deconstruct books, curricular materials, and popular classroom materials to bring to light bias, prejudice, and anti-mixed race beliefs and biases, using the various instruments and approaches discussed in this chapter and Chapter 7.

Provide lots of opportunities for students to develop and create accurate curricular materials for the classroom. Older students can also create materials for younger students.

Be creative in constructing unique approaches to teaching required materials. Francis Wardle has often visualized designing a U.S. history or social studies unit, from pre-Civil War to the present time, using as the core texts Frederic Douglass's three wonderful autobiographies (Douglass, 1994), a biography of Paul Robeson, and James Earl Jones's delightful autobiography. Each of these books brings a minority perspective to our history, and each of these famous people was very involved in many important aspects of our country's history: slavery, abolition, women's suffrage, reconstruction, the Civil War, the Spanish Civil War and World War II, the cold war, the **McCarthy era**, Jim Crow laws, civil disobedience, and various civil rights accomplishments (Frederic Douglass' meeting with John Brown immediately before Harper's Ferry is a classic historical episode) (Douglass, 1994). Each has a connection to multiethnic and multiracial issues—Douglass, of course, was multiracial and married a White woman (and wrote affirmatively about multiracial identity); Paul Robeson was the first Black Othello to kiss a White Desdemona, and his son married a White (Jewish) woman; James Earl Jones proudly acknowledges his Irish heritage and his White Irish American wife.

Conclusion

Teachers are instrumental in setting the climate for all children in the school. While they lack full control of the curriculum—and have less and less influence on pedagogy—they still dictate the attitudes, values, and the quality of interactions that occur in the classroom. Teachers also define and control the amount and quality of interactions they have with parents, which is critically important for each child's school success. Teachers must be aware of this power and must understand how their own race, ethnicity, and culture affect their interactions with these students and parents—especially those whose backgrounds are different from their own. Thus teachers need to carefully assess their own ethnicity, culture, and worldview. Because multiethnic and multiracial students are almost always totally invisible in schools, teachers must be particularly sensitive to their needs and learn instructional approaches that will both enhance their positive self-identity and increase their social and academic success. Finally, teachers must never allow students who are different—including multiethnic and multiracial students—to experience harassment, hostility, and/or put-downs from students and school staff.

Questions/Projects

1. Examine the "Forms of Bias in Curricular Materials and Programs" (Sadker & Sadker, 2002) and how each is reflected in the schools' curricula.

2. Discuss one form of bias, "invisibility," that particularly affects multiethnic and multiracial children.

3. Reflect back on your own school experience. Are there times when a teacher did or said something that you believe was biased, racist, and/or insensitive?

4. Discuss how biases and stereotypes affect all students: females, males, minority students, multiethnic and multiracial students, and mainstream White students. Give specific examples.

5. Visit a school and walk through while observing signs of the forms of bias. How are they represented? What messages do you think they convey to the children attending that school?

6. Use the Materials and Activities checklist to examine children's storybooks for biases. Discuss how you could use these stories to help your students understand biases. Discuss ways you can get unbiased books into your classroom.

Resources

Article

Loren Katz, L. (2002). Know your roots. *Raising Black and Biracial Children*, 7 (1), 32–33.

Website

Multicultural resources
http://www.eastern.edu/publications/emme (volume 3, #2)

9

Teaching Teachers

The establishment of a firm, healthy, and positive self-identity in children is strongly influenced by parents, extended family, peers, and teachers. Each plays a major role in facilitating a child's acceptance and security in all aspects of his or her identity, including gender, ethnicity, and race. Teachers are influential in the presentation of information crucial to a child's identity development, as well as nurturing and expecting supportive peer interaction in the classroom. As has been widely said, "A teacher sets the cultural climate of the classroom," which can support or devastate children. Although the National Council for Accreditation of Teacher Education (NCATE) established a multicultural standard for the accreditation of programs for teacher education, little progress has been made in preparing teachers to handle the increasing demands posed by an ever more diverse student population. A survey of 255 elementary, middle, and high school principals showed that principals believe preservice teachers need better preparation for working effectively with diverse students, particularly in urban settings (Truog, 1998). Few teacher education programs prepare teachers to work effectively with diverse students, their families, and communities.

This chapter examines some of the challenges faced in preparing teachers in cross-cultural competency and presents suggestions for ways to prepare teachers who are more aware of and sensitive to diverse student populations. Further, our focus is on ways to extend these approaches to prepare teachers to affirm and support multiethnic and multiracial students and to celebrate all interethnic and interracial diversity, including their own. While this chapter focuses on preparing P–12 teachers to effectively implement curricula for multiracial and multiethnic children, we believe that it takes the entire school community—teachers, paraprofessionals, administrators, and other professional staff—to create a healthy, empowering school climate.

Focus Questions

1. Who should teach multicultural education to college students preparing to become teachers?

2. Why have traditional multicultural classes failed to prepare teachers to provide for the needs of multiracial and multiethnic children and their families?

3. How does the fact that most teachers are White, middle-class women affect our ability to meet the needs of the increasing number of children of color in our schools?

4. Why are minority teachers often insensitive and unknowledgeable about supporting multiracial and multiethnic children and their families?

5. How can we place multicultural education at the center of teacher preparation programs?

The Nature of Public Education

Francis Wardle spent time in the Highlands of Guatemala working with the Mayan Indians after the devastating earthquake of 1976. While his main role was to assist in rebuilding a village destroyed by the earthquake, his interests in education and culture led him to examine the local educational process. One day he observed a social studies class in the local public elementary school. To his amazement, both the book used by the class and the teacher's lecture placed the small country of **Belize** (formerly British Honduras) within the political borders of Guatemala. Belize has been independent since it was granted freedom from Britain; before that it was part of the British Commonwealth. It has never been a part of Guatemala. However, because Belize was part the old Spanish Colonial Empire from which Guatemala wrestled its freedom in 1863, Guatemalan children are still taught that Belize belongs to Guatemala (Wardle, 1976).

Public schools teach the political view of a country as codified by the country's decision makers. In all societies education has been considered the preferred vehicle for indoctrinating the next generation, in this society as anywhere else. Today our contemporary curricular content is academic basics, computer skills, and a view of history based on and perpetuated by those who lead the country—determined by national standards, national initiatives, and state legislation. In this light, multicultural education is not seen as a necessity, and opponents of multicultural education contend that "*it*" detracts from the important content that needs to be taught. Thus, because multicultural education is not seen as an integral and natural part of the curriculum, teachers tend to describe multicultural education as "doing *it*" (Nieto, 1994). It is usually an add-on to the curriculum, something extra that has to be done with not enough time or resources, after the official, important curriculum is covered, resulting in many teacher education programs across the nation deemphasizing the subject and requiring minimal multicultural education courses.

College curricula for future teachers are devised by state education experts and college professors, and not by participating students. These experts tend to have several basic views of public education and the role of public institutions in preparing teachers:

1. Curriculum is about content.
2. We must teach teachers how to teach to the average student.
3. The needs of any student who is not average—special needs students, English as a second language students, and minority students—are to be met by specific courses on how to adapt or "compensate" the prototype curriculum to their needs. In other words these students are viewed as having deficits compared to "normal" students (Wardle, 2003).

Thus, it is not surprising that many students entering teacher multicultural education courses still expect to start by learning all about how to do "*it*," how to teach children who are not as proficient or prepared as they were. They are always surprised and confused when told that first they are going to study themselves: their gender, racial, ethnic, cultural, socioeconomic, and physical (ability, disability, and appearance) socialization. As long as mainstream Whites— and educational curricula and materials—continue viewing Whites as the norm— the standard—against whom all others must be judged and measured, and then expecting others to explain themselves, they will not be prepared to work with diverse students.

Clearly, the lack of an emphasis on providing future teachers with information and skills to assist them in working effectively with diverse student populations is a direct reflection of our society's views about education. Not surprising, since this country still does not even acknowledge that multiethnic and multiracial students even exist, teachers are not taught how to how to meet their needs!

Preparing Future Teachers

Looking the Monster in the Eye

Frykholm (1997), Ooka Pang (2001), and many others endorse radical changes in the way teachers are prepared for working with diverse student populations. Advocates believe education programs that prepare future teachers should assist their students' introspection and self-awareness. These suggestions are based on two ideas: (1) People cannot affirm diversity in others until they affirm their own, and (2) there can be no educational equity without a deep understanding of what constitutes equity and diversity. Further, issues of equity involve an understanding of social inequities and how to create learning environments that are fair and accessible for all students, regardless of social and/or other backgrounds. Educational preparation programs need to demand critical analysis and personal reflections that challenge how people view the world and their position within it—and, as teachers, their position within the educational world (Goodman, 1997).

Many college students are often very defensive and resistant to multicultural classes (Ooka Pang, 1994). This resistance is primarily from students who have had little, if any, exposure to curricular content dealing with diversity and/or multiculturalism in P–12 education (Goodman, 1997; Howard, 1993). Most of these students are mainstream Whites, who will remain the numerical majority of teachers in the foreseeable future. Another problem with multicultural education is the assumption by many that its only purpose is to enable students of color to study, be exposed to, and learn from persons and groups of color. Whites are seen as not needing multicultural education (Banks & Banks, 1997). Thus, it is only needed in schools having "diverse" students, or students of color. Additionally, even when multicultural education courses are offered and/or required, most fail to address ethnically and racially mixed children—one of our fastest growing student populations.

Teachers of Teachers

Almost all teacher preparation courses are taught by faculty with graduate degrees. However, nationally there are very few institutions that offer graduate degrees, particularly doctorates, in multicultural education. As a result, many people who teach multicultural education courses lack adequate preparation

Chapter Feature
Teacher Preparation Programs

Based on adult learning concepts, teacher education should include the following:

- Students need to be empowered by the instructor to evaluate their strengths, weaknesses, and professional goals, and then plan their learning.
- A variety of methods should be used by the instructor to enable students to evaluate their experiences critically and to grow from them in working with children, families, and communities.

- Learning should be planned around the specific tasks professionals face—planning, working with parents, discipline issues, managing the classroom, and so on.
- The content of the curriculum must start with immediate professional concerns of the educator, placed within the context of theoretical perspectives and examined under the microscope of critical pedagogy.

From Wardle (2003).

Chapter Feature
Student Profile: Monica

Monica is a Latina Black. Both of her parents are from Mexico, but her mother is White Mexican and her father is Black Mexican. She considers herself biracial; however, she sometimes identifies as Black/African American, "if I have to choose," because she has always been rejected by the Mexicans. Although Monica is living proof to the contrary, Mexican Americans often challenge her, "There are no Black people in Mexico." "In Mexico there are plenty others just like me," Monica adds. Monica feels that part of the problem is that in the United States, people, including Mexicans, want to be as mainstream White as possible. The darker people are, the more they are a reminder of how much farther they have to go. "The lighter you are the more stripes you have. They see me as Black, and they don't want to be Black."

Monica had a reputation for being in fights "all through school" and being openly aggressive and defiant with teachers and other adults. In high school she remembers a Latino/White teacher commenting to another teacher, right in front of her, that, "she really is not Latina. Latinos [Hispanics] are persons whose lineage is from Spain. Being from a Spanish-speaking country does not make her Latina [Hispanic]." Mexican students always teased Monica, "They would call me 'nigger' or something derogatory and make fun of my hair. They said that my mom was not really my mom." Yet the Black/African American students did not like her either, "because I am light-complected, have long hair, and look mixed. They said that the teachers treated me like I was better than them and that I talked like a White girl, just because I don't talk like them." Monica feels that the Mexican students were the cruelest, more so than the African American and mainstream White students.

Monica is also very angry that teachers at her schools knew about the harassment, overheard it, but did nothing about it. Monica feels that most persons in U.S. society are afraid to deal with diversity because it reminds them of who they are. She concludes, "We are all racially mixed. Look at the history of Europeans mixing with the Indians. Whites [mainstream] don't want to admit that; Latinos don't want to admit that; nobody does because everyone wants to be White. I know people, including teachers, who are not White, but they deny it and say they are White, White, White."

(Cruz-Janzen, 2000). Further, a graduate degree in multicultural education is usually from a college department of single-race studies—African American, Latino, Asian, etc. (or a combination of education, psychology, sociology, and a single-race department). There are no departments of multiracial/multiethnic studies in our universities. Also people who provide diversity training at the school district level—principals, curriculum developers, and staff development experts—are also poorly versed in multicultural education.

Many mainstream White faculty often express fear and apprehension about teaching diversity and multicultural content and/or in raising discussions about equity (Ayvazian, 1997; Cruz-Janzen, 1997; Gonsalves-Pinto, 1997). Further, students of all backgrounds perceive mainstream White professors as not being prepared and/or interested enough to teach diversity and multiculturalism and lacking credibility. "I always felt the professor was disconnected from the subject." Most mainstream White professors that students experienced treated the subject as trivial and expected students of color in their courses to serve as the "diversity experts": "There were these group presentations and the students go through their own experiences." Conversely, many minority professors know little about minority groups beyond their own and often concentrate on issues of hatred, discrimination, and White guilt—providing teachers with little in the way of culturally competent approaches to working with all sorts of diverse students. Almost no diversity professors—including minorities—know anything of the needs of multiethnic and multiracial students.

Students add that all educators must experience diversity and discrimination within authentic contexts: *So they can speak from a perspective of knowing*. However, race or ethnicity should not be a barrier to teaching multicultural education to future teachers. Anyone with enough commitment and effort could become knowledgeable, understanding, and empathetic—to teach other students. Tragically, many often expect that only persons of color are qualified, or equipped, to teach about racial and ethnic diversity, which often gives students the impression that this is the only class they are qualified to teach. Francis Wardle believes that being White enables him to extract discussions and confessions from White students without their feeling defensive, guilt ridden, or attacked. Further, as a European White man who has learned about racism and discrimination, he feels a particular empathy with other mainstream White teachers whom he wishes to influence.

Even when there are official multicultural courses in colleges, they often provide little valuable information. They deal with diversity and multiculturalism perfunctorily by simply covering the [one and only] chapter in the text and then moving on to "business as usual": "There is one chapter in the book that is multicultural. Our professor talked about multicultural education issues but never did anything. It is not put into practice in the education courses. The next day you are told to do it. We are told, 'Do as I say, not as I do.'"

Critical Pedagogy

As we discussed in Chapter 8, student teachers should discover who they are and should have ample opportunities to explore their own race/ethnicity, to investigate power and privilege, and to understand how people develop into racial beings (Derman-Sparks & Phillips, 1997; Howard, 1999; Wiest, 1998).

Paulo Freire (1970), the great Brazilian adult educator, developed the concept of **critical pedagogy**—the idea that while students are learning the basics of a skill or trade, in this case, teacher education, they must be critical thinkers of what they are learning *at the same time*. He believed critical pedagogy involved thinking about the power relationships in a society that create and maintain socially constructed knowledge. Thus, teacher candidates should continually examine both the content of what they are learning and the way they are teaching it, as they relate to the education and success of all their students—including minority and multiethnic and multiracial students (Ooka Pang, 1994; Truog, 1998). Teachers must also examine the role of the public school teacher within society and determine to what extent teachers perpetuate unequal and unjust educational approaches—in expectations, special education, gifted programs, athletics, segregation within the school, and the hidden curriculum.

Curricular Content

Even student educators who attended urban high schools demonstrate alarming ignorance of even the most minimal knowledge of non-Eurocentric content. Students of color who were recent high school graduates state, "You are taught as soon as you get in the schools that Europe's way is everything. No other group is ever included in a text. So it's kind of subliminal but you know it's there" (Cruz-Janzen, 1997, p. 172); and, "I didn't ever learn about any Blacks that did things that achieved . . . I don't remember sitting in one history class and learning about anybody but White men achieving" (p. 203). Contributions of women in history are also often ignored—in science, politics, the arts, and literature (Sadker & Sadker, 1994). Understandably, most student teachers cannot name any important person, dead or alive, who is multiethnic and/or multiracial, since these people are either invisible in the school's curricula or labeled only with the person's minority or lowest status heritage. For example, there's a wonderful little museum at O'Hare Airport dedicated to famous women. The biological sketch of the famous ballet dancer Maria Tallchief accurately mentions her Osage chief father but simply ignores her mother (Irish/Scottish White).

Everyone must have positive role models—including role models in literature and history—and teachers can play an important role in providing children of all backgrounds with the information they need to establish themselves as valued and contributing members of society. A participant in a study expressed this view:

> I think for me what's really important is history, knowing how people came here and what contributions they've made. For example, the African American experience is different. But after that experience, what contributions? What did happen? [What about] the Latino experience of the Western Movement and how land was taken from the Latinos as well as from the Native Americans? Not just sixth grade but through college. Encompassing. How the Asians have their own Ellis Island—an island in the South Pacific that most Asian Americans came through. The Japanese internment in the 1940s is two pages in a history book, if that. The Alamo is a column and a half. These are some of the little things that ultimately I think would make a difference for everyone, not just biethnic, biracial, bicultural, but everyone. Understanding who they are. (Cruz-Janzen, 1997)

Chapter Feature
Student Profile: Russell

Russell, Navajo and African American, now 29 years old.

Russell is the first child in the family born outside the Navajo Reservation. He has a younger sister who was also born off the reservation as well as five older siblings. His mother is Navajo Native American and his father is African American. Both sides of the family maintained close contact with each other until his paternal grandmother died and his grandfather remarried an African American woman who is "not interested in Indians." Russell self-identifies as both Navajo and Black. Physically, he could be considered Native American, African American, Asian, Hawaiian, Samoan, or Middle Eastern. "People find it amazing that I say that I am Black and I am Indian. A lot of them are real fascinated that they are actually in the presence of someone of that combination."

"I know some Indian people who want nothing to do with Indian ways because they think it's dirty, they think

it's low. Our kids are conditioned from an early age that they have to select one, and that's part of the problem."

As a child, Russell thought that he was the only African American Navajo in the world besides his brothers and sisters. In elementary school he was pressured by his peers to choose only one of his backgrounds. "We were in class, in first grade, I remember sitting down and the Mexican kids kind of went their way and the White kids their way. I knew I was Indian so I separated myself. During that time it was hard and I didn't have anybody older than me explaining what I was going through." His peers would tell him that he was more African American than Native American and therefore he was African American.

With his parents' and family's support, he stood firm and felt comfortable saying: "I'm Black and here's my dad to prove it, but I am also Navajo and here's my mom."

Sociopolitical Construction of Multiethnic and Multiracial Persons

"What are you?" Multiethnic and/or multiracial children are constantly harassed with this question. The implication is that they are not normal. "What do you mean? Am I a dog? Am I a boy or what?" These are too often the thoughts such questioning brings forth. Children's behavioral and psychological development is impaired when they are not able to establish a healthy and firm sense of personal identity, which is strongly grounded in an individual's social context—especially in school—and includes gender, social class, ethnicity, race, and physical appearance (Morrison & Bordere, 2001). If a person's identity is not clear to others, then maybe it will not be clear to him or her. A person of mainstream White and Latino parentage explains,

Maria Luiza's father is Spanish (White), her mother is Morena (mixed), and she speaks Portuguese. What is her identity? How should teachers support it?

Multiethnic and multiracial children struggle to establish a firm self-identity in a society highly polarized and antagonized along an unrelenting Black versus White dichotomy. They are often caught in the difficult dilemma of juggling the ethnicity and/or race of each parent without compromising either one and feeling guilt and shame for betraying one parent. Lack of information and knowledge about persons like themselves makes many multiethnic and multiracial children feel abnormal, isolated, and unfit, unable to fit in or belong anywhere. Biethnic and biracial children develop low self-esteem because they don't have a "real good hold on what they are. Not a real good, clear self-concept about what the two sides mean, what that means to you, what that means to the rest of the world." One of their biggest challenges is trying to find a way to "fit in."

Experts within the mental health field believe that children with multiple heritages experience added difficulties developing ethnic and racial self-identity and self-concept, including difficulty adjusting to educational settings (Bradshaw, 1992; Funderburg, 1994; Nishimura, 1995; Olumide, 2002). Some professionals, in fact, perpetuate the view of the marginal, dysfunctional, degenerate multiethnic and multiracial child. Francis interviewed Alvin Poussaint, the Black psychiatrist and *Cosby Show* consultant, about his view on this topic. Francis asked him why he had changed his view of multiethnic and multiracial children from one of being dysfunctional and confused to one of being potentially very successful. He replied that his initial view was based on what he had been taught in his graduate studies in psychiatry. His new view was based on his own experience and studies of multiethnic and multiracial students (Poussaint, 1984). Another reason why many experts believe multiethnic and multiracial children face problems is that all identity models used in psychology and psychiatry are for single-race and single-ethnicity people. Thus, the field has no "body of knowledge" to use in working with these children and their families; therefore, they must be abnormal (as compared to single-race people).

There are, however, more and more highly successful and competent multiethnic and multiracial children, as Poussaint (1984) discovered, who are very popular at school, experience academic and athletic success, and have extremely high self-esteem. RaEsa, the Black/White daughter of Francis Wardle, is a 17-year-old in the International Baccalaureate Program, the National Honor Society, and the lacrosse team. She has a part-time job, visits friends in France, Hollywood, and New York, and is very much a typical social 17-year-old girl. Currently, she is applying for college in Colorado, the East Coast, and England.

Multiethnic and Multiracial Students Need to See Themselves in Their Curricula

Multiracial and multiethnic students—including students in college—need to see and read about people who are like them. They are often surprised when they learn that highly acclaimed people such as Alexandre Dumas, the most famous author in France during the 1800s; Mexican muralist Diego Rivera, the most acclaimed painter of the "Spanish Americas"; Antonio Francisco Lisboa, the most prominent colonial artist in Brazil; Jose Campeche (Puerto Rican); and other important people in history are multiracial. Few students are told that Frederick Douglass is multiracial, let alone that his second wife was White (Stephens, 1999). When multiracial and multiethnic students find out these truths, they feel both elated and robbed: "I tried to do the work but a lot of times I didn't have the role models, the characters who looked like me or looked like my friends."

When multiethnic and multiracial children learn about people like them, they often say, "I wish I had known. I wish I had learned about other people like me. I wouldn't have felt so abnormal." A person of mainstream White and Latino White parents expressed her feelings:

> In college my [African American] roommates would talk about light skin, dark skin, and the dark-skinned [students] felt they were more superior because they weren't mixed. I could not understand that, so I was always interested to know whether people were mixed. Finding other mixed people gave me an empowering sense of identity. When I found other German and Spanish mixed people, we got together and created the "Spermans." We thought it was cool because we were alike, we had a group to identify with, [and] we had our own name. It was great! I think it's important to have someone who is just like you.

Another person of African American and Latino Indian ancestry shared her perspective:

> The greatest disadvantage is the identity issue. Not faceless but in a sense you feel like you are faceless. I didn't know who I was. My whole life it was my quest to understand, being isolated as a child, being a child [with] that burden. Interest in finding about other biethnic and biracial persons was always a priority, especially for those who were also African American and Mexican, like myself. They represented the desperately needed role models I craved—people that I could identify with. I wanted to know what their life experiences had been. Had they also been through the same as me?

A person of mainstream White and Latino White heritage also wrote:

> I might have learned about people who were biethnic or biracial. As a matter of fact, I just remembered one kid in elementary school who was half Black and half White. Somehow I couldn't understand it. It didn't make any sense to me. I think it would have helped me to learn that there are other or more mixtures than just Black-White. That didn't fit my experience.

Multiethnic and multiracial children, and all children of color, need to feel accepted. They need to see that their experiences also represent an "American," worldwide, and cosmopolitan view. Furthermore, they need to be educated, along with everyone else, about the richness of their dual and/or multiple heritages. Colleges of education, multicultural instructors, and people providing in-service diversity training in schools across the country must find ways to support, celebrate, and affirm these children and their families.

Teachers Need to Affirm Multiracial and Multiethnic Students' Strengths

The study of individuals from multiethnic and multiracial backgrounds requires a paradigm shift that emphasizes the positive aspects of multiple heritages. Many believe that these persons possess a broader and more diverse repertoire of conceptions of reality (Fish, 2002; 1994; Olumide, 2002; Wardle, 1996b). Contrary to general perceptions, these persons do not manifest personal maladjustment or identity confusion. They often demonstrate greater ability to reconcile different cultural norms, the ability to identify with more than one group, thus enjoying their own ethnic heritage as much as those of other groups, along with developing an enhanced intergroup tolerance and a facility with languages spoken by their own groups (Stephan, 1992).

According to Brown (1990), children of multiple heritages "typically possess more insight and sensitivity" to the groups in their background than single-race children. They know first-hand what each identity implies. Unfortunately, this awareness often comes from being questioned about "what" and "who" they are from an early age. Finding their self-identity at odds with the way others insist on defining them raises their awareness of and sensitivity to racial issues within society at large and to the willingness of people and society to stereotype people and their behaviors. Further, as one multiracial adolescent put it, "I soon learned to do what I want to do, not what my peers want me to do (based on racial group belonging). If they don't like it, that's their problem!" We could all wish for this kind of independent thinking and behavior—especially for our children.

Further, multiethnic and multiracial individuals can exhibit different group orientations over time (Poston, 1990, p. 153). Persons with multiple heritages may hold fluid ethnic and racial identities and be capable of adjusting their self-perception to different cultural contexts (Miller, 1992) or to changes in roles and situations. Stephan (1992) referred to this as situational identity and found that some individuals may feel part of one group in one situation while part of another group in other situations. Root (1992) calls this context identity. Hence, ethnic and racial identities are not rigid but fluid and do not require conscious selection; individuals do not select systematically to be of one group one moment and some other group later. They tend to express past experiences and memberships within more than one group—a skill that we are now seeing as positive. This ability to move between groups liberates multiethnic and multiracial children and adults from the rigid rules and racial/ethnic behavioral expectations, allowing them both more choices and freedom and at the same time challenging our race/ethnicity status quo.

What Teachers Must Know and Be Able to Do

The first step in preparing teachers to explore all aspects of diversity, including their own, is self-understanding (Banks 2001; Spring, 2001). This is also crucial for understanding multiethnic and multiracial identity development, particularly because many people with a single-race background have strong biases about interracial relationships and multiracial and multiethnic children. Prospective teachers must first detach themselves from the "box mentality" (Cortes, 1999; Cruz-Janzen, 1997) of identity development.

The reality is that all persons, regardless of where they live, are individuals foremost, even when they exist within overlapping layers of diversity. Each person is unique, unlike any other person on earth. And, as Bronfenbrenner so accurately points out, each of us constructs our own, independent, unique reality (1979, 1989), based on a variety of overlapping factors, including but not limited to race, ethnicity, gender, occupation, education, age, socioeconomic status, learning styles and intelligences, abilities and disabilities, background, and communities. As well, students must come to grips with their own mixed racial and ethnic histories. We must accept that there is no pure race anywhere in this planet. We are all the product of some form and degree of mixing (Zack, 2002).

Chapter Feature
Who Am I?

25 Questions

This document can be used for a variety of class-related activities for college students preparing to become teachers.

Adopted students should use information about their biological parents, if they have it. This is particularly important for foreign adopted children. All students, as they go back in history, will obviously have an increasing number of relatives on both sides of their family tree. Include all relevant information that you know of.

1. Name.
2. Both parent's last names.
3. Linguistic/national origin of both last names.
4. Original meaning of these last names, if you know them.
5. Was either or both of these names radically changed at some point in your family history? If so, why was it changed? What was it before it changed? Or, as in the case of many Black families, was your last name adopted from a White family/person after your relatives were freed? Do you know why this name was chosen?
6. Where are you from in the United States?
7. Where do you currently live?
8. What is the structure of your current living arrangement—home, dorm, fraternity/sorority, apartment, etc.?
9. Where did your family/relatives originally come from before coming to the United States? Or were they always here?
10. Where did your family/relatives come from before living in the country from which they immigrated to the United States (for example, from Scandinavia before moving to England, from Portugal before moving to Brazil, from Jamaica before moving to India), or were they always there?
11. What language(s) did your family speak before learning English? Do you still speak this language? Do your parents or grandparents speak it?
12. How long has your family lived in what is now the United States?
13. What race/ethnicity/mixed race do you consider yourself?
14. What other races/ethnicities are in your background?
15. Are there any minority races in your background, if you identify as White; or any White or other minorities in your background, if you identify as a minority?
16. If there are any minority heritages in your (White) background or any White (and minority) heritages in your minority background, where did they enter your family tree?
17. Have you ever experienced interpersonal conflict because of your race, ethnicity, gender, mixed race, religion, or language? Have you ever tried to hide part of your heritage? Have you discovered that your parents/grandparents tried to hide it from you? If so, please describe the conflict. Were these issues resolved? How?
18. Are you now comfortable embracing your total heritage—including non-mainstream White parts or White/other minorities if you are a minority?

Chapter Feature   **Continued**

19. Are you comfortable with your racial and ethnic identities? Do you feel positive and affirmative about them? Explain.

20. Are you interested in further exploring your full background, including those parts that don't match your current racial/ethnic identity? This is both for people who identify as White and those who identify with a single racial/ethnic minority identity.

21. What are ways you can use knowledge about your own racial, ethnic, religious, national, and/or language heritage to assist and support multiethnic and multiracial students and their families in your classrooms?

22. What are ways you can use knowledge about your own racial, ethnic, religious, and national heritage to help all students under-

stand the rich history of intermarriage, interfaith marriages, and linguistic interchange, and deconstruct the orthodoxy of single race/ethnic groupings?

23. Do you currently engage in activities to gain further knowledge about your background or celebrate some part of your heritage: reading, group membership, church attendance, learning a language, visiting your family's country of origin, learning folk dances, etc.? Describe and show how they relate to your background.

24. If you could, would you like to interview a relative (dead or alive) about some aspect of your past? Why?

25. What part of your background would you like to know more about? Why? How could you find this information?

Brazilian children in Diamantina, MG, illustrate that there are no pure biological races anywhere on the planet.

Twenty-Five Recommendations for Teachers, Education Professors, and Educational Leaders

These recommendations are for all teachers, including mainstream White teachers and teachers of color. All teachers must carefully examine these points to become more supportive and inclusive of all students in their teaching. These recommendations are primarily for teachers of children in grades P–12 but are also applicable to many college teachers. Application of these ideas in school-related settings requires careful adjustment for the developmental age of the students.

1. Admit that racism still exists throughout the world and is re-emerging in some places. Develop skills for combating racism in society and the schools. Understand the subtle and not-too-subtle expressions of racism in our early childhood programs and schools, such as Head Start programs that disproportionately place minorities and minority boys in special education programs and assumptions that mixed-race children will have more psychological and emotional problems than single-race students.

2. Understand the historical development of racial classifications around the world and how they continue to perpetuate conquest and exploitation. As Jill Olumide suggests, "In the most profound sense, anti-racism . . . must endeavor to be anti-*race*. Nothing else will do" (2002, p. 5).

3. Understand the historical development of racial categories in this country and its connection to the enslavement of Africans in the "New Hemisphere"— the United States, the Caribbean countries, Brazil, and the Spanish colonial empire. Understand that continuing racial categories helps perpetuate racism and inequality.

4. Become globally competent and understand how we are all connected; that what happens in one country has an impact on other parts of the world. Understand factors that force people to leave their homelands and how prejudice and racism are transported around the globe, informally by individuals and formally through the mass media, propaganda, and political/social intuitions. While U.S. racism is transported worldwide through Hollywood, commercialism, and capitalism, racial, religious, gender, and other prejudices enter this country with new immigrants: for example, Vietnamese prejudice against Amerasian children, strict gender roles and limitation of many Muslim countries, and genital mutilation within some African groups (King, 1999).

5. Understand that racial mixing has been common throughout the history of humankind, there is no pure race anywhere in the world—even the Europeans have a long history of racial mixing prior to coming to the Western Hemisphere (Zack, 2002). Help each student examine the rich variety of his or her own ancestry—language, national origin, and political and religious affiliations, with a stress on how people have compromised, blended, mixed, and combined elements of these factors.

6. Recognize that every person is foremost an individual unlike any other— with strengths, challenges, idiosyncrasies, joys, expectations, and fears. According to Olumide (2002), because of the shifting, developing, and overlapping nature of social groups, all of us are subject to conflicting social designations through multiple affiliations with variously constructed groups. As such, a person might be both privileged and marginalized in different situations—in this sense, we are all mixed in our range of identity-making materials (p. 7). Thus, each of us is continually structuring and reconstructing our social realities.

7. Recognize that as individuals we all live within overlapping spheres of diversity that cannot be separated from each other. Each person exists within his or her own unique spheres of diversity and is entitled to simultaneous respect and acknowledgment of them all. We must stop placing persons in rigid and mutually exclusive diversity boxes; we must never assume one characteristic or attribute—say race or disability—is more important than another.

8. Understand various theories of racial and ethnic identity development, particularly during early childhood and adolescence, and especially as they apply to healthy multiethnic and multiracial development. Further, understand that many professionals' views of multiethnic and multiracial identity are based on single-race identity constructs and an unwritten belief that a single-race identity is somehow natural, proper, and normal (Gibbs, 1987; Olumide, 2002; Wardle, 1989). Never, ever, assume an anti-multiethnic or multiracial view is correct simply because it is expressed by an "expert."

9. Understand their own past socialization, including gender, race, ethnicity, physical appearance, religion, and social class. Understand how they perceive themselves as members of these groups in addition to how they feel about others who are not like them. Explore what they have learned, good and bad, about people with all sorts of diversity and what they have learned about mainstream White people. This is equally important for White students and student of color. For example, in one of Francis Wardle's graduate classes, three Black students indignantly expressed the belief that all mainstream White parents are very permissive, irresponsible, and never provide appropriate discipline for their children; further, that White students all suffer from a lack of the use of corporal punishment by their parents.

10. Understand their own ethnic and racial identity development. College students should engage in activities to explore their complex background, such as which country their parents came from and the various racial and ethnic contributions to their family. Tied closely to everyone's identity is religious background. How does a person's religion shape the way he or she sees the world? Has that person ever questioned his or her religion or religious upbringing? Why—and what was the result?

11. Understand that the only way to deal with prejudice is by admitting that it exists and confronting it. Students must begin by genuinely and sincerely exploring and admitting their own prejudices in relation to persons who are not like them ethnically, racially, linguistically, nationally, or religiously. There is a great deal of within-group discrimination and prejudice in each of the large population groups in this country, including the mainstream White group and each minority group. Students must ask themselves: "Am I prejudiced?" and "How did I become

this way?" As well, they must ask, "How do I change my prejudiced attitudes and behaviors so I don't inadvertently hurt children who depend on me for guidance and nurturance?"

12. Understand how racial classifications are sociopolitical, rather than biological and genetic, and how they maintain a social power structure that benefit a few at the expense of many. Investigate ways to deconstruct race and racial categories, both at the college or university level and in public schools. How does the hidden curriculum reinforce racial classifications: Are there minorities at every level of the staff or just at the bottom levels (janitor and paraprofessionals)? Does the program engage in single-race celebrations and use the contribution approach to multicultural education? Are there classes and extracurricular activities that are only for students who belong to specific single-race/ethnic groups?

13. Acquire skills to be able to confront ethnic and racial harassment directly. Admit that racial harassment occurs every day in our P–12 schools and that children of all ages and races/ethnicities engage in this damaging behavior. Admit that adults in the schools, including parents, administrators, teachers, and other professional staff engage in these behaviors as well (Wehrly, Kenney, & Kenney, 1999). Children should never be told to "ignore" their tormentors. While this has become an issue under the new anti-bullying programs in schools throughout the country, it cannot be ignored for racial harassment—including put-downs and insults of multiethnic and multiracial students and their family members.

14. Recognize that multiethnic and multiracial persons are normal rather than pathological and/or confused. Society places undue stress on these individuals as a result of lack of information, misconceptions, and unreasonable expectations. Student teachers must become aware of multiethnic and multiracial persons' skills and their ability to develop understandings that many single-race-minded persons lack. Multiracial/multiethnic students can move in and out of various cultures effectively and present cultural bridges we can all learn from.

15. Believe in your heart that minority children and multiethnic and multiracial children have an equal capacity to succeed, the same as mainstream White and Asian children.

16. Find all the ways you can to support multiracial and multiethnic families—resources, referrals to competent professionals, creating support groups and websites.

17. Pressure companies that develop curricula, book publishers, and educational supply companies to expand their multicultural offerings and to make sure all children, including multiethnic and multiethnic children, are well represented in all school materials. Maybe, as college students, you can begin a campaign with several school supply companies or textbook companies to address this issue. Do a needs assessment of what the companies currently offer (use instruments scattered throughout this book), then mount a campaign for change.

18. Make sure that any conferences, training, or in-service training that focuses on multicultural or diversity issues address the unique needs of multiethnic and multiracial children and their families. As Cortes (2000) so eloquently says, talking about diversity without addressing multiethnic and multiracial diversity is no longer acceptable.

19. Learn about multiethnic and multiracial people from history, literature, the arts, mathematics, medicine, and governments. Teachers cannot teach multiethnic and multiracial children about role models if they don't know about them. One of the best ways to do this, of course, is to learn about different racial and ethnic influences in your own background. You may also have national, regional, linguistic, and religious diversity in your past.

20. Make sure you never provide activities, lessons, or projects that require multiethnic and multiracial children to reject, hide, or devalue any part of their heritage. A conscious effort must be made to think and act outside of the traditional racial categories we have all learned to use and think with. This is particularly difficult because all curricular materials, especially multicultural ones, are designed, structured and categorized around conventional racial/ethnic boxes.

21. Learn how to provide lots of opportunities for multiethnic and multiracial children in your classroom to explore their complex and rich backgrounds and to have these unique backgrounds reinforced. Understand these children need concrete opportunities at their development level to develop a healthy self-identity. Develop a resource file, discover helpful books, list Internet sites, and discover if there are local support groups.

22. Never, ever, expect multiethnic and multiracial children to select one category on school forms; never try to convince them that selecting one of the many options is somehow more politically correct or responsible. Explore a variety of approaches to having the school adopt a multiethnic/multiracial category on its forms (Graham, 1996); maybe investigate ways a class can take on this project as an anti-bias class activity (Derman-Sparks, 1989).

23. Continually deconstruct any curricular goal, objective, or content that implies one group of people is somehow better than another group in activities, abilities, proficiencies, or intelligence. The first goal of education, P–12, must be that each student is free to choose his or her destiny—based on interests, abilities, likes and passions, ***not based on*** gender, race, ethnicity, mixed ethnicity/race, or ability/disability. No child should ever believe she or he can't do something because, "I'm a girl," "I'm mixed race," "I'm White," etc.

24. Critically examine all curricular materials for bias, stereotype, and misinformation. Further, research ways to actively include multiethnic and multiracial people and their accomplishments in the curriculum, while also exploring universal human activities, values, arts and culture.

25. Find ways to include real and symbolic multiethnic and multiracial people in your curriculum. Again, because we have ignored the existence of multiethnic and multiracial people in our country's history, in world history, and in our contemporary reality, teachers and future teachers will have to do considerable study and research to find this information. College students might begin by exploring and unearthing some of the wonderful famous multiethnic and multiracial people in our past and present.

The first goal of education must be that each student is free to choose his or her destiny.

Clearly, before university faculty can effectively teach others and help prepare them to develop and implement curricula that are diverse, equitable, and truly multicultural, they must explore their own identities, roles in society, and the needs of all students in our schools, including students of color and multiethnic and multiracial students. It would also help if universities established departments of multiethnic and multiracial studies, included content on multiethnic and multiracial students in multicultural classes, and provided multiethnic and multiracial student support groups within their overall diversity efforts.

Conclusion

While we recognize that teachers often do not determine the curriculum, establish the school climate, or create the overall school philosophy, we believe teachers in early childhood programs and schools have a vital role in supporting the healthy identity development of multiethnic and multiracial children and in supporting their drive toward academic success. To do this, however, teachers must receive a different and improved kind of teacher preparation that should include self-reflection, understanding the history of racism, understanding the negative power of racial categories, and being informed about the history of multiethnic and multiracial people and the normalcy and potential of multiracial and multiethnic children. Reformed teacher preparation programs must begin with the reeducation of college faculty; it would also be greatly enhanced by universities' establishing departments of multiethnic and multiracial studies, and providing multiethnic/multiracial support groups and activities.

Questions/Projects

1. Interview the multicultural coordinator of a school. Focus questions on how the staff addresses the needs of multiethnic and multiracial students and their families and whether it supports single-race activities.

2. Interview teachers and ask them what racial issues they encounter in their schools. Does the district or school have a policy for addressing negative speech/behavior? Does it cover multiethnic and multiracial children?

3. Interview the person in charge of multicultural training at a college that prepares teachers. Focus questions on how the college prepares teachers to meet the needs of multiracial and multiethnic children.

4. Visit a children's library or bookstore. Determine how many books are about minority people, heroes, families, and children, and how many are about multiracial or multiethnic heroes, families, and /or children.

5. Analyze an elementary social studies text (content and pictures) to determine how often the topic of multiracial and multiethnic heritage is addressed. Is it positive, negative, or neutral?

Resources

Websites

Interracial Voice e-Magazine
http://www.Interracialvoice.co

MAVIN. National Organization for Multi-ethnic and Multiracial Students
http://www.mavin.net/

Mixed Initiatives
Mixed race students and transracially adopted students
http://www.umich.edu/~themix/

New People Magazine
http://www.Newpeoplemagazine.com

Appendix A

Age-Related Issues for Interacial and Interethnic Families

	Environment (Home and School)	Working with Professionals/Teachers
Pre-marriage	Expose each other to both your environments—home, neighborhoods, favorite eating places, etc. Learn to feel comfortable in each others environment.	Openly discuss interracial/interethnic marriage. Don't allow professionals to interject subjective arguments. Deal realistically with possible consequences, including loss of friends and relatives.
Marriage	Many home issues are the same as all newly married: affordability, size, location, neighborhood. Try to live in an integrated neighborhood, one that supports both of you.	If marriage conflict requires counseling/therapy, don't let race/ethnicity become a major issue. Look at interpersonal problems, relatives, etc. Isolate racial/ethnic issues from other issues.
Birth and infertility. 0- to 2-year-old child (biological/ adopted)	Mirrors to view self. Make house child-safe. Get quality child care. Evaluate child care for support of multiracial children. Books, dolls, pictures, and materials must reflect all races/ethnicities.	Biracial babies (Black/White) may be smaller than White babies and very light. Make sure your professionals respond to your child as an individual, not a stereotyped category. Many professionals make race-based assumptions.
2- to 5-year-old child (biological/ adopted)	Mirrors to view self. Multiracial/multiethnic dolls, books, posters, puzzles. If in child care, try to find one with caregivers with a variety of racial backgrounds—also children. Look for mixed-race/ethnicity friends for children, if possible.	Let professionals know your child is multiracial or multiethnic. If adopted, also insist professionals respond to child's mixed identity. Don't let professionals assume problems are automatically caused by adopted mixed status.

	Environment (Home and School)	Working with Professionals/Teachers
5- to 11-year-old child (biological/ adopted)	School should have staff and students with various racial/ethnic backgrounds. Have art and books around the home and school that reflect various peoples and country of origin of adopted child.	Monitor professionals' support, both of multiracial/multiethnic identity and adoptive status. Remove child if this is not occurring. Educate teachers and others.
Adolescence/ Dating	Try to have child attend an integrated school and choose clubs and groups based on interest, not racial/ethnic makeup. Encourage membership in groups away from school that complement the school environment.	If child needs therapy or is in counseling, don't assume a professional of color is necessarily supportive of multiracial and multiethnic identity. If a therapist feels the child is denying his or her minority status, examine carefully.
Young Adult	At this time, your child will probably be on his or her own. Your involvement will be very limited—listening, advice, etc.	If the young adult seeks psychological help, don't allow the professional to blame you, the parent, for his or her problems, especially in the area of identity.

	Physical Care of the Child	Relatives
Pre-marriage	Find out what's important to your companion, based on his or her cultural and family background.	Be open with relatives. Try not to avoid or dismiss relatives. Even if they disapprove, they are your relatives and will not go away. Try to develop a relationship. Your children need them.
Marriage	Learn about the care methods used by the culture of your spouse or the minority side of adopted child's background.	Invite all—even those who have expressed objection. Try not to shut the door on those who object—leave it open.
Birth and infertility. 0- to 2-year-old child (biological/ adopted) (*cont.*)	Learn how to care for child's hair. Also skin, if it tends to get dry or flaky. Know about dark marks that some minority children get that are mistaken for bruises (abuse).	Many reluctant grandparents fall for their new grandchildren. Expose children often to both sets of grandparents and uncles/aunts. Don't let past disagreements get in the way.

	Physical Care of the Child	Relatives
2- to 5-year-old child (biological/ adopted)	Learn various hairstyles for your child's hair. Understand that your children can get sunburned. Find clothes that look good with their color skin.	Continue as much exposure as possible. Request gifts that represent all cultures, races, and ethnicities. Emphasize the genetic and individual characteristics of both sets of grandparents in children. Don't devalue either background.
5- to 11-year-old child (biological/ adopted)	Help with hair and dry skin. For some girls, hair becomes a major struggle at this age. Help with selecting complimentary clothes. Help your child to select fashion style unique to him- or herself.	As much exposure as possible, have relatives talk to your children about their heritage and what's important to them. See if relatives can help with children's research projects, including through use of the Internet.
Adolescence/ Dating	Help with appropriate hairstyles, fashion choices, and makeup. Address dry skin, if a problem. Provide oils for dry hair. Find a stylist who can cut and style your child's hair.	Time visiting various relatives will give your child a good sense of diversity. Regular correspondence is also helpful.
Young Adult	Stress the need for self-respect, especially in the area of sex. Also discuss the negative effects of drugs.	Support the young adult's contact with relatives he or she has grown to trust and enjoy. This is very healthy.

	Talking with Spouse and Children	Identity/Support
Pre-marriage	Discuss society's and relatives' response to your possible marriage. Discuss how you will handle discrimination. Talk about how you will raise your children.	Support each other's ethnic, racial, and cultural background. Feel proud of who you are. Don't give up your background to fit that of your spouse. Don't feel guilty. Start developing your own unique culture.

	Talking with Spouse and Children	**Identity/Support**
Marriage	Don't let society's opposition either stop you or force you to do something out of stubbornness. Know there are many successful interracial marriages.	Discuss your identity as an interracial couple and how people respond. Feel good about this collective identity. Join a support group of other interracial couples. Read material.
Birth and infertility. 0- to 2-year-old child (biological/ adopted)	Discuss possible religious conflicts (example baptism); also how to respond to insensitive comments from strangers. How do you tell them your child is adopted or multiethnic/ multiracial? Talk about it.	Be proud of your child's total identity, don't hide any of it. Be comfortable talking to others about it. Expose children to other adopted and multiracial/multiethnic children.
2- to 5-year-old child (biological/ adopted)	Talk to children about similarities and differences, how we get physical characteristics and other traits from both sides of the family. Respond to any questions of your children.	This is the usual time when children are curious about hair texture, eye shape, skin color, etc. Talk openly about being proud to be different and to have a mixed heritage.
5- to 11-year-old child (biological/ adopted)	Be open to your children about their adoptive status, and anything you know about their birth parents. Talk about the naturalness of multiethnic/ multiracial children—both adopted and biological.	Children this age need labels and words to help them. Biracial, mixed, multiethnic, adopted all help. Help them articulate their identity and feel good about it.
Adolescence/ Dating	Talk about dating and how you experienced it as a child. Help child view people as individuals, not categories. Help him or her select dates that have similar interests, etc.	Child's identity will be challenged by Black students, White students, and teachers. Help child educate these people and articulate who they are! Help child understand he or she does not have to justify who he or she is, or racial choice.
Young Adult	The young adult will rarely seek your advice. When he or she does, assure your child of your support and the rightness of his or her identity choice.	Identity challenge should be viewed as a problem of the challenger, not your son or daughter. Help your child see he or she does not have to prove who he or she is.

	Materials (Books, etc.)	Racial/Ethnic Categories
Pre-marriage	Read books about interracial/interethnic marriage (for example, *Mixed Blood*, by P. Spickard). Read articles—academic and in the popular press. Contact web sites.	Discuss with each other the question of your own racial/ethnic identity and the label you use to represent that identity. If your heritage includes Native American, Black, Latino, and/or Asian, how do you define and label yourself?
Marriage	Find out what each of you enjoys, and what you can learn from each other—music, dance, art, literature—without being phony.	Discuss the question of the official label for your birth or adoptive child. What are your choices? Will you accept one of the labels provided by the government, or refuse to select from the limited government choices?
Birth and infertility. 0- to 2-year-old child (biological/adopted)	Read books about interracial/interethnic families. Listen to lullabies from various cultures, such as Paul Robeson's "My Curly Headed Baby." Read articles and books about multiethnic/multiracial children and minority children.	Many states will request identity of child for the birth certificate. Also, if you take out SS card at this time, it also asks for your child's racial/ethnic identity. Insist your child is multiracial/multiethnic.
2- to 5-year-old child (biological/adopted)	Provide books about interracial families and adoption, dolls of various races, puzzles and posters of interracial/interethnic families, etc. Avoid materials that break down world into distinctive races and groups.	Preschools, Head Start, child care programs, etc. all request the racial category of your child. Insist on multiracial. If they refuse, check "other," refuse to fill out forms, or do what both of you are comfortable with.
5- to 11-year-old child (biological/adopted)	Collect artifacts, pictures, calendars, books, brochures, etc. of a variety of cultural groups: Native American, West Indian, African, etc. and materials about smaller groups: Guatemalan Indians, Polish, Kenyan.	During this age, children have to fill out their own categories. Discuss with your child—biological or adopted—what categories to use and what to do if officials make it difficult.

	Materials (Books, etc.)	**Racial/Ethnic Categories**
Adolescence/ Dating	Provide reading books on adoption, racial/ethnic identity, racism, and interracial families. Provide material about heroes who are mixed or adopted. Show children TV programs and articles in popular press that address adoption and mixed people.	Discuss openly the category your child believes he or she belongs to—or his or her dislike for the whole notion. Can your child force a change in his or her school? Can he or she talk to the press? Can he or she develop a multiracial/ multiethnic student group?
Young Adult	Books about any successful person who has challenged society, especially autobiographies. For example, Paul Robeson, James Earle Jones, Maria Tallchief, Betty Okino, Dan O'Brian.	At this time your child probably will have selected a category that meets his or her needs. Support that choice. Some children this age feel the government has no right to label them with any label.

Source: F. Wardle (1999) from *Tomorrow's Children*. Used by permission, Center for the Study of Biracial Children.

Glossary

Acculturation The way people and cultures change and adapt as they are exposed to other peoples and cultures, leading to the dynamic, ever-changing nature of societies.

African American According to the Census, a person "having origins in any of the Black racial groups of Africa. It includes people who indicate their races as 'Black, African American, or Negro,' or provides written entries such as African American, Afro American, Kenyan, Nigerian, or Haitian" (U.S. Bureau of the Census, 2000). Note: The Census asks for self-identification.

Anglo Saxon Anglo is English; Saxon a small tribe in Germany. The combined term has come to be associated with the dominant religious, legal, and cultural values brought from England to this country and other British colonies throughout the world.

Anti-Bias and Ecological Model of Multicultural Education A diversity model developed by Wardle that is designed to help teachers focus on each student's individual context, including race, ethnicity, culture, gender, socioeconomic status, ability/disability, family, and community.

Anti-miscegenation laws Laws prohibiting interracial, and often interethnic, marriage.

Asian Self-identification among people of Asian descent. There are seventeen detailed Asian race and ethnic categories used in displaying data from Census 2000: Asian Indian, Bangladeshi, Cambodian, Chinese —except Taiwanese, Filipino, Hmong, Indonesian, Japanese, Korean, Laotian, Malaysian, Pakistani, Sri Lankan, Taiwanese, Thai, Vietnamese, other Asian.

Assimilation The expectation that new immigrants will shed their own culture and language to become fully American. Also the expectation that minorities within the country will assume mainstream White cultural values.

Authoritarian parenting style A parenting style characterized by a severe and inconsistent disciplinary approach.

Authoritative parenting style A parenting style characterized by a firm and consistent disciplinary approach that involves verbal explanation and involvement by the child in discipline matters.

Belize A Central American country with a British colonial history and English as the official language; formerly called British Honduras.

Biethnic A child or person of parents from two U.S. Census ethnic categories, such as mainstream White and Latino White.

Biracial A child of parents of two different races, such as White and Black.

Black Irish Irish people with darker complexions and dark hair, who are either descendants of the people shipwrecked from the Spanish Armada or descendants of people directly from Spain.

Blanqueamiento A common term in Latin American countries with a Spanish colonial past, meaning whitening of society.

Blood quantum The federally mandated amount of blood required to be a member of an Indian tribe; differs from tribe to tribe.

Cephalic index The study of people by comparing the size and shape of their heads.

Cholo Person of Black/Indigenous mix—used in countries south of the United States.

Cognitive developmental stages The stages children progress through as they make sense out of the world; specifically Piaget's four stages of mental representation.

Colorism A system of hierarchy within Black communities—and other communities, including Latinos—based on the color of the person's skin and other preferred European characteristics—facial features, hair texture, and others.

Coloureds   Mixed race/ethnicity people living in South Africa; also includes Asians.

Concept formation   Process used by children and adults to learn new concepts. One common approach is by determining positive and negative instances—what something is, and what it is not.

Concrete Operations Stage   The third Piaget stage, from approximately 6 or 7 to 11 or 12 years old. This stage is characterized by more sophisticated abstract thinking, the ability to handle more than one piece of information at a time, and logical problem solving.

Content integration   A curricular approach that spreads content across all curricular domains—for example, including multicultural content in math, art, science, literature and physical education.

Contributions Approach   The first level in Banks' *Integration of Multicultural Content*, focusing on heroes, holidays, and discrete cultural elements.

Critical pedagogy   An approach to education developed by the Brazilian educator, Paulo Freire, that argues students can learn new concepts and deconstruct the power relationships behind those concepts *at the same time.*

Cross-cultural competency   The ability to function effectively with people from a variety of cultural and other backgrounds; the ability of mainstream White teachers to teach minority students.

Cultural literacy   The curricular content all U.S. children should learn, according to E.D. Hirsch.

Culture   The way people view the world, acquired by people as members of various groups, and representing their orientation to all living things—their worldview.

Decision Making and Social Action Approach   The final level of Banks's *Integration of Multicultural Content*, in which students make decisions on important social issues and take action to address these issues.

Developmental age   The skills, concepts, and abilities a child has that correspond to other children his or her age, such as walking and speaking. Learning based on development.

Developmental stages   The concept of developmental psychology that argues that children develop through distinct stages as they mature. Each stage has unique characteristics that separate it from other stages. Piaget and Erikson have created stage models.

Diversity   All the ways in which people are different, including individual, group, and cultural differences (Bucher, 2000).

Diversity of diversity   The variability and differences within traditional ethnic, racial, gender, disability, and other traditional groups.

Domestic adoption   Adoption of U.S. children by U.S. families.

Durante vita   For life; slavery for the entire life of the person without the ability to acquire freedom.

Ecological components   Components of Wardle's developmental model that relate to the child's physical and human environment.

Ecological context   A term derived from Bronfenbrenner's ecological theory: the various social impacts that affect a person, such as family, community, school, peer group, and others.

Educational standards   Educational expectations that stipulate the content, skills, and concepts each student should know in each subject area, at specific time periods (for example, the literacy skills and knowledge a student should have at the end of third grade).

Empowering Social Culture and Social Structure—One of Banks's *Approaches to Multicultural Education.*

English Language Learners—Another name for LEP children in U.S. schools.

Equity Pedagogy   One of Banks's *Approaches to Multicultural Education.*

Essentialism   Focusing on one small aspect of a biological variation and using this variation to fallaciously postulate an ideal type—in this case, race.

Ethnic Additive Approach   The second level of Banks's *Integration of Multicultural Content*, focusing on adding content, themes, and perspectives without changing the curricular structure.

Ethnic group   A group with several distinguishing characteristics that enable both its own members and members of other groups to identify members. These characteristics might be cultural, linguistic, historical, social/political, or a combination. Ethnic groups are often targets of racism and discrimination.

Ethnicity   A shared cultural worldview and/or geographic origins. Members of ethnic groups, such as Latinos in the United States, may not share common distinguishing cultural, racial, language, or other characteristics but are joined together by a U.S.-designated category based on their world region/countries of origin.

Eugenics movement A popular movement in the early part of the twentieth century that believed certain people should be killed or sterilized to keep races and humanity from being contaminated by impure genes. Led to the Nazi attempt to exterminate the Jews.

Eurocentric A focus—including that of school curricula—based on European values, history, culture, and traditions.

Folk category The way people in individual cultures categorize people—differing from other cultures and from a scientific basis for race (which does not exist). In the United States the official and folk categories are pretty much the same.

Foreign adoption Adoption of children from other countries by U.S. families.

Formal Operations Stage The last of Piaget's stages, occurring after age 11 or 12. Involves sophisticated problem solving and the ability to hypothesize about potential results that have not been directly experienced by the person.

Gatekeeper An entity that prevents something from getting through, such as a gate in a fence. In the case of multiethnic/multiracial issues, gatekeepers are people, organizations, and institutions that prevent positive and affirming information about multiethnic and multiracial children from reaching the public and professionals.

Genotype The genetic makeup of a person—the code the person carries in the genes that makes up his or her physical nature—including hair texture and color, eye shape and color, skin color, facial feature, body type, and height.

Goals 2000 The six national educational goals that have led to national standards, which many believe will lead to a national curriculum.

Hidalgo In the tradition of Spain, the son of a nobleman, descendant of royalty.

Hidden curriculum Aspects of a curriculum children learn that are not specified in a curriculum document. For example, certain classes, programs, groups, and athletic teams are only for students of specific racial groups.

Hispano The preferred term for someone living primarily in the U.S. Southwest and claiming direct, uninterupted descendance from Spain.

Hybrid degeneracy The idea that a person of more than one racial/ethnic background would be physically, emotionally, psychologically, and morally weaker than a person of one racial or ethnic background.

Hypodescent The social system that maintains the fiction of single-race identification of individuals by assigning a racially mixed person to the racial group in his or her heritage that has the least social status (Root, 1996).

Iberians People originally from Spain and Portugal.

IDEA, Individuals with Disabilities Education Act (1990) The federal legislation that provides free education, in the least restrictive environment, for children with disabilities, infants to 21 years old.

Identity development models Theoretical attempts to describe how children develop a sense of their unique identity; they tend to be dominated by single-race views of identity.

Identity versus Role Confusion Erikson's stage that corresponds to adolescents, in which they must develop a sense of role identity, including gender, race/ethnicity, and a future career.

Industry versus Inferiority The Erikson stage (6 to 12 years old) in which children are mastering a vast amount of new skills and learning to be competent in many areas.

Initiative versus Guilt One of Erikson's psychosocial stages (3 to 7 years old) in which the child must learn to initiate actions on his or her own.

Issei First-generation Japanese Americans who came to this country after 1861. Most came to earn enough money to return to Japan and rejoin their families.

Jim Crow system The system of rules, laws, and accepted behaviors that discriminated against Blacks after the Civil War.

Knowledge Construction Process—One of Banks's *Approaches to Multicultural Education*. The process by which each individual constructs his or her view of the world. It's highly influenced by family, culture, society, the media, and schools.

Know-Nothing Party A White, Anglo-Saxon, Protestant group that advocated anti-immigrant policies.

Latino A self-designated classification for people whose origins are from Spain, the Spanish-speaking countries of Central or South America, and the Caribbean region, mostly used by people in the United States. Origin can be viewed as ancestry, nationality, or country of birth of the person or person's parents or ancestors prior to their arrival in the United States (U.S. Bureau of the Census, 2000).

Learning environments The classroom, school, curricular materials, playground, and people that surround a child's formal education.

Life-span theory A theory of human development that spans a person's entire life, birth to death. Erik Erikson's theory of psychosocial development is a life-span theory.

Limited English Proficiency (LEP) Children in our schools with limited skills (speaking, understanding, reading, writing) in the English language.

Macroculture The dominant culture in the United States.

Mainstream Whites According to the 2000 Census, a White person is someone who self-identifies as "having origins in any of the original people of Europe, the Middle East, or North Africa. It includes people who indicate their race as 'White' or report entries such as Irish, German, Italian, Lebanese, Arab, or Polish" (U.S. Bureau of the Census, 2000).

Marginalized/marginalization A term coined by Stonequist to describe multiethnic and multiracial people; now used in a more broader context: someone who operates on the edge of one or more social groups.

Marginal Whites White immigrants who initially were not considered part of the White population because they were not WASPs, but are now viewed as American Whites—Irish, Jews, Poles, Italians, and others.

McCarthy era The period in U.S. history in the 1950s where people's lives and careers were destroyed by someone accusing them of being a communist. The career of Paul Robeson, the great singer and actor, was destroyed by the hearings on the Committee on UnAmerican Activities, organized by the senator from Wisconsin, Joe McCarthy.

Mejorando la raza The concept prevalent in Latin American countries with a Spanish colonial past of marrying someone lighter to improve the race.

Mestizo In Puerto Rico, and most Spanish-connected Latin America, mestizo means White and Indian. The term is used to deny African heritage when applied to apparent Latinos of African ancestry.

Mission/Indian boarding schools Schools for Native American children organized and funded by various religious organizations, including Mormons, ostensibly to "civilize" Native Americans and make them good Christians.

Moreno/morena—In Brazil, a person with brown or black hair that is curly but not tight curly, tan skin, a nose that is not narrow, and lips that are not thin—lighter than a mulatto in Brazil (Fish, 2002, p. 121). In the United States, Latinos use *moreno* to refer to dark-skinned African Americans—as a derogatory term. It means a person with brown-tan skin color, curly hair, and apparent African ancestry.

Mulatto The folk word for a mixed-race person of Black/White parentage. Most multiracial people dislike the term, because in Spanish a *mulatto* is a mule, an animal that cannot procreate.

Multicultural (anti-bias) education—An educational movement designed to make sure students from diverse racial and ethnic groups, genders, economic backgrounds, and special needs, have equal opportunity to succeed in schools and universities (Banks & Banks, 1997).

Multiculturally competent Same as culturally competent.

Multiethnic In this book we use the term multiethnic to represent a person whose acknowledged identity includes two or more of the U.S. Census ethnic categories.

Multiracial In this book we use the term multiracial to represent a person whose acknowledged identity includes two or more of the U.S. Census racial categories.

Nativist Anglo-Saxon Protestants born in the United States and deeply concerned with keeping their race pure.

Nisei Second-generation Japanese Americans. Almost all were interned in camps during WWII.

Noncustodial parent A biological parent who does not have legal—or part legal—custody of his or her child.

Octoroon A person with one-eighth Black parentage.

OMB categories The categories developed by the Office of Management and Budget, for schools, universities, and all federal contracts. Usually based on the Census categories, although as yet the OMB categories do not correspond to the 2000 Census categories.

One-drop rule   The uniquely U.S. approach to race that maintains that anyone with "one drop" of African blood is Black. The rule also includes people with other mixtures, with the race or ethnicity of the lowest status defining the person's racial or ethnic identity.

Out marriage   A term used by sociologists to describe people who marry "out of their group (race/ethnicity/nationality)." In the view of the authors, a somewhat negative term.

Permissive parenting style   A parenting style characterized by a lax and inconsistent disciplinary approach.

Phenotype   The physical appearance of a person—physical characteristics, particularly skin color, facial features, eye shape, and hair texture.

Physiognomy   The practice of trying to judge character and mental qualities through the physical appearance of a person, especially facial features.

Pre-Color Constancy   A concept in Jacob's developmental model that suggests children develop certain skills, attitudes, and concepts needed before they can understand that a person's skin color is constant—it does not change.

Prejudice Reduction   One of Banks's *Approaches to Multicultural Education.*

Preoperational Stage   The second of Piaget's stages, from age 2 to 6 or 7, characterized by egocentrism, centrism, and a predominance of real perceptual information over symbolic data.

Psychosocial Stages   Name given to Erikson's eight stages that make up his theory of lifespan development.

Quadroon   A person with one-fourth Black parentage.

Race   A socially constructed way of grouping people, which differs from society to society and has no biological basis.

Racial purity   The essentialist notion that a minor biological difference causes people to be grouped into exclusive groups based on race. The one-drop rule perpetuates this concept by placing a person with any Black heritage into the Black racial group.

Sansei   Third-generation Japanese Americans, born and raised in suburban, integrated communities, many of whom married non-Japanese Americans.

Support groups   Local groups created to provide support, friendship, and role models for interracial families. Some have newsletters, websites, and organize conferences. The groups were instrumental in creating the national multiracial movement.

Taino Indians   Indigenous or Native Americans of Puerto Rico.

Third-culture children   Children who have more that one citizenship—U.S. and some other country; children who are truly citizens of two or more countries.

Tokenism   A minimal effort of integration; for example, employing one women, one Black person, and one Latino; or, in a classroom, having one Black doll, one Hispanic doll, and one Native American doll, and then claiming to be diverse. Exhibiting tokenism shows the lack of true understanding of diversity. One problem of tokenism is that it puts tremendous pressure on the token to be perfect.

Traditional Census categories   The U.S. Census Bureau categories that are also generally the folk categories of the United States. However, the Census changes categories over time.

Transformative Approach   The third level of Banks's *Integration of Multicultural Content,* in which the structure of the curriculum is changed to enable students to view content, issues, and concepts from the view of diverse ethnic, racial, and cultural groups.

Treaty of Guadalupe Hidalgo   The treaty signed between Mexico and the United States that ceded land from Mexico to the United States under specific conditions (that were not fulfilled).

Trigueña   Wheat-colored—a description for a person's skin color.

U.S. Census Categories   The racial and ethnic categories used by the Census to collect demographic information. The 2000 Census allowed people to select more than one race/ethnicity for the first time.

Zambo   Person of Black/Indigenous mix—a term used in countries south of the United States.

References

Aboud, F. E. (1987). The development of ethnic self-determination and attitudes. In J. S. Phinney & M. J. Rotheram (Eds.), *Children's ethnic socialization: Pluralism and development* (pp. 29–55). Newbury Park, CA: Sage.

Alejandro-Wright, M. N. (1985). The child's conception of racial classification: A socio-cognitive model. In M. B. Spencer, G. K. Brookins, & W. R. Allen (Eds.), *Beginnings: Social and affective development of black children*. Hillsdale, NJ: Erlbaum.

Allen, T. W. (2000). Race and ethnicity: History and the 2000 census. *Kansas State University 9th Annual Cultural Studies Symposium: Who counts? What counts? And how?* Panel on "Color lines: Nation, state, and the proliferation of race," March 9–11, 2000.

Alves-Silva, J., Santos, M. S., Guimaras, P. E. M., Ferreira, A. C. S., Bandelt, H. J., Pena, S. D. J., & Prado, V. M. (2000). The ancestry of Brazilian mtDNA lineages. *American Journal of Human Genetics, 67,* 444–461.

Andrews, G. R. (1980). *The Afro-Argentines of Buenos Aires, 1800–1900.* Madison: The University of Wisconsin Press.

Ayvazian, A. (1997, Summer). Faculty fears: Barriers to effective mentoring across racial lines. *Multicultural Education, 4,* (4), 13–17.

Bandura, A. (1965). Behavioral modification through modeling practices. In L. Krasner & L. Ullman (Eds.), *Research in behavior modification.* New York: Holt Rinehart and Winston.

Banks, J. A. (1995). Multicultural education: Historical development, dimensions, and practices. In J. A. Banks & C. A. McGee Banks (Eds.), *Handbook of research on multicultural education* (pp. 3–24). New York: Macmillan.

Banks, J. A. (2001). *Cultural diversity and education: Foundations, curriculum, and teaching.* Boston: Allyn and Bacon.

Banks, J. A. (2002). *An introduction to multicultural education* (3rd ed.). Boston: Allyn and Bacon.

Banks, J. A., & Banks, C. A. (1997). *Multicultural education: Issues and perspectives* (3rd ed.). Boston: Allyn and Bacon.

Barry, E. (2002, November 29). Descendants learn of breeding study. *Rocky Mountain News,* p. 62.

Bazin, G. (1975). *A Arquitetura Religiosa Barroca no Brazil.* Rio de Janeiro: Record.

Beane, H. (2001). *Raising healthy, happy interracial children: Supporting your biracial children.* Brochure. Washington, DC: Author.

Benjamin-Wardle, M. (1994). 14 year old speaks out, proving that teens have concerns, too. *New People, 1* (16), 6.

Berlak, H. (1999, Spring). Standards and the control of knowledge. *Rethinking School, 13* (3), 1–11.

Bigelow, B. (1999, Summer). Standards and multiculturalism. *Rethinking Schools, 13,* (4), pp. 1–7.

Bowles, D. D. (1993). Biracial identity: Children born to African American and White couples. *Clinical Social Work Journal, 21* (4) 417–428.

Bradshaw, C. K. (1992). Beauty and the beast: On racial ambiguity. In M. P. P. Root (Ed.), *Racially mixed people in America.* Newbury Park, CA: Sage Publications.

Brandell, J. R. (1988, October). Treatment of the biracial child: Theoretical and clinical issues. *Journal of Multicultural Counseling and Development, 16,* 176–186.

Bredekamp, S., & Copple, C. (Eds.). (1997). *Developmentally appropriate practice* (rev. ed.) Washington, DC: NAEYC.

British Association for Adoption and Fostering (BAAF). (1995). *Practice notice #13.* London, England: Author.

Brown, N. G., & Douglass, R. E. (1996). Making the invisible visible: The growth of community network organizations. In M. P. P.

Root (Ed.), *The multiracial experience: Racial borders as the new frontier* (pp. 323–240). Thousand Oaks: Sage

Brown, P. M. (1990, August). Biracial identity and social marginality. *Child and Adolescent Social Work*, 7, (4), 319–337.

Bronfenbrenner, U. (1979). Context of child rearing: Problems and prospect. *American Psychologist*, 34, 844–850.

Bronfenbrenner, U. (1989). *The developing ecology of human development*. Paper presented at the biannual meeting of the Society for Research in Child Development, Kansas City, MO.

Bruner, J. S. (1972). The nature and uses of immaturity. *American Psychologist*, 27, 687–708.

Bruner, J. S., Goodnow, J., & Austin, G. (1956). *A study of thinking*. New York: Wiley.

Bucher, R. D. (2000). *Diversity consciousness. Opening our minds to people, culture, and opportunities*. Upper Saddle River, NJ: Prentice-Hall.

Carnes, J. (1995). *Us and them: A history of intolerance in America*. Montgomery, AL: Southern Poverty Law Center.

Clark, B. (1997). *Growing up gifted* (5th ed.). Upper Saddle River, NJ: Merrill.

Comas-Diaz, L. (1996) LatiNegra: Mental health issues of African Latinas. In M. P. Root (Ed.), *The multiracial experience: Racial borders as the new frontier* (pp. 167–190). Thousand Oaks, CA: Sage Publications.

Cortes, C. E. (1999). Mixed-race children: Building bridges to new identities. *Reaching Today's Youth*, 3 (2), 28–31.

Cortes, C. E. (2000). The diversity within: Intermarriage, identity, and campus community. *About Campus*, 5 (1), 5–10.

Covin, S. A., & Wiggins, F. (1989, July). An antiracism training model for white professionals. *Journal of Multicultural Counseling and Development*, 17, 105–114.

Crohn, J. (1995). *Mixed matches: How to create successful interracial, interethnic and interfaith relationships*. New York: Fawcett Columbine.

Cross, W. E. (1987). A two factor theory of black identity development in minority children. In J. S. Phinney & M. J. Rotheram (Eds.), *Children's ethnic socialization* (pp. 117–134). Newbury Park, CA: Sage.

Cruz-Janzen, M. I. (1997). *Curriculum and the self-concept of biethnic and biracial persons*. Dissertation, University of Denver. Ann Arbor, MI: UMI Dissertation Services.

Cruz-Janzen, M. I. (1997–98). Invisibility: the language bias of political control and power.

In F. Schultz (Ed.), *Annual editions: Multicultural education* (article #37; 225–228) Guilford, CT: Dushkin/Mcgraw Hill.

Cruz-Janzen, M. I. (1998). Culturally authentic bias. *Rethinking Schools*, 13(1), 5.

Cruz-Janzen, M. I. (2000, April). Preparing preservice teacher candidates for leadership in equity. *Equity and Excellence in Education*, 33 (1), 94–101.

Cruz-Janzen, M. I. (2001). Y tu abuela, a'onde esta? *SAGE Race Relations Abstracts*, 26 (1), 7–24.

Curry, N. E., & Johnson, C. N. (1990). *Beyond self-esteem: Developing a genuine sense of human value*. Washington, DC: NAEYC.

Daniel, G. R. (1992). Passers and pluralist: Subverting the racial divide. In M. P. Root (Ed.), *Racially mixed people in America*. Newbury Park, CA: Sage.

Davidman, L., & Davidman, P. T. (1997). *Teaching with a multicultural perspective: A practical guide* (2nd ed.). White Plains, NY: Longman Publishing.

Davis, F. J. (1998). *Who is Black? One nation's definition*. University Park: Pennsylvania State University Press.

Derman-Sparks, L. (1989). *Anti-bias curriculum: Tools for empowering young children*. Washington, DC: NAEYC.

Derman-Sparks, L. & Phillips, C. B. (1997). *Teaching/learning anti-racism: A developmental approach*. New York: Teachers College.

Diaz, C. F. (2001). (Ed.). *Multicultural education in the 21st century*. New York: Longman.

Doll, R. (1970). *Curriculum improvement* (2nd ed.). Boston: Allyn and Bacon.

Douglass, F. (1994/1845/1855/1893). *Autobiography: Narrative of the life. My bondage and my freedom. Life and times*. New York: Library of America.

Dworetzky, J. P. (1995). *Human development: Life span approach* (2nd ed.). St. Paul, MN: West.

Epstein, J. L. (1984). *Single parents and the school: The effects of marital status on parent and teacher evaluation* (Report #353). Baltimore, MD: Center for Social Organization of Schools, Johns Hopkins University.

Epstein, J. L. (1985). Home and school connections in schools of the future: Implications of research on parent involvement. *Peabody Journal of Education*, 62, 18–41.

Erikson, E. (1963). *Childhood and society* (2nd ed.). New York: Norton.

Fish, J. M. (2002). (Ed.). *Race and intelligence: Separating science for myth*. Mahwah, NJ: Lawrence Erlbaum Associates.

Flores, L. (1995, December 25). California issue is anything but Black and White. *The Denver Post*, A 29.

Forbes, J. (1993). *Africans and Native Americans: The language and evolution of Red-Black peoples.* Champaign: University of Illinois Press.

Freire, P. (1970). *Pedagogy of the oppressed.* New York: The Seabury Press.

Frykholm, J. (1997, September). A stacked deck: Addressing issues of equity with preservice teachers. *Equity and Excellence in Education, 30* (2), 50–58.

Gallup Poll. (1991, August). For the first time, more Americans approve of interracial marriage than disapprove. *Gallup Poll Monthly, 311,* 60–64.

Gardner, H. (1983). *Frames of mind.* New York: Basic Books.

Gay, G. (1995). Curriculum theory and multicultural education. In J. A. Banks & C. A. McGee Banks (Eds.), *Handbook on multicultural education.* New York: Macmillan.

Gay, K. (1987). *The rainbow effect: Interractial families.* New York: Franklin Watts.

Gibbs, J. T. (1987). Identity and marginality: Issues in the treatment of biracial adolescents. *American Journal of Orthopsychiatry, 57* (2), 265–276.

Gibbs, J. T. (1989). Biracial adolescents. In J. T. Gibbs, L. N. Huang, et al. (Eds.), *Children of color: Psychological interventions with minority youth* (pp. 322–350). San Francisco, CA: Jossey-Bass.

Gibbs, J. T., & Hines, A. M. (1992). Issues for Black-White biracial adolescents. In M. P. P. Root (Ed.), *Racially mixed people in America* (pp. 223–238). Newbury Park, CA: Sage.

Gilliland, H. (1995). *Teaching the Native American* (3rd ed.). Dubuque, IA: Kendall/Hunt.

Gonsalves-Pinto, L. (1997, Summer). Voices from the trenches: Students' insights regarding multicultural teaching/learning. *Multicultural Education, 4* (4), 44–48.

Gonzalez, P. & Rodriguez, R. (2002), March). I.N.S. disbands, census eliminates 'Hispanic' category. Universal Press Syndicate. Column of the Americas. March 29, 2002.

Goodman, D. (1997). Understanding and addressing resistance to social justice issues. *Democracy and Education, 12* (1), 20–23.

Goodman, M. E. (1964). *Race awareness in young child.* New York: Collier.

Gordon, A. (1964). *Intermarriage: Interethnic, interracial, interfaith.* Boston: Beacon Press.

Graham, L. O. (2000). *Our kind of people: Inside America's Black upper class.* New York: Harper Perennial.

Graham, S. (1996). The real world. In M. P. P. Root (Ed.), *The multiracial experience* (pp. 37–48). Newbury Park, CA: Sage.

Grant, C. A., & Sleeter, C. E. (1998). *Turning on learning: Five approaches for multicultural teaching plans for race, class, gender, and disability* (2nd ed.). Upper Saddle River, NJ: Merrill.

Grant, M. (1916). *The passing of the great race: The racial basis of European history.* New York: Charles Scribner's Sons.

Haizlip, S. T. (1994). *The sweeter the juice.* New York: Simon and Schuster.

Hall, C. C. I. (1980). *The ethnic identity of racially mixed people: A study of Black-Japanese.* Unpublished doctoral dissertation, University of California at Los Angeles.

Herring, R. D. (1992). Biracial children: An increasing concern for elementary and middle school counselors. *Elementary Guidance and Counseling, 27,* 123–130.

Herrnstein, R. J., & Murray, C. (1994). *The bell curve: Intelligence and class structure in American life.* New York: The Free Press.

Hetherington, E. M., Cox, M., & Cox, R. (1978) The aftermath of divorce. In J. H. Stephens, Jr. & M. Mathews (Eds.), *Mother-child, father-child relations.* Washington, DC: National Association for the Education of Young Children.

Hirsch, E. D. (1987). *Cultural literacy: What every American needs to know.* Boston: Houghton Mifflin.

Hirsch, E. D. (1996). *The schools we need.* New York: Doubleday.

Hodgkinson, H. (2002/03). Educational demographics: What teachers should know. Article 1. *Multicultural Education: Annual Editions 02/03.* Guilford, CT: McGraw-Hill.

Holmes, S. A. (2000, March). New policy on census says those listed as white and minority will be counted as minority. *New York Times*, p A-9.

Howard, G. R. (1993, September). Whites in multicultural education: Rethinking our role. *Phi Delta Kappan, 75* (1), 36–41.

Howard, G. R. (1999). *We can't teach what we don't know: White teachers, multiracial schools.* New York: Teachers College Press.

Jacobs, C. (1977). Black/white interracial families: Marital process and identity development in young children. *Dissertation Abstracts International, 38* (10–13), 5023.

Jacobs, J. H. (1992). Identity development in biracial children. In M. P. P. Root (Ed.), *Racially mixed people in America* (pp. 190–206). Newbury Park, CA: Sage.

Johnson, D. J. (1992). Developmental pathways: Toward an ecological theoretical formulation of race identity in Black-White biracial children. In M. P. Root (Ed.), *Racially mixed people in America*. Newbury Park, CA: Sage.

Johnson, S. (1990, January). Toward clarifying culture, race, and ethnicity in the context of multicultural counseling. *Journal of Multicultural Counseling and Development, 18*, 41–50.

Jones, A. C. (1985). Psychological functioning in Black American: A conceptual guide for use in psychotherapy. *Psychotherapy, 22*, 363–369.

Kaeser, G., & Gillespie, P. (1997). *Of many colors: Portraits of multiracial families.* Amherst: University of Massachusetts Press.

Katz, P.A. (1982). A review of recent research in children's racial acquisition. In L. Katz (Ed.), *Current topics in early childhood education* (pp. 17–54). Norwood, NJ: Ablex.

Katz, W. L. (1997). *Black Indians: A hidden heritage.* New York: Simon and Schuster.

Katz, W. L. (2002). Know your roots. *Raising Black and Biracial Children, 7* (1), 32–33.

Kennedy, R. (2003). *Interracial intimacies: Sex, marriage, identity and adoption.* New York: Pantheon Books.

Kerwin, C., & Ponterotto, J. G. (1995). Biracial identity development: Theory and research. In J. G. Ponterotto, J. M. Casas, L. A. Suzuki, & C. M. Alexander (Eds.), *Handbook of multicultural counseling* (pp. 199–217). Newbury Park, CA: Sage.

King, E. (1999). *Looking into the lives of children: A worldwide view.* Albert Park, Australia: James Nicholas Publishers, Ltd.

King, E., Chipman, M., & Cruz-Janzen, M. I. (1994). *Educating young children in a diverse society.* Boston: Allyn and Bacon.

Kitano, H. H. L. (1976). *Japanese Americans* (2nd ed.). Englewood Cliffs, NJ: Prentice Hall.

Knepper, P. (1995, Winter). The prohibition of biracial legal identity in the United States and the Nation: An historical overview. *State Constitutional Commentaries and Notes, 5* (2), 14–20.

Kohlberg, L. (1963). The development of children's orientations toward a moral order. Sequence in the development of moral thought. *Vita Humana, 6*, 11–33.

Kunesh, T. P. (1984). *The myth of the Black Irish: Spanish syntagonism and prethetical salvation.*

[http://www.hypertext.com/BlackIrish.html], [tpkunesh@hypertext.com].

Lewit, E. M., & Baker, L. G. (1994). Race and ethnicity—changes for children. *The Future of Children, 4* (3), 134–144.

Livingston, L. C. (1997). *American Indian ballerinas.* Norman: University of Oklahoma Press.

Loewen, J. (1995). *Lies my teacher told me.* Carmichael, CA: Touchstone Books.

Mandelbaum, P. (1990). *You be me, I be you.* Brooklyn, NY: Kate/Miller.

Manning, M. L. (1999/2000, Winter). Developmentally responsive multicultural education for young adolescents. *Childhood Education*, 82–87.

McCullough, D. (2001). *John Adams.* New York: Touchstone.

McGarrity, G., & Cardenas, O. (1995). Cuba. In Minority Rights Group (Ed.), *No longer invisible: Afro Latin Americans today* (pp. 77–108). London, England: Minority Rights Publications.

McIntosh, P. (1988). *White privilege and male privilege: A personal account of coming to see correspondence through work in women's studies.* Unpublished paper #189. Wellesley, MA: Wellesley College, Center for Research on Women.

McRoy, R. G., & Freeman, E. (1986). Racial identity issues among mixed-race children. *Social Work in Education, 8*, 164–174.

Melina, L. R. (1989). *Making sense of adoption.* New York: Harper and Row.

Meyerhoff, M. K., & White, B. L. (1986, September). Making the grade as parents. *Psychology Today*, 38–45.

Miller, R. L. (1992). The human ecology of multiracial identity. In M. P. Root (Ed.), *Racially mixed people in America.* Newbury Park, CA: Sage.

Morrison, J. W., & Bordere, T. (2001, Spring). Supporting biracial children's identity development. *Childhood Education. Association for Childhood Education International, 77* (13), 134–141.

Muhammad, J. S. (1995). Mexico and Central America. In Minority Rights Group (Ed.), *No longer invisible: Afro-Latin Americans today* (pp. 163–180). London, England: Minority Rights Publications.

Nakashima, C. L. (1992). An invisible monster: The creation and denial of mixed-race people in America. In M. P. Root (Ed.), *Racially mixed people in America.* Newbury Park, CA: Sage.

Nieto, S. (1994). Moving beyond tolerance in multicultural education. *Multicultural Education, 1* (4), 9–38.

Nishimura, N. J. (1995). Addressing the needs of biracial children: An issue for counselors in a multicultural school environment. *The School Counselor, 43,* 52–57.

Nobles, W. W. (1976). Black people in white insanity: An issue for black community mental health. *Journal of Afro-American Issues, 4* (1), 21–22.

Nobles, W. W. (1980). *African philosophy: Foundations for Black psychology* (2nd ed.). New York: Harper and Row.

Oboler, S. (1995). *Ethnic labels, Latino lives: Identity and the politics of (re)presentation in the United States.* Minneapolis: University of Minneapolis Press.

Ogbu, J. U. (1978). *Minority education and caste.* New York: Academic Press.

Ogbu, J. U. (1991). Low school performance as an adaptation: The case of Blacks in Stockton, California. In M. A. Gibson & J. U. Ogbu (Eds.), *Minority status and schooling: A comparative study of immigrant and involuntary minorities.* New York: Garland Publishing.

Olumide, J. (2002). Raiding the gene pool. In *The social construction of mixed race.* Sterling, VA and London: Pluto Press.

Ooka Pang, V. (2001). *Multicultural education: A caring-centered, reflective approach.* San Francisco, CA: McGraw-Hill.

Ormrod, J. E. (1999). *Human learning* (3rd ed.). Upper Saddle River, NJ: Merrill.

Paley, V. G. (1979). *White teacher.* Cambridge, MA: Harvard University Press.

Phinney, J. S. (1993). A three stage model of ethnic identity development in adolescence. In M. E. Bernal & G. P. Knight (Eds.), *Ethnic identity: Formation and transmission among Hispanic and other minorities* (pp. 61–79). Albany, NY: SUNY Press.

Phinney, J. S., & Rotheram, M. J. (Eds.). (1987). *Children's ethnic socialization: Pluralism and development.* Newbury Park, CA: Sage.

Piaget, J. (1963). *The origins of intelligence in children.* New York: Norton (originally published in 1936)

Poussaint, A. P. (1984). Study of interracial children presents positive picture. *Interracial Books for Children Bulletin, 15* (6), 9–10.

Poston, W. S. C. (1990, November/December). The biracial identity development model: A needed addition. *Journal of Counseling & Development, 69,* 152–155.

Powell, A. (1988). Raise your child with ethnic pride. *OURS, 21* (6), 26–29.

Powell, D. R. (1998). Reweaving parents into the fabric of early childhood programs. *Young Children, 53* (5), 60–67.

Programs for Educational Opportunity. (1996). Abolishing harassment: Equity coalition for race, gender, and national origin. *Equity Coalition, 4* (1).

Rasberry, W. (2002). We're OK. Mixed-race children launch healing trend. *Raising Black and Biracial Children, 6* (5), 12.

Register, C. (1990). *Are these children yours? American families with children adopted from other countries.* New York: Free Press.

Root, M. P. P. (1990). Resolving "other" status: Identity development of biracial individuals. In L. S. Brown & M. P. P. Root (Eds.), *Diversity and complexity in feminist Therapy* (pp. 185–205). New York: Haworth.

Root, M. P. P. (Ed.). (1992). *Racially mixed people in America.* Newbury Park, CA: Sage.

Root, M. P. P. (1996). (Ed.). *The multiracial experience: Racial boundaries as the new frontier.* Thousand Oaks, CA: Sage.

Root, M. P. P. (1997). Multiracial Asians: Models of ethnic identity. *Amerasian Journal, 23* (1), 29–41.

Root, M. P. P. (1998). Multiracial Americans: Changing the face of Asian America. In L. C. Lee & N. W. Zane (Eds.), *Handbook of Asian American psychology* (pp. 261–281). Thousand Oaks, CA: Sage.

Root, M. P. P. (2003). Issues and experiences of racially mixed people. *Multiracial Child Resource Book.* Seattle, WA: Mavin Foundation.

Rosenblatt, P. C., Karis, T. A., & Powell, R. D. (1995). *Multiracial couples: Black and White voices.* Thousand Oaks, CA: Sage.

Russell, K., Wilson, M., & Hall, R. (1992). *The color complex: The politics of skin color among African Americans.* New York: Doubleday.

Sadker, D., & Sadker, M. (1994). *Failing at fairness: How America's schools cheat girls.* New York: Charles Scribner's Sons.

Sadker, D., & Sadker, M. (2002). *Teachers, schools, and society* (6th ed.). New York: McGraw Hill.

Samhan, H. H. (1997). *Not quite White: The Arab American experience.* Paper presented at a symposium on Arab Americans by the Center for Contemporary Arab Studies, Georgetown University, Washington, DC.

Sample, S. (1993, March/April). The American Indian child. *Child Care Information Exchange, 90.*

Scales-Trent, J. (1995). *Notes of a White Black woman*. University Park: Pennsylvania State University Press.

Schmitt, E. (2001, March 13). For 7 million people in census, one race category isn't enough. *The New York Times*, pp. A1, A14.

Sebring, D. L. (1985). Considerations in counseling interracial children. *Journal of Non-White Concerns in Personnel and Guidance, 13*, 3–9.

Sickels, R. J. (1972). *Race, marriage, and the law*. Albuquerque: University of New Mexico.

Smedley, A. (2002). Science and the idea of race. In J. M. Fish (Ed.), *Race and intelligence* (pp. 145–176). Mahwah, NJ: Erlbaum.

Spencer, M. B., & Markstrom-Adams, C. (1990). Identity process among racial and ethnic minority children in America. *Child Development, 61*, 290–310.

Spickard, P. (1989). *Mixed blood: Intermarriage and ethnic identity in twentieth century America*. Madison: University of Wisconsin Press.

Spickard, P. R. (1992). The illogic of American racial categories. In M. P. Root (Ed.), *Racially mixed people in America*. Newbury Park, CA: Sage.

Springer, J. (2001). *Deculturation and the struggle for equality: Brief history of the education of dominated cultures in the United States* (3rd ed.). Boston: McGraw Hill.

Stachowski, L. L. (1998, Summer). Student teachers' efforts to promote self-esteem in Navajo pupils. *Educational Forum*, 341–346.

Steel, M. (1995, Spring). New colors. *Teaching Tolerance*, 44–49.

Stephan, C. W. (1992). Mixed-heritage individuals: Ethnic identity and trait characteristics. In M. P. P. Root (Ed.), *Racially mixed people in America*. Newbury Park, CA: Sage.

Stephens, G. (1999). *On racial frontiers: The new culture of Frederick Douglass, Ralph Ellison, and Bob Marley*. Cambridge, UK: Cambridge University Press.

Stonequist, E. V. (1937). *The marginal man: A study in personality and culture conflict*. New York: Russell & Russell.

Sullivan, P. (1998, February). What are you? Multiracial families in America. *Our Children*, 34–35.

Tatum, B. D. (1992, Spring). Talking about race, learning about racism: The application of racial identity development theory in the classroom. *Harvard Educational Review, 62* (1), 1–23.

Tatum, B. D. (1999). Why are all the black kids sitting together in the cafeteria?

Thompson, W. C. (1999). *The use of popular media multicultural education: Stressing implications for the black/non-black biracial North American student*. Unpublished dissertation. Syracuse University: Syracuse, NY.

Thornton, M. C. (1992). The quiet immigration: Foreign spouses of U.S.A. citizens, 1945–1985. In M. P. P. Root (Ed.), *Racially mixed people in America*. Newbury Park, CA: Sage.

Toplin, R. B. (1976). *Slavery and slave relations in Latin America*. Westport, CT: Greenwood Press.

Truog, A. L. (1998). Principals' perspectives on new teachers' competencies: A need for curricular reform. *Teacher Educator, 34* (1), 54–69.

U.S. Bureau of the Census. (1990). *U.S.A. Census 1990*. Washington, DC: Author.

U.S. Bureau of the Census. (1992, March). Marital status and living arrangements. *Current Population Reports, Population Characteristics, Series P20-468*, December. Washington, DC: U.S. Government Printing Office.

U.S. Bureau of the Census. (1997, October 30). *Office of Management and Budget revisions to the standards for the classification of federal data on race and ethnicity*. (Pp. 58782–58790; p. 58792). Washington, DC: Author.

U.S. Bureau of the Census. (2000). *U.S.A. Census 2000*. Washington, DC: Author.

U.S. Bureau of the Census. (2001, March). *Census 2000 shows America's diversity*. Washington, DC: Author. Retrieved from www.census.gov 4/19/01.

Valverde, K. C. (1992). From dust to gold: The Vietnamese Amerasian experience. In M. P. P. Root (Ed.), *Racially mixed people in America*. Newbury Park, CA: Sage.

Wardle, F. (1976, November) A first look at education of Guatemala Indians in post earthquake Guatemala. *New Schools Exchange, Newsletter, 136*, 12–15

Wardle, F. (1977, October). Do they still kill cowboys? *Early Years for Teachers through Age 8*, 32.

Wardle, F. (1987). Are you sensitive to interracial children's special identity needs? *Young Children, 42* (2), 53–59.

Wardle, F. (1988). Who am I? Responding to the child of mixed heritage. *PTA Today, 13* (7), 7–10.

Wardle, F. (1989). Children of mixed heritage: How can professionals respond? *Children Today, 18* (4), 10–13.

Wardle, F. (1990). Endorsing children's differences: Meeting the needs of adopted minority children. *Young Children, 45* (5), 44–46.

Wardle, F. (1991, May/June). Are we shortchanging boys? *Child Care Information Exchange, 74* (5), 48–51.

Wardle, F. (1992). *Biracial identity: An ecological and developmental model.* Denver, CO: Center for the Study of Biracial Children.

Wardle, F. (1993, November/December). Spreading misinformation about biracial kids. *New People,* 7.

Wardle, F. (1994). What about other kids in the neighborhood? *New People, 4* (5), 10–19.

Wardle, F. (1994b, January/February). Give biracial teens a chance to overcome their own challenges. *New People,* 7.

Wardle, F. (1996a). Multicultural education. In M. P. P. Root (Ed.), *The multiracial experience: Racial borders as the new frontier.* Thousand Oaks, CA: Sage.

Wardle, F. (1996b). Proposal: An anti-bias and ecological model for multicultural education. *Childhood Education, 72* (3), 152–156.

Wardle, F. (1999). *Tomorrow's children: Meeting the needs of multiracial and multiethnic children at home, in early childhood programs, and at school.* Denver, CO: CSBC.

Wardle, F. (2001a). Supporting multiracial and multiethnic children and their families. *Young Children,* 56(6), 38.

Wardle, F. (2001b). We win, we win, we win. *New People E magazine.* http://www.newpeoplemagazine.com

Wardle, F. (2002a). In a racist society, biracial children need two parents. *New People E Magazine.* http://www.newpeoplemagazine.com.

Wardle, F. (2002b, February). Is the multiracial movement soft on civil rights? *New People E magazine.* http://www.newpeoplemagazine.com.

Wardle, F. (2002c). Notes from the field. *New People E Magazine.* http://www.newpeoplemagazine.com

Wardle, F. (2002d, July). Single White women raising multiethnic and multiracial children. *New People E Magazine.* www.newpeoplemagazine.com

Wardle, F. (2003). *Introduction to early childhood education: A multidimensional approach to child-centered care and learning.* Boston: Allyn and Bacon.

Wehrly, B., Kenney, R. K., & Kenney, M. E. (1999). *Counseling multiracial families.* Thousand Oaks, CA: Sage.

Wells, H. G. (1961). *The outline of history.* Garden City, NY: Garden City Books.

West, M. M. (2001). Teaching the third culture child. *Young Children, 56* (6), 27–32

Wiest, L. R. (1998, November). Using immersion experiences to shake up preservice teachers' views about cultural differences. *Journal of Teacher Education, 49* (49), 358.

Wiles, J., & Bondi, J. (1998). *Curriculum development. A guide to practice* (5th ed.) Upper Saddle River, NJ: Prentice Hall.

Williams, G. (1995). *Life on the color line: The true story of a White boy who discovered he was Black.* New York: Dutton.

Wilson, A. (1984). "Mixed race" children in British society: Some theoretical consideration. *British Journal of Sociology, 35,* 41–61.

Wilson, T. P. (1992). Blood quantum: Native American mixed bloods. In M. P. Root (Ed.), *Racially mixed people in America.* Newbury Park, CA: Sage.

Winn, N. N., & Priest, R. (1993). Counseling biracial children: A forgotten component of multicultural counseling. *Family Therapy, 20,* 29–35.

Wolfman, I. (1991). *Do people grow on family trees? Genealogy for kids and other beginners.* New York: Workman.

Wright, M. A. (1998). *I'm chocolate, you're vanilla: Raising Black and biracial children.* San Francisco, CA: Jossey Bass.

York, S. (1991). *Roots and wings.* St. Paul, MN: Redleaf Press.

Zack, N. (2002). American mixed race: The U.S. 2000 Census and related issues. Guest editorial. *Interracial Voice E Magazine.* http://www.Interracialvoice.com. Retrieved June 22, 2002.

Zeichner, K. (1996). Educating teachers for cultural diversity. In K. Zeichner, S. Melnick, & M. Gomez (Eds.), *Currents of reform in preservice teacher education* (pp. 133–175). New York: Teachers College Press.

Author Index

Aboud, F.E., 13, 14, 109, 110, 115, 150
Alejandro-Wright, M.N., 113
Allen, T.W., 35, 61, 82
Alves-Silva, J., 88, 97
Andrews, G.R., 63
Austin, G., 38
Ayvazian, A., 207

Baker, L.G., 37
Bandura, A., 155, 183
Banks, C.A., 2, 3, 9, 18, 34, 58, 125, 205
Banks, J.A., 2, 3, 9, 18, 24, 30, 34, 35, 39, 40, 53, 55, 58, 59, 80, 125, 205, 213
Barry, E., 59
Bazin, G., 168
Beane, H., 137
Benjamin-Wardle, M., 17, 122
Berlak, H., 179
Bigelow, B., 179
Bondi, J., 179
Bordere, T., 76, 78, 209
Bowles, D.D., 22, 103, 123, 136
Bradshaw, C.K., 73, 91, 210
Bredekamp, S., 152
Bronfenbrenner, U., 112, 118, 125, 126, 174, 213
Brown, N.G., 13, 125, 142
Brown, P.M., 212
Bruner, J.S., 38, 195

Cardenas, O., 64
Carnes, J., 56, 59, 67
Chipman, M., 29
Clark, B., 194, 195
Comas-Diaz, L., 64
Copple, C., 152

Cortes, C.E., 15, 16, 34, 101, 150, 152, 156, 166, 177, 186, 213, 218
Covin, S.A., 124
Cox, M., 121
Cox, R., 121
Crohn, J., 120, 132, 133
Cross, W.E., 13, 126
Cruz-Janzen, M.I., 13, 25, 29, 43, 44, 45, 50, 62, 63, 67, 80, 123, 135, 182, 185, 193, 206, 207, 208, 213
Curry, N.E., 103

Daniel, G.R., 123, 129
Davidman, L., 24, 197
Davidman, P.T., 24, 197
Davis, F.J., 70, 79, 81, 90, 94
Derman-Sparks, L., 207
Diaz, C.F., 24
Doll, R., 169
Douglass, F., 69, 169, 200
Douglass, R.E., 13, 125, 142
Dworetzky, J.P., 115

Epstein, J.L., 182
Erikson, E., 112, 113, 115, 126, 146

Fish, J.M., 10, 23, 28, 35, 44, 53, 55, 57, 89, 94, 95, 165, 212
Flores, L., 100
Forbes, J., 190
Freeman, E., 12, 13, 113, 116, 120, 121, 122
Freire, P., 42, 207
Frykholm, J., 204

Gallup Poll, 1
Gardner, H., 38, 173, 180, 194, 195

Gay, G., 100
Gibbs, J.T., 12, 13, 14, 103, 116, 122, 217
Gillespie, P., 199
Gilliland, H., 198
Gonzalez, P., 86
Goodman, D., 205
Goodman, M.E., 113
Goodnow, J., 38
Gordon, A., 132
Graham, L.O., 91, 92
Graham, S., 219
Grant, C.A., 153
Grant, M., 48, 54, 55, 56, 78, 79, 80, 88

Haizlip, S.T., 51, 87, 88, 89, 91, 92
Hall, C.C.I., 118
Hall, R., 91
Hernstein, R.J., 57
Hetherington, E.M., 121
Hines, A.M., 12, 14
Hirsch, E.D., 179
Holmes, S.A., 87
Howard, G.R., 26, 27, 186, 205, 207

Jacobs, C., 103, 109, 112
Jacobs, J.H., 14, 103, 109
Johnson, C.N., 103
Johnson, D.J., 88
Johnson, S., 120, 123
Jones, A.C., 119, 123, 125

Kaeser, G., 199
Karis, T.A., 73
Katz, P.A., 113
Katz, W.L., 42, 190, 195
Kennedy, R., 198
Kenney, M.E., 12, 13, 16, 109, 120, 122, 135, 136, 139,

Kenney, M.E. (*cont.*), 140, 142, 144, 167, 183, 218
Kenney, R.K., 12, 13, 16, 109, 120, 122, 135, 136, 139, 140, 142, 144, 167, 183, 218
Kerwin, C., 110, 112
King, E., 29, 216
Kitano, H.H.L., 65
Knepper, P., 52, 53, 62, 78, 87, 88
Kohlberg, L., 113
Kunesh, T.P., 57

Lewit, E.M., 37
Livingston, L.C., 156
Loewen, J., 189

Mandelbaum, P., 199
Manning, M.L., 39
Markstrom-Adams, C., 37
McCullough, D., 54
McGarrity, G., 64
McIntosh, P., 124
McRoy, R.G., 12, 13, 113, 116, 120, 121, 122
Melina, L.R., 139
Meyerhoff, M.K., 121
Miller, R.L., 90, 92, 213
Morrison, J.W., 76, 78, 209
Muhammad, J.S., 63
Murray, C., 57

Nakashima, C.L., 58, 68, 73, 87, 91, 92, 100
Nieto, S., 24, 203
Nishimura, N.J., 137, 210
Nobles, W.W., 123, 125

Oboler, S., 60
Ogbu, J.U., 64, 88
Olumide, J., 12, 34, 44, 58, 91, 117, 118, 120, 122, 138, 139, 141, 167, 210, 212, 213, 217
Ooka Pang, V., 24, 204, 205, 208
Ormrod, J.E., 161, 194

Paley, V.G., 186
Phinney, J.S., 13, 14, 103, 109, 114
Piaget, J., 112
Ponterotto, J.G., 110, 112
Poston, W.S.C., 108, 112, 119, 120, 213
Poussaint, A.P., 211
Powell, A., 139, 182
Powell, D.R., 180
Powell, R.D., 73
Priest, R., 73
Programs for Educational Opportunity, 41

Rasberry, W., 90
Rodriquez, R., 86
Root, M.P.P., 1, 3, 10, 11, 14, 15, 16, 51, 73, 88, 98, 99, 111, 112, 117, 118, 126, 129, 196, 213
Rosenblatt, P.C., 73
Rotheram, M.J., 13, 14, 103, 109, 114
Russell, K., 91

Sadker, D., 183, 188, 208
Sadker, M., 183, 188, 208
Samhan, H.H., 80, 84, 85
Sample, S., 173
Santos, M.S., 88, 97
Scales-Trent, J., 51, 58, 89, 90, 91, 100
Schmitt, E., 76
Sebring, D.L., 123
Sickels, R.J., 58
Sleeter, C.E., 153
Smedley, A., 55, 79
Spencer, M.B., 37
Spickard, P., 36, 50, 54, 55, 57, 58, 59, 60, 64, 65, 66, 70, 88, 91, 189
Springer, J., 23, 54, 57
Stachowski, L.L., 184, 186, 198
Steel, M., 58, 88, 96
Stephen, C.W., 76, 212, 213
Stephens, G., 156, 169, 211

Tatum, B.D., 58, 110, 116, 147, 162
Thompson, W.C., 11
Thornton, M.C., 62, 73
Toplin, R.B., 68
Truog, A.L., 202, 208

U.S. Bureau of the Census, 1, 3, 8, 9, 35, 76, 82, 83

Valverde, K.C., 58, 74

Wardle, F., 12, 13, 14, 15, 16, 17, 18, 20, 21, 22, 28, 33, 35, 39, 45, 46, 89, 103, 112, 115, 116, 117, 119, 120, 121, 123, 124, 125, 130, 133, 134, 138, 139, 140, 141, 143, 144, 147, 151, 152, 153, 155, 161, 164, 165, 167, 170, 173, 180, 182, 183, 203, 204, 205, 212, 217
Wehrly, B., 12, 13, 16, 109, 120, 122, 135, 136, 139, 140, 142, 144, 167, 183, 218
Wells, H.G., 55, 79
West, M.M., 3, 46, 112, 119, 126, 141, 170, 174
White, B.L., 121
Wiest, L.R., 207
Wiggins, F., 124
Wiles, J., 179
Williams, G., 51
Wilson, A., 28, 123
Wilson, M., 91
Wilson, T.P., 88, 89, 90, 91, 139
Winn, N.N., 73
Wright, M.A., 137

York, S., 13

Zack, N., 18, 23, 35, 44, 49, 51, 58, 80, 82, 86, 87, 88, 89, 90, 97, 99, 100, 156, 165, 213, 216

Subject Index

Acculturation, 23
Adoptive families, school support for, 140–141
African Americans, definition of, 23
American Family Association (AFA), 139
Anglo Saxon, definition of, 23
Anti-Bias and Ecological Model of
    Multicultural Education, 170–177
  ability/disability, 173
  application of the model, 176–177
  community, 173–174
  culture, 172–173
  family, 174
  figure, 171
  gender, 173
  race/ethnicity, 170–172
  socioeconomic status, 174, 176
Anti-bias education, 9
Anti-Japanese sentiment, 64–65
Anti-miscegenation, 52
Asians, 35
Assimilation, process of, 26–27

Banks, James
  multicultural education, approaches to,
    40–43
  multicultural education, dimensions of, 36–39
Belize, 203
Bias and prejudice, teachers' addressing,
    185–186
Biased instructional materials and programs,
    188–194
  culturally authentic bias, 192
  forms of, 188–192
    cosmetic bias, 192
    fragmentation and isolation, 190
    imbalance and selectivity, 189
    invisibility, 189
    linguistic bias, 190–192
    stereotyping, 189
    unreality, 189–190
  making learning meaningful, 193–194
Biethnic, 3

Bill of rights for racially mixed people, 11
Biracial, 3
Black History Month, 20
Black Irish, 57
Blanqueamiento, 63
Blended families, 142
  school support for, 143–144
Blood quantums, 90
British Association for Adoption and Fostering
    (BAAF), 139
Brown v. Board of Education of Topeka (Kansas)
    (1954), 71–72

Categorization of people, 76–101
  after the Civil War, 91–93
    attempts to classify blacks differently,
      91–92
    mainstream Whites, 92–93
  Latinos, 85–87
  legacy of slaves and slave owners, 96–97
  maintaining the color line, 97–99
    group solidarity, 98–99
  in other nations, 93–96
    Latin America and the Caribbean, 94–96
    South Africa, 93–94
  race, racism, and, 78–83
    current racial categories, 82–83
    justifying racial labels, 82
    shifting identities, 80–81
    slavery, 79
  the race myth, 87–91
    multiethnic and multiracial Native
      Americans, 89–90
    passing as White, 88–89
    problem with race, 88
    supporting the one-drop rule, 90–91
    theory of hybrid degeneracy, 87–88
  today's multiracial and multiethnic children,
    99–100
  new visibility, 100
Center for the Study of Biracial Children, 12,
    127, 234–238

243

Cephalic index, 56
Chinese Exclusion Act, 67
Cholo, 23
Civil Rights Act (1964), 71
Civil rights movement, 68
Colonialists, 50
Colorism, 92
Color line, maintaining, 97–99
Coloureds, 93
Community, 173–174
Concept formation, 161
Concrete Operations Stage, 115
Content integration, 36–38
Contributions approach, 40–42
Cosmetic bias, 192
Critical pedagogy, 207–208
Cultural literacy, 179
Culturally authentic bias, 192
Culture, 172–173
  definition of, 28–29
  diversity and, 33–35
  teachers as products of, 184–185
Curricular approaches, 149–177
  early childhood (up to 8 years old),
    149–153
    curricular content, 151–152
    curricular materials, 152–153
    goals for early childhood curricula, 150
    learning environment, 151
  hidden curriculum, 169–170
  high school, 161–164
    curricular content, 167–168
    curricular materials, 168–169
    goals, 165–166
    learning environment, 166–167
  late elementary school (8 to 11 years old),
    153–161
    curricular content, 156
    curricular materials, 156, 161
    goals, 154
    learning environments, 155
  middle school, 161–164
    curricular content, 162–163
    curricular materials, 163–164
    goals, 161–162
    learning environment, 162
  multicultural model, 170–177
    ability/disability, 173
    application of the model, 176–177
    community, 173–174
    culture, 172–173
    family, 174
Curricular content, 151–152, 156, 162–163,
    167–168, 208

Curricular materials, 152–153, 156, 161,
    163–164, 168–169
  bias in, 188–192

Decision-making and social action approach,
    42–43
Desegregation, 71
Developmental age, 40
Development of a racial system, 50–54
  colonialists, 50
  false equality, 54
  immigration acts and court rulings, 53–54
  preoccupation with race, 50–52
  racial boundaries, 52–53
Diversity, 8–13, 9–11, 22–24, 33–35
  in the classroom, 8–13
    increasing advocacy, 12–13
    interracial patterns, 13
    multicultural education, 9–11
  and culture, 33–35
  of diversity, 23
  within traditional racial groups, 22–24
Domestic adoption, 138–139
Durante vita, 52

Ecological components, 118–119
  integrating, 126
Educational equity, 18
Educational standards, 179
Empowering school culture and social
    structure, 39–40
English Language Learners (ELL), 71
Equal Education Opportunities Act (EEOA),
    72
Equity pedagogy, 38
Essentialism, 10
Ethnic additive approach, 42
Ethnicity and race, role of teachers,' 183–184
Eugenics movement, 59
Eurocentric, 20

False equality, 54
Families and communities, 128–148
  different family structures, 138–147
    blended families, 142
    foster families, 141–142
    grandparents raising children, 145–146
    single-parent families, 144–145
    teen parents, 146–147
    transracial adoption, 138–141
  multiethnic and multiracial families, 129–136
    child's ethnic or racial identity, 129–132
    religion, 132–134
    school support for, 135–136

selecting schools and early childhood programs, 134–135
Family, 120–122, 128–148, 174
Folk categories, 89
Foreign adoption, 140
Formal operations stage, 112
Foster families, 141–142
school support for, 141–142
Fragmentation and isolation, 190

Gatekeepers, 12
Geary Act (1892, 1902), 67
Gender, 173
Genotype, 28
Grandparents raising children, 145–146
school support for, 146
"The Great Compromise," 81
Group antagonism, 122–123
Group membership, 29–33
group acceptance and multiethnic/multiracial identity, 32–33
non-Whites, 32
Group solidarity, 98–99

Hidalgos, 78
Hidden curriculum, 169–170, 182–184
teachers and, 182–184
Hispanic, 60–62
Historical developments, 48–75
changes and improvements in education, 71–72
desegregation, 71
language proficiency and rights of disabled students, 71–72
development of a racial system, 50–54
colonialists, 50
false equality, 54
immigration acts and court rulings, 53–54
preoccupation with race, 50–52
racial boundaries, 52–53
immigration, 62–69
civil rights movement, 68
Japanese American immigrants, 64–67
new restrictions, 69
opposition to non-white immigrants, 67
Puerto Rican and Filipino immigrants, 68
Latinos, 60
term "Hispanic," history of, 60–62
multicultural education, 74
origins of U.S. racism, 54–57
Irish Americans, 56–57
proving racial superiority, 56
racial hierarchies, 55
today's racism, 57

racism and segregation, 69–70
legal segregation, 70
World War II, 70
rejection of racial mixing, 57–60
Japanese racial purity, 59–60
negative influences, 58–59
Hybrid degeneracy, theory of, 87–88

Iberians, 80
Identity development, 102–127
defining, 102–103
models, 103–112
Jacob's developmental model, 108–109
Kerwin-Ponterotto's model, 110
Phinney's model of ethnic identity in adolescents, 109–110
Poston's developmental model, 108
Root's approach, 111–112
Wardle's developmental and ecological model, 112–126
community, 125–126
cultural contexts, 123–125
development stages, 112–118
ecological components, 118–119
family, 120–122
group antagonism, 122–123
integrating the ecological components, 126
of multiracial and multiethnic children, 102–127
Identity *versus* Role Confusion Stage, 161
Imbalance and selectivity, 189
Immigration, 62–69
acts and court rulings, 53–54
civil rights movement, 68
Japanese American immigrants, 64–67
new restrictions, 69
opposition to non-white immigrants, 67
Puerto Rican and Filipino immigrants, 68
Immigration Act, 53, 67, 69
Immigration and Naturalization Act, 67
Individuals with Disabilities Education Act (IDEA), 9, 72
Industry *versus* Inferiority Stage, 115
Initiative *versus* Guilt, 114–115
Institutional change, increasing advocacy for, 12–13
internet sites, 12
research, 12–13
Instruction, impacts of standards on, 179–180
Instructional strategies, 178–201
biased instructional materials and programs, 188–194
culturally authentic bias, 192

Instructional strategies, (*cont.*)
forms of, 188–192
making learning meaningful, 193–194
impacts of standards on instruction, 179–180
influence of the teacher, 180–188
addressing bias and prejudice, 185–186
changing teachers attitudes, 187–188
implementing the hidden curriculum,
182–183
parent/teacher disagreement, 182
role of teacher's ethnicity and race,
183–184
teachers as products of culture, 184–185
understanding racism, 186–187
techniques, specific suggestions for, 194–201
challenging students, not stereotyping,
199–200
confronting biased behavior or language,
198–199
creating appropriate instructional
materials, 200–201
creating small groups and cooperative
learning, 199
different learning styles, 194
exploring race and racism, 199
healthy racial identity development, 194,
197
providing role models and using the
community, 197–198
treating child as unique individual, 198
Interracial patterns, 13
Invisibility, 189
Irish Americans, 56–57

Jacob's identity developmental model, 108–109
Japanese American immigrants, 64–67
anti-Japanese sentiment, 64–65
the Nisei, 65–66
the Sansei, 66–67
settling down, 65
Japanese racial purity, 59–60
Jim Crow system, 92

Kerwin-Ponterotto's identity development
model, 110
Knowledge construction process, 37–38
Know-Nothing Party, 67
Ku Klux Klan, 57

Language proficiency and rights of disabled
students, 71–72
Latin America and the Caribbean, 94–96
Latinos, 60, 85–87
term "Hispanic," history of, 60–62

Learning environment, 151
Life-span theory, 112
Limited English Proficient (LEP), 71
Linguistic bias, 190–192
Loving v. State of Virginia (1967), 1, 72, 76

Macroculture, 23
Mainstream Whites, 23, 92–93
Marginalization, 10
Marginal Whites, 93
MAVIN, 12, 19, 221
McCarthy era, 200
Mejorando la raza, 63
Mestizo, 3
Mill v. Washington, DC Board of Education, 72
Mission/Indian boarding schools, 182
Morena, 94
Mulatto, 3
Multicultural education, 9–11, 36–43, 149–177,
202–221
approaches (Banks), 40–43
contributions approach, 40–42
decision-making and social action
approach, 42–43
ethnic additive approach, 42
transformative approach, 42
changes and improvements in, 71–72
desegregation, 71
language proficiency and rights of disabled
students, 71–72
curricular approaches, 149–177
five dimensions of (Banks), 36–40
content integration, 36–38
empowering school culture and social
structure, 40
equity pedagogy, 38–39
knowledge construction process, 38
prejudice reduction, 39–40
historical developments in, 74
reforming, 43–46
problems with traditional approaches,
43–45
truly inclusive multicultural curricula,
45–46
single-race/ethnicity approach, 21–22
teaching teachers, 202–221
traditional approach, 20–47
approaches to teaching, 36–43
diversity within traditional racial groups,
22–24
getting on the same page, 33–36
diversity and culture, 33–35
race and ethnicity, 35–36
group membership, 29–33

group acceptance and multiethnic/
multiracial identity, 32–33
non-whites, 32
race, ethnicity, and culture, 24–29
definition of culture, 28–29
definition of race, 28
process of assimilation, 26–27
understanding, 25–26
reforming multicultural education, 43–46
single race/ethnicity approach, 21–22
Multicultural education movements (1980s,
1990s), 74
Multiculturally competent people, 26
Multiethnic and multiracial children, 1–19,
209–213
characteristics of, 2–3
dealing with group antagonism, 122–123
diversity in the classroom, 8–13
ethnic and racial identities, 7–8
identity development of, 102–127
needs of, 13–18
responsibility of the schools, 15–18
personal journeys, 4–6
in schools, historical developments, 72–74
sociopolitical construction of, 209–213
importance of students' learning about
themselves, 211–212
teachers' affirming students' strengths,
212–213
supporting, 17
today, 99–100
new visibility, 100
Multiethnic and multiracial families, 129–136
child's ethnic or racial identity, 129–132
how schools can support, 135–136
religion, 132–134
selecting schools and early childhood
programs, 134–135
Multiracial Activist, 12

National Association for the Advancement of
Colored People (NAACP), 80
National Association of Black Social Workers
(NABSW), 139
National Council for Accreditation of Teacher
Education (NCATE), 202
Native Americans, 89–90
Nativists, 59
Nazi ideology, 57
New Pluralism, 74
The Nisei, 65–66
Noncustodial minority parent, 121
Non-White immigrants, opposition to, 67
Non-Whites, definition of, 32

Octoroon, 91
OMB categories (Office of Management and
Budget), 16
One-drop rule, 53, 88–89
supporting, 90–91
Out marriage, 58

*Pennsylvania Association for Retarded Children v.
Commonwealth*, 72
People v. Hall (1854), 52
Phenotype, 10, 28
Phinney's model of ethnic identity in
adolescents, 109–110
Physiognomy, 35
Plessy v. Ferguson (1896), 52
Poston's identity developmental model, 108
Potato famine, 163
Prejudice reduction, 38–39
Preoperational stage, 114
Public education, nature of, 203–204
Puerto Rican and Filipino immigrants, 68

Quadroon, 91

Race, 7–8, 14, 24–29, 32–33, 50–53, 82–83,
87–91
defining, 28
ethnicity, and culture, 24–29
understanding, 25–26
myth, 87–91
multiethnic and multiracial Native
Americans, 89–90
passing as White, 88–89
problem with race, 88
supporting the one-drop rule, 90–91
theory of hybrid degeneracy, 87–88
preoccupation with, 50–52
Racial
boundaries, 52–53
categories, 82–83
and ethic identities, 7–8, 14, 32–33
development of, 14
group acceptance and, 32–33
hierarchies, 55
labels, justifying, 82
mixing, rejection of, 57–60
Japanese racial purity, 59–60
negative influences, 58–59
purity, 58
superiority, 56
Racism, 54–57, 69–70, 187–188
origins of U.S., 54–57
and segregation, 69–70
legal segregation, 70

Racism, (*cont.*)
   World War II, 70
   teachers' understanding, 186–187
   today, 57
Refugee Act of 1980, 69
Religion, 132–134
Research, 12–13
Rice v. Gong Lum (1927), 53
Root's approach, 111–112

The Sansei, 66–67
School forms, 16–18
Schools, responsibility of, 15–18
   educational equity, 18
   school forms, 16–18
Shifting identities, 80–81
Single-parent families, 144–145
   school support for, 145
Single-race/ethnicity approach to multicultural
      education, 21–22
Slavery, 79
Slaves and slave owners, legacy of, 96–97
Socioeconomic status, 174, 176
South Africa, 93–94
Stereotyping, 189
Student profiles, 15, 24, 49, 61, 77, 117, 151,
      154, 162, 164, 167, 181, 206, 209
Support groups, 13

Taino Indian, 5
Teachers, 180–189
   attitudes, changing, 187–188
   bias and prejudice, addressing, 185–186
   ethnicity and race, role of, 183–184
   hidden curriculum, implementing, 182–184
   parent/teacher disagreement, 182
   preparing future, 204–209
      critical pedagogy, 207–208
      curricular content, 208
      dealing with diverse student populations,
         204–205
      faculty of the teachers, 205–207
   as products of culture, 184–185
   racism, understanding, 186–187
   and sociopolitical construction of
         multiethnic/multiracial children,
         209–213
   teachers' responsibilities, 213

twenty-five recommendations for, 216–220
Teen parents, 146–147
   how schools can support, 147
Third-culture children, 3
Tokenism, 192
Transformative approach, 42
Transracial adoption, 138–141
   domestic, 138–139
   foreign, 140
   school support for adoptive families, 140–141
Treaty of Guadalupe Hidalgo, 60
Trigueña, 5

Unreality, 189–190
U.S. Census categories, 3, 82
U.S. racism, origins of, 54–57
   Irish Americans, 56–57
   proving racial superiority, 56
   racial hierarchies, 55
   today's racism, 57

Wardle's developmental and ecological model,
      112–126
   community, 125–126
   cultural contexts, 123–125
      majority/higher status context, 124–125
      minority/lower status context, 123–124
   development stages, 112–118
      avoid focusing on racial/ethnic groups
         (adolescence), 116–117
      concrete operations stage (transition
         period), 115
      industry *versus* inferiority stage (transition
         period), 115
      initiative *versus* guilt stage (early
         childhood), 114–115
      join non-race-specific groups
         (adolescence), 117–118
      preoperational stage (early childhood), 114
   ecological components, 118–119
   family, 120–122
   group antagonism, 122–123
   integrating the ecological components, 126
WASP (White Anglo Saxon Protestants), 23
White supremacists, 54–55
World War II, 70

Zambo, 23